SEVEN DECADES OF RURAL SOCIAL WORK

From Country Life Commission to Rural Caucus

Emilia E. Martinez-Brawley

Foreword by
Ralph Pumphrey

PRAEGER SPECIAL STUDIES • PRAEGER SCIENTIFIC

Library of Congress Cataloging in Publication Data

Martinez-Brawley, Emilia E   1939-
    Seven decades of rural social work.

    Bibliography: p.
    Includes index.
    1. Social service, Rural--United States. I. Title.
HV91.M32   361'.973   80-24185
ISBN 0-03-058027-7

Published in 1981 by Praeger Publishers
CBS Educational and Professional Publishing
A Division of CBS, Inc.
521 Fifth Avenue, New York, New York 10017 U.S.A.

© 1981 by Praeger Publishers

123456789   145   987654321

Printed in the United States of America

FOREWORD

Now that most of the population of the United States is no longer
rural, social work, along with government and some other business
and professional groups, is becoming conscious of rural life, its values
and problems. As Dr. Emilia E. Martinez-Brawley points out, this
Johnny-come-lately effort often ignores the wealth of experience, research, and writing from the past that would give three-dimensional
substance to today's concerns and attempts to deal with them.

How many social workers today, even those in rural areas,
know that Theodore Roosevelt appointed a Rural Life Commission in
1908? Or that the American Red Cross extended its World War I services to the families of military personnel into a nationwide network
of social service agencies reaching into most rural counties? Or
that county or multiple-county juvenile courts provided a prototype
for later administration of other social welfare programs?

Why did some of those early efforts to deal with rural problems
fade into oblivion, while others are still with us? Present-day workers would do well to try to find answers to this question as they seek
solutions to the problems before them. In many cases they would find
past and present interrelated.

In Seven Decades of Rural Social Work, Dr. Martinez-Brawley
provides an excellent introduction of such searching. It is organized
to tell its story both topically and sequentially; furthermore, it is
well written so the thought can be followed easily. All social workers,
whatever their special fields, should appreciate her contribution to
the history of the profession.

CONTENTS

INTRODUCTION

RURAL SOCIAL WORK:
THE REBIRTH OF A SPECIALTY

During the past few years there has been a resurgence of the field of social work practice in rural communities as an area that deserves the special concern of social work practitioners and educators. The 1973 Annual Program Meeting of the Council on Social Work Education (CSWE) in San Francisco included, for the first time in many years, a forum for the discussion of rural concerns.[1] An outcome of that meeting was the establishment of the Council on Social Work Education Task Force on Rural Practice with nationwide representation.[2] In July 1976 on the occasion of the First National Institute for Social Work in Rural Areas, the Rural Social Work Caucus, with representation from practitioners and educators, was formed in Knoxville, Tennessee.[3] The caucus sees as its mission continued advocacy for sensitivity to rural people and their problems, and hopes to serve as a unified point of reference in the development of the social work response to rural areas.

The caucus called for the development and dissemination of educational material on rural social work.[4] The caucus, which has been instrumental in encouraging dialogue between practitioners and educators concerned with rural communities, secured program time for a session at the Twenty-Third Annual Program Meeting (APM) of the Council on Social Work Education in Phoenix, Arizona,[5] a few meetings at the 1978 APM in New Orleans, and a whole day of sessions devoted to rural themes at the 1979 APM in Boston.[6] The caucus also sponsored, in conjunction with the University of Wisconsin-Extension, a Second Annual Institute on Social Work in Rural Areas in Madison in July 1977, a Third Annual Institute in Morgantown, West Virginia, in 1978, and a Fourth Institute in Laramie, Wyoming, in 1979. The caucus played a key role in the passage of a national "Policy on Social Work in Rural Areas" by the delegate assembly of the National Association of Social Workers (NASW) in July 1977,[7] and in the establishment of an NASW Rural Task Force in 1979.

In spite of these commendable current efforts to enhance rural social work practice, a historical outlook on the field has been clearly missing. The 1977 National Association of Social Workers' "Policy on Social Work in Rural Areas," which charts the path of action of social workers on public policy issues, states:

> Schools of Social Work and human service organizations have
> focused practitioner education and training on urban
> settings to the point the curriculum materials for educat-
> ing practitioners for rural settings are practically non-
> existent. [8]

Although this indictment of social work education is for the most part
correct, historical research would reveal that there have been ante-
cedent efforts at developing such materials. Yet it appears that the
national policy has been formulated in oblivion of the past. The policy
statement continues:

> Two small texts have been published that relate specifi-
> cally to social work in rural communities—one in 1933
> and one in 1976. There are less than twenty articles that
> relate specifically to social work practice in non-metro-
> politan settings. [No date suggested][9]

On the matter of texts, the national policy statement is pre-
sumably referring to Josephine Brown's The Rural Community and
Social Casework (1933)[10] and to Leon Ginsberg's Social Work in Rural
Communities (1976). [11] Although those two works have been seminal,
they were by no means the only contributions to the rural social work
literature in the past. As far as other publications are concerned, the
student of the history of rural social work would find that just during
the single peak period that preceded the New Deal, there were more
than 50 articles published in social work journals and magazines.
Activity during the New Deal years was intense, and writings were
even more numerous.

The National Association of Social Workers' "Policy on Social
Work in Rural Areas," while serving to refocus national attention on
this area of practice, makes evident the need for further research in
the field. An account of the status of social work in rural communities
from its inception to the present should serve practitioners and educators alike to look at the developments in the field from the vantage
point of a historical perspective.

It will be the purpose of this volume to describe the status of
social work in rural communities from 1908 until 1979, by addressing
the following basic questions whose answers help capture the important landmarks in the development of the field: What was the genesis
of social work practice in rural areas? What impact did the depression and the New Deal years have on social work practice in rural
areas? What were the consequences of World War II for the rural
specialty? What is the status of current social work practice in rural
communities?

These questions have been examined from a historical–descriptive perspective and constitute not only the headings of succeeding sections but also the focuses around which the narrative of events is organized. The sources of the data have, for the most part, been published documents and archival material. Personal interviews were used to corroborate and supplement the data when printed information was incomplete or unavailable.

Each one of the periods in the development of the rural social work field discussed in this volume can be best illustrated by selected originals written during those years. Another historical volume by the author, Pioneer Efforts in Rural Social Welfare: First Hand Views since 1908 (Pennsylvania State University Press, 1980), presented several works up to 1939. The present volume contains an Appendix in which a selection of works, written after 1940, has been included. The articles in the Appendix are not easily available to students in the field. Some of them were published in journals now defunct (such as Survey), others are available in the proceedings of conferences seldom perused by today's students (such as the former National Conference on Social Work), and still others are originals that were never published. The reader is encouraged to peruse the material chosen for the Appendix since those documents will add significant meaning to statements and descriptions found in the text.

THE MEANING OF RURAL
AND RURAL SOCIAL WORK

The author acknowledges that there exists controversy in the utilization of the terms rural social work and social work in rural communities. Although references have been made to this controversy as a historical event, this volume does not attempt to deal with this unresolved dilemma. The term social work in rural communities, rather than rural social work, was the preferred one in the text, except when rural social work appeared in quoted excerpts, or when style required a shorter expression to refer to rural practice. It is the thrust of this volume to imply that rural practice is a specialty within social work, a specialty developed due to contextual differences in the practice. As Nancy Humphreys suggested at the Fourth National Institute on Social Work in Rural Areas, a specialty might be derived in one of three ways: by the uniqueness of the population served (for example, social work with alcoholics); by the uniqueness of the method employed (for example, the traditional casework, group work, and community organization approaches or the new generalist); or by the uniqueness of the context of practice (for example, rural, urban, suburban, and so on).[12]

The author further acknowledges that there is controversy around what constitutes a rural community. The author has addressed the definitional quandaries of social work and rurality in a paper presented at the 1979 NASW National Symposium in San Antonio, Texas.[13] The problem of what rural means to social work practitioners has not yet been resolved. Consequently, a flexible definition of ruralness along the lines of that set up by Fred Hines and his associates has guided this investigation.[14] On the basis of Hines's method, a range of ruralness (for example, from least to most rural) can be inferred by population size of either counties or cities outside those that are clearly metropolitan areas.

THE NEED FOR HISTORY IN RURAL SOCIAL WORK

Elliot Eisner has addressed the influence of the scientific-efficiency movement in schooling, tracing it from the works of Thorndike in the 1920s through the works of Ralph Tyler in the 1930s, to the present days of measurement and accountability. In describing the influence of scientificism in educational and curricular practices, Eisner stated:

> To do research has come to mean to do scientific inquiry, and to do such scientific inquiry in education has meant to do inquiry in which variables are identified, measured, and analyzed statistically. The desired image of the educational researcher is that of a hard scientist, someone who as far as possible emulates his colleagues in the natural sciences. To engage in other forms of inquiry, to do history, or critical analysis of existing educational or social problems, to engage in philosophic inquiry, is not to do research.[15]

A similar situation has existed in social work research. The emergence of scientifically oriented research frameworks that have tried to emulate the model of the physical sciences has produced a humanistic vacuum in social work research. This volume does not pretend to fill that gap. What this volume attempts to do is bring into a historical perspective recent discoveries in the rural field. Many of those "discoveries" represent, in fact, a revival of core statements of days past.

When Pennsylvania State University Press decided to publish Pioneer Efforts in Rural Social Welfare: First Hand Views since 1908, some colleagues who had read the manuscript before publication suggested that what was needed after Pioneer was another historical volume that would cover, with a bird's-eye view, the broad history of the rural field from 1908 until the present. These colleagues felt Pioneer needed a companion volume to place those original early documents into a frame of reference that included recent events. This volume is an attempt to provide such a framework. Seven Decades of Rural Social Work is intended to provide a summary of where we came from and how we survived the decades in rural social work. Seven Decades is intended to offer an overview of the rural field for all practitioners, rural and urban. The author trusts the volume to be history in a very contemporary and dynamic sense. Seven Decades is meant to offer the reader history and description for present reference and present use.

NOTES

1. Council on Social Work Education (CSWE) Program, Nineteenth Annual Program Meeting, San Francisco, February 25-28, 1973, p. 40.

2. Stephen A. Webster, "A Report from the Rural Social Work Caucus," mimeographed (Madison: University of Wisconsin, February 24, 1977).

3. Ibid.

4. Ibid.

5. Council on Social Work Education Program, Twenty-Third Annual Program Meeting, Phoenix, Arizona, February 27 to March 2, 1977, pp. 10, 12.

6. For details, see CSWE, APM programs for Twenty-Fourth and Twenty-Fifth Annual Meetings, New Orleans and Boston, 1978, and 1979, respectively.

7. NASW News 20 (July 1977): 38-39.

8. Ibid., p. 38.

9. Ibid.

10. Josephine C. Brown, The Rural Community and Social Casework (New York: Family Welfare Association of America, 1933).

11. Leon H. Ginsberg, ed., Social Work in Rural Communities (New York: Council on Social Work Education, 1976).

12. Nancy A. Humphreys, "Keynote Address to the Fourth National Institute on Social Work in Rural Areas," Laramie, Wyoming, July 29, 1979.

13. Emilia E. Martinez-Brawley, "The Myth of Rural Social Work and the Reality of Rural Practice: Toward a Practice Definition of Rurality" (Paper presented at the Sixth NASW Professional Symposium, San Antonio, Texas, November 17, 1979).

14. Fred K. Hines, David L. Brown, and John M. Zimmer, Social and Economic Characteristics of the Population in Metro and

Non-Metro Counties, 1970 (Washington, D.C.: Economic Research Service, U.S. Department of Agriculture, 1975), pp. 3-6.

 15. Elliot Eisner, "The Curriculum Field Today: Where We Are, Where We Were, and Where We Are Going," mimeographed (Paper presented to the Society for Professors of Curriculum, 1976), pp. 16-17.

1
THE GENESIS OF RURAL SOCIAL WORK: FROM COUNTRY LIFE COMMISSION TO PREDEPRESSION YEARS

THE COUNTRY LIFE COMMISSION AND RURAL WELFARE

The genesis of rural social work can be traced to the Country Life Commission of 1908 appointed by Theodore Roosevelt, "the first president in the industrial age to acquire a sympathetic understanding of modern farm problems,"[1] and to the National Conference on Charities and Corrections of the same year. The nineteenth-century idyllic vision of the country as a problem-free environment dwindled during its last decade and the first decade of the twentieth century.

In July 1873 disillusioned farmers had banned together to form the first farm organization, the Patrons of Husbandry, or the Grange, "against the oppression by the railroad monopoly which had established an absolute tyranny . . . 'unequalled to any monarchy of the Old World.'"[2] Rural clergymen were seeing the country churches as "dying institutions" and the laity as "degenerate and declining in numbers," and the Committee of Twelve, which made an indelible mark on rural and urban education, was "merciless in its evaluation of the cherished one-room country schools."[3] Unflattering reports of rural life were being issued by 1908, and the members of the Country Life Commission and, later, the Country Life Movement were among those instrumental in developing public awareness of the needs of rural communities.[4] They were the real rural social workers of those early days and they came from all walks of life. They were presidents of agricultural and mechanical colleges, directors of rural work for religious organizations, rural educators, journalists, and so on.

Apprenticeship training for social workers had begun as early as 1870 with the efforts of Zilpha Drew Smith of the Boston Associated Charities.[5] The charity organization movement of the nineteenth cen-

1

tury had established the principle of "scientific charity," with the corollary that skill and training were essential for philanthropic work. Formal professional education was initiated with the first full year's course offered by the New York School of Philanthropy in 1904 and the opening of the Chicago School of Civics and Philanthropy in 1908.[6] But social work training efforts, like the efforts of professional practitioners, were restricted to the cities.

The remediation of the ills of rural areas was left to that group of men and women who came to be known as "country lifers." In his study of the Country Life Movement, Merwin Swanson suggested:

> In the first decade of the twentieth century the leaders of this group began to argue that something was seriously amiss with rural life, something more subtle than economic injustices. They believed that the growing numerical and cultural dominance of urban America and the increasing discrepancy between rural and urban standards of living were debilitating rural society and, at the same time, were distracting national attention from the rural degeneration; without remedial measures country life would die.[7]

In his 1908 address to the National Conference on Charities and Corrections, at that time the most recognized and reputable forum of social work opinions in the nation, Liberty Hyde Bailey, president of the Country Life Commission and director of the New York State College of Agriculture at Cornell, stated:

> One of the great needs of the time in social studies is that we discover the rural country. There is a city phase and a rural phase of application to all questions of education, truancy, public health, pauperism, immigration, charities, correction, civic relations, labor, density of population, moral standards. We have made the serious mistake in treating some of these questions as separate problems for the city and rural districts, largely, however, by disregarding the one. . . . The so-called rural question is not a new or separate question, but only an overlooked or neglected question.[8]

In his statement, Bailey was addressing not only the social welfare needs of the country but also suggesting that they were the counterparts of urban questions. But Bailey was a pragmatist, and he highlighted remedies for the rural problem. He saw education and the development of country institutions as the crux in the solution of

country problems. Bailey ended his historical address with the following recommendations to the assembled social workers:

> I shall mention no specific things to be done, but indicate
> points of view to be established.
> 1. Extend your customary efforts to all people, irrespec-
> tive of where they live, and let them apply equally every-
> where. Recognize the fact that your work is broadly hu-
> man.
> 2. Aim to create a public sentiment that shall aid in re-
> moving the disabilities under which the farmer works and
> that shall allow him his share of the benefits of the prog-
> ress of the race.
> 3. Advise the organization of good public health super-
> vision for both the people and their domestic animals.
> You should be cautioned, however, that this supervision
> should have due regard to existing rural conditions and not
> be imposed as a piece of theoretical legislation.
> 4. Endeavor to interest good countrymen in the work that
> you are doing, bringing them into your organizations,
> making them in effect your local agents and representa-
> tives; this is very much better than to attempt to reach
> the problem by merely sending persons into the country. [9]

The report of the Country Life Commission lent national cre-
dence to the statements of country lifers. On February 9, 1909,
Theodore Roosevelt transmitted the report of the commission with a
special message to Congress. Roosevelt had already gained much
goodwill among farmers with his annual message to Congress in 1902,
when he had announced that rural free delivery was to become a fixed
policy, and with his 1907 address in Lansing, Michigan, entitled "The
Man Who Works with His Hands." In 1909 Roosevelt spoke directly
about general welfare matters affecting rural people:

> It would be idle to assert that life on the farm occupies as
> good a position in dignity, desirability and business results
> as the farmers might easily give if they chose. One of the
> chief difficulties is the failure of country life as it exists at
> present to satisfy the higher social and intellectual aspira-
> tions of country people. [10]

Although Roosevelt's main welfare theme was the overall enhancement of the quality of life of country people rather than any direct
remediation, he suggested that "the welfare of the farmer is of vital
consequence to the welfare of the whole community," and recommended

that the Department of Agriculture should become the Department of
Country Life, "fitted to deal not only with crops but also with all the
larger aspects of life in the open country."[11]

With their legitimacy undoubtedly confirmed by the president's
message, country lifers tried to interest social workers in their platform. However, the emergent social work profession was too preoc-
cupied with the development of its own casework techniques to become
engaged in the broader community-based approach proposed by the
country lifers. Although social work in the early settlement houses
had been imbued with a community-minded approach to social problems, the scientific investigation and treatment of specific cases had
soon become the clearer target of trainers:

> Casework provided the lion's share of field and vocational
> opportunities. Equally important, it seemed the most
> clearly defined technique in social work, and appropriate
> to the requirements of all educational institutions. Like the
> professional association, the professional school was shaped
> by case workers as an instrument of control in the profes-
> sional subculture and contributed to making casework the
> nuclear skill in social work.[12]

The relationship between social work and country life movements was cordial but unproductive. Survey, perhaps the most influential social work periodical of the time, continued to publish articles
on the rural theme; the National Conference on Charities and Corrections continued to include rural sessions in its meetings; and country
lifers made attempts at offering summer seminars for rural social
workers at the Massachusetts Agricultural College in Amherst.[13]
But the marriage of the two groups, country life and emergent professional social work, was never consummated: "The two groups talked
amicably with each other but did not listen to each other's message."[14]

Till its demise in the 1940s, the country life movement kept true
to the platform that had been laid down in 1908 by the first commission's report.[15] The report had emphasized the need for developing
a highly organized rural society able to rise to the challenge of the
cities by a reevaluation and redirection of its institutions, a society
where the farmer would be kept on his land through the enhancement
of all rural resources. Country lifers' commitment to community development had been clear. They spoke the language of organization
rather than of individual amelioration to which the social work profession at that time seemed exclusively tuned.

FOCUSING PUBLIC ATTENTION ON RURAL
PROBLEMS: THE BUDDING SOCIAL WORK EFFORTS

In spite of the fact that social work did not become immersed in
rural themes, there were between 1908 and 1917 a number of sporadic
efforts initiated by social workers on behalf of rural people. For the
most part, these efforts attempted to focus public attention on the social problems of the country.

In 1909 John C. Campbell of the Russell Sage Foundation of
Demorest, Georgia, presented to the National Conference of Charities
and Corrections a stirring paper entitled "Social Betterment in the
Southern Mountains." Campbell highlighted for the predominantly urban audience the dilemmas of southern Appalachia and of the rural
South in general. Besides addressing specific problems such as health,
nutrition, and education, he issued a plea for better understanding of
the rural South:

> This question of the mountain dweller is a national ques-
> tion. You have it in your New England hills, with less
> hope of solution it is sometimes felt, and although it is a
> larger question in the South, it is, after all, only a ques-
> tion of intensified rural conditions. If you cannot altogether
> understand the South, may we not hope for your patience
> and for your sympathy? [16]

During the same decade, Survey published a number of articles
highlighting crucial topics within the rural problems theme. In 1911
Charles L. Chute of the National Child Labor Committee wrote "The
Cost of the Cranberry Sauce."[17] In this article, Chute discussed in
a very dramatic fashion the problems of migrant farm workers in
New Jersey. "The system itself is intolerable,"[18] said Chute of the
practice of removing whole Italian and Portuguese families from the
neighboring states to labor in the cranberry fields. "The wholesale
removal of these families is not for an outing in the New Jersey
pines . . . but to labor for the support of their families in a region
where there are no restrictions as to age, sex, hours, and conditions
of labor."[19]

"Children in Rural Districts" was the subject of J. J. Kelso's
article in Survey in October 1911.[20] Although Kelso was a Canadian,
his experiences in rural Ontario were applicable to the vast rural in-
lands of the United States. Kelso admonished that "an important social work" was being left undone when children of rural areas were
abandoned by all authorities to grow in deprived environments.[21] He
indicted city charities for disregarding the welfare of rural districts:

Wealthy and influential city charities should exercise some oversight over the nearby rural districts. Some charities actually draw a line around the city and refuse to touch any case, no matter how urgent, that happens to be outside that line. [22]

In 1912 "Tragedies of Village Slums," by Katherine Piatt Bottorff, discussed the housing problems of small villages throughout America: [23]

Let me show you the homes of the poor in one beautiful Indiana town. Let me lead you from cabin to hovel and show you the close relation existing between physical and moral degradation; let me point out how much the environment means to a family of children, who reflect, inevitably in conduct and character, every phase of the descent in social and moral scale. I want you to cry, Enough! These conditions must be remedied by legislation, and it must be immediate and thorough. [24]

There were still other articles depicting rural problems. The rural church was a stronghold of activity and hope, and rural leaders were described as performing many social work tasks with varying degrees of success. In 1913, however, the Country Life sponsored "Conference of Rural Social Workers" at Amherst changed its name to "Conference of Rural Community Leaders," thus symbolically marking the beginnings of a clearer distinction between those who performed social work tasks in rural areas and professional social workers. [25]

By 1917 professional and nonprofessional social workers had amply described the detrimental conditions of many rural areas. The myth of the country as a problem-free environment had, for the most part, been dispelled. But the actual interventions of social workers in rural areas did not amount to much. In 1917 William T. Cross, general secretary of the National Conference of Social Work, described for the conference the lack of organized social work involvement in the rural areas:

Heretofore, the established welfare agencies have had little enough to offer the country. Their programs have stopped short at the city gates. Constructive schemes of recreation, social centers, nursing have been developed in a limited way. Rural education has received great stimulus in recent years and the problems of the country church have had a flood of illumination. In scientific agriculture

and economic co-operation, the chief gains seem to have
been registered. Thus, the progress that has been made
has occurred mainly in directions that do not correspond
closely to the lines of discussion in the National Conference of Social Work. [26]

Cross suggested that the lack of trained workers in rural areas
paralleled the lack of organized welfare efforts. In his message,
Cross anticipated the calls for regional or county level organization
of the rural social services that were to become commonplace in the
1920s. Furthermore, Cross also attempted to set forth some ideas
as to what constituted for him "rural social work." His emphasis
was on the different environmental conditions affecting social work in
the country:

> The various factors underlying poverty occur in different
> order and potency. The same is true of other social ills.
> Remedies for these ills must have peculiar adaptation.
> The usual ruralite differs characteristically from the man
> in the city. There is said to be a typical rural mind. [27]

He also addressed what the nature of the practice he deemed appropriate for rural areas was:

> Programs of social work for the country must be simple.
> . . . Unification must be taught at the outset. . . . Even-
> tually every rural district must face the question, are we
> to have one trained leader, or five specialists? Already
> in the larger cities a movement to federate and amalgamate
> social service, even down to individual case treatment, has
> set in; why should the error of dissipation of effort and re-
> sources be perpetuated in the country? [28]

WORLD WAR I AND THE AMERICAN RED CROSS

In 1917 the United States entered World War I. The war became a central national concern and rural activities were affected by
wartime organization. The Home Service of the American Red Cross,
which had been created to serve soldiers' families, was a significant
force in developing a regional approach to social service delivery in
the interior of the country. Even during the war years, the Home
Service extended its scope to cover civilian families. After the war,
those extended services became their raison d'être. Many of the
names associated with the Home Service of the Red Cross—Jesse
Steiner, Henrietta Lund, Josephine Brown—continued to be leading
national figures in rural social work for many years.

In 1918 <u>Survey</u> published an article by W. Frank Persons, director general of civilian relief of the American Red Cross. "Home Service in One Rural County" described "what a group of untrained volunteers did in developing Home Service for the Red Cross in a territory innocent of social agencies."[29] The manpower needs of the local Home Service sections required concerted efforts on the part of the national office. <u>Survey</u> reported on "Training for Home Service" in May 1919.[30] From the beginning, the Red Cross had asked for the cooperation of schools of social work to prepare their workers. Institutes, conferences, and chapter courses of a duration of about six weeks each, carried out by the schools of social work, had been the usual training procedure. "The Red Cross supplemented the teachings, procured field work opportunities . . . carried the overhead expense and recruited the students." By 1919 the Red Cross had entered into cooperative agreements for expanded courses for rural workers with many schools and agricultural colleges, which were deemed "the natural resources for training rural workers for whom there is now great demand." But the Red Cross was not satisfied with the length of the courses or the nature of the sponsorship of rural training. The same 1919 report indicates that the Red Cross hoped to have the training of rural workers, in time, "taken over entirely" by the educational institutions and to achieve the lengthening of the basic six week training to a minimum of twelve weeks, "with additional advanced courses covering a period of one year or more."[31]

The aspirations of the Red Cross for expanded courses and outreach, although alive through the 1920s, did not materialize. The Home Service sections continued to be opened for a few years after the war, but eventually the local Red Cross offices either lost interest in them or simply dissolved them.[32] The efforts of the Home Service in establishing professional ideals for social work services in rural communities accomplished more lasting results than the brief life of their local Home Service sections. As Swanson pointed out, the participation of established leaders, such as Alice Higgins Lathrop of the Family Welfare Association (now Family Service Association of America [FSAA]) and Jesse Frederick Steiner, head of the Red Cross Bureau of Training for the Home Service, ensured the continuation of rural social work efforts beyond those of the Red Cross. Thanks to the Red Cross, the social welfare community became more aware of rural social ills.

THE NATURE OF RURAL SOCIAL WORK:
LAUNCHING A LONG-LASTING DIALOGUE

In 1921 <u>The Family</u> published Henrietta L. Lund's "Case Work in Rural Communities." Lund was supervisor of rural social work for the northern division of the American Red Cross. From the point of view of a practitioner, Lund launched a dialogue on the nature of rural social work practice that was to last for many years:

> It has been emphasized that family social work methods must be proved capable of coping with the peculiarities of rural people. Human nature is the same the world over. The very principle of family social work, the very training with which a worker is prepared, makes it mandatory upon her to give treatment to fit the individual situation. [33]

Beyond emphasizing the applicability of "casework" (social work) to rural communities, Lund introduced the notion of nuances in the application of the method. The question of whether the method was the same and only the environment differed between urban and rural areas was a hard one to answer. For Lund the crux of the distinction appeared to lie in the environmental differences as well as in the personality characteristics that rural practice required of the worker:

> The future of family social work is largely with the individual worker who is going to present it to the rural districts. The harvest is ripe—are we going to falter because of lack of laborers? The social worker of the rural district is a pioneer builder of a big movement; she must have the love of the people and the country at heart; she must understand the psychology of the country store; she must bunk with the squatter's family in the one room shack if need be; she must go to the movies with the town's scapegoat to get her chance to talk to him—if she can do all this and still be human, then her possibilities for service are unlimited. [34]

One interesting phenomenon that was occurring in the field of rural sociology at the time had repercussions for rural social work since it attempted to throw light upon the dilemma of the nature of rural social work and the applicability of the case approach. By the 1920s the emerging emphasis on rural social research had begun to exert pressure on rural sociologists who had been, up to that time, more concerned with amelioration than research. Whatever discoveries rural sociologists had offered to rural welfare had come from the "commission inquiry and report method," [35] a method that was falling out of favor by the late 1920s. By 1927 "the social survey was undoubtedly the most commonly used instrument of rural social research." [36] George H. Von Tungeln addressed the National Conference of Social Work on the contributions the social survey method had to make to rural welfare practice. According to Von Tungeln, the survey method had unearthed, in a scientific fashion, a number of truths that up to then had been only speculative. One of those truths concerned the nature of the social services desired or required by farmers:

> The farmer . . . thinks in terms of community organiza-
> tion, community work, or cooperative work rather than
> case work. Once this has been genuinely understood, the
> running quarrel between the community organizationists
> and the social case workers as to which should be devoured
> or vanquished by the other will cease to be a quarrel, or
> even a serious argument. Case work is quite the proper
> thing in the city, with its heterogeneity of people and occu-
> pations, while community work is probably quite as proper
> in the country. . . . The city . . . needs its social case
> experts as the country needs its community experts.[37]

But Von Tungeln's position was far from being unambiguous. In his opinion, there was one possible place where the case method might be more applicable due to the heterogeneity of the farm population: "Community work is probably quite as proper in the country, where there is homogeneity of occupation and also of people to a large extent except in the South where there are two races on the farm."[38]

And so discussions about the essence of rural practice and how it differed from its urban counterpart were launched in those early days of the Home Service to continue unresolved and controversial through future decades.

PROFESSIONALIZATION AND RURAL PRACTICE

During the 1920s, because of the movement toward professionalization, social workers began to feel more acutely than ever the pull between professional standards of practice, as were being taught in the schools of social work, and local community values and ideas. Nowhere were these dilemmas more evident than in the rural areas, where workers were but few voices amidst crowds of laymen serving on county welfare boards. This pull of forces often earned social workers the enmity of local leaders. It also widened the distance between community-oriented sociologists and adjustment-oriented social workers.

All subjects began to be discussed from this new perspective of professionalism, and voices rose in favor of the trend as well as against it. Social workers, by now being called case workers to denote both their training and ameliorative method orientation, were indicted for their detachment from community ideals. This was the

theme of Walter Burr's "The Philosophy of Community Organization:
The Rural Community Ideal," presented by this professor of sociology
from Kansas to the National Conference on Social Work in 1925:

> The status of the community at any given time is the result,
> up to that time, of certain living moving factors peculiar to
> that community. The social worker is likely to have fixed
> his ideal as the result of experiences and observations of
> other social phenomena in entirely different communities.
> The fact that one rural community is not like another or a
> group of others does not tell anything about that community
> being ideal or not being ideal. . . . Because a cooperative
> cheese factory makes an ideal basis for economic and social
> success in certain communities in Wisconsin, a Wisconsin
> worker comes down to certain livestock or wheat sections
> of Kansas, and assumes that the cooperative cheese factory
> would make the economic basis for community success
> there also.[39]

The rigidity and prescriptive orientation of those early case
work remedies enraged free-minded spirits such as Burr:

> To enforce upon a community from the outside the ideal
> of any individual or organization is decidedly harmful. It
> is establishing a benevolent tyranny. Social workers are
> usually the worst sort of benevolent tyrants. Rural people
> have especially been tyrannized in this regard by their well-
> meaning institutional friends. They are continually being
> offered "the benevolent end of despotism."[40]

What many failed to see was that such despotism was also enraging
to many rural social workers, but they did not begin to verbalize their
ideas until they felt more secure in their identities in the days of the
New Deal.

Some of the names that were to become familiar to rural workers in later years were involved in those early discussions of practice
issues. Josephine Brown, at that time general secretary of the Dakota
County Welfare Association in Minnesota, later author of Social Casework and the Rural Community (1933), discussed at the 1922 National
Conference on Social Work the utilization of volunteers. In "The Use
of Volunteers in Rural Social Work," Brown attempted to bridge the
gap between theoretical training and community mores by advocating
the intelligent utilization and cooperation of local volunteers by flexible case workers who could be ready to abandon, in emergencies,
their most precious theories. Brown had anticipated the potential

problems of a rigid orientation in the practice of case work in rural communities:

> The city worker today enters a field where case-work precedent is already established. Her work is carefully defined as she follows well-marked lines of procedure in selecting and putting to work volunteers whether on committees or in more personal kinds of service. With varying degrees of success the volunteer fits into the office of this case-working agency, gives certain hours to the work and receives a more or less definite course of instruction. The trained worker who has been accustomed to working with volunteers in this fashion will do well when she enters the rural field to dispossess her mind of all preconceived ideas on the subject. If she does not know before she begins her county work she will soon learn that her status here is quite different from that of the case worker in town. There the volunteer while desirable was optional. In the country, the volunteer is a necessity. In town the volunteer is on trial. In the country it is the social worker who is in that equivocal position. . . . She must realize that the case by right of long acquaintance and treatment belongs to the volunteer, not to her. She is welcomed as an advisor, not as a dictator, and it is her privilege to sift the salient points . . . and later direct the discussion of the case to the point where the volunteer will herself make a reasonable diagnosis and possibly plan the very treatment the social worker has in mind. [41]

Another problem of which rural social workers became cognizant during this period of incipient professionalization was that of continued professional development. In the cities, where the supervisory system had taken strong hold, workers were to grow from the wisdom of the more experienced as well as from exposure to colleagues. But in the rural areas, the isolation of trained workers made for a very different situation. The worry became not only to train rural workers adequately, through the inclusion of appropriate content in allied subjects such as rural sociology, but also to maintain their interest in their own development once they were practicing in isolated regions.

Jesse Frederick Steiner addressed the issue of appropriate content to be included in the training of rural social workers in a paper entitled "Rural Sociology—Indispensable or Merely Desirable?" presented at the professional standards and education section of the 1927 National Conference on Social Work in Des Moines. This article by Steiner touched upon a spot that was to remain tender for many decades, and which, in the minds of many still represents a delicate matter of balance: the relationship between sociology and social work, most particularly rural sociology and rural social work:

> During the past decade, the relation between sociology and social work has been a favorite topic for discussion at various meetings and conferences without apparently leading to any generally accepted principles or policies for the guidance of curriculum makers. . . .
> The social worker has no time to give to sociology if it does not provide direct aid in solving the specific problems he faces. The sociologist, in his turn, ignores the social worker because the latter seems to be wrapped up entirely in the matter of securing practical results. [42]

For Steiner, the preparation of rural social workers was a matter that needed to transcend those often inaccurate rivalries based on an obsolete understanding of teritorial matters by members of both fields:

> Only a few of the professional schools give particular attention to the training of rural social workers, and these are not agreed concerning the subjects of study to be emphasized or the type of work experience that would be most valuable. Certainly, the well prepared rural worker should possess, in addition to social work technique, a keen insight into the characteristics of rural life and a well rounded knowledge of rural people. While many elements must enter into the acquirement of this thorough understanding of rural situations, the study of rural sociology would seem indispensable, for it represents the aspect of social science which during the past twenty-five years has attempted to recognize in a systematic manner our constantly growing knowledge of the social forces at work in rural communities. [43]

Harold J. Matthews addressed the problem of the continuing development of rural workers in an article appearing in Social Forces in September 1927, entitled "Special Problems of Rural Social Work." Matthews exhorted lonely rural workers to attend state conferences, to subscribe to the professional journals, and even to "read and refer to Social Diagnosis and other reliable books on case work." [44] Social Diagnosis was, of course, Mary Richmond's 1917 treatise on social diagnosis and social investigation. Richmond had been a long-time proponent of scientific charity, and Social Diagnosis was held by case workers as evidence of the professionalization of social work through scientific investigation and functional specificity. Although Matthews's article was a prime example of the exaggerated concern with professionalism during the period—a concern quite unrealistic in the rural areas—it goes beyond that topic to provide a summary of the state of the art and a listing of practical suggestions and answers to the dilemmas of rural practice.

GROUP WORK AND THE RURAL AREAS

Two other landmark developments must be included in any description of rural social work efforts prior to the depression. They are the recreational group work efforts and the various attempts to organize and/or regionalize social services by units larger than the rural towns or villages.

During the first decade of the twentieth century, the cities witnessed the emergence of group work as a popular form of social intervention. The settlement house movement, spearheaded by Jane Addams, established the groundwork upon which later social group work practice grew. Social participation, association and interaction of peers, democratic processes, and impact upon surrounding environmental conditions were key principles that survived the decline of settlement houses.

The rural areas of the United States did not remain immune to group work influences. Although the progressive and reform-oriented efforts of the settlement house movement were not felt in the country, the recreation programs that became important in the cities after the war years were the major thrust of group work organizations in the country during and after the war.

The Country Life Commission had emphasized church-based service and recreation programs for rural areas. The war efforts provided the backbone of governmental resources to organizations like the United States Boys' Working Reserve.[45] The reserve included boys between 16 and 21 years of age who, having passed at least a cursory physical examination, were found fit to work on farms where their labor had been requested. They lived in camps under semimilitary discipline. The farms and other rural establishments that employed them were investigated by the Department of Labor. The system of supervision varied from state to state, but in Wisconsin, for example, where an elaborate system emerged, about three hundred school principals, clergymen, teachers, and other rural leaders volunteered as supervisors. What the reserve did was to develop a new core of people interested in understanding rural problems.

No agricultural-recreational organization has endured the test of time as has the U.S. Department of Agriculture Extension sponsored

4-H club. Although the clubs had been in operation before World War
I, the war-strengthened communal spirit gave them a boost. The
4-H clubs thrived throughout the 1920s. Neither the United States
Boys' Working Reserve nor the 4-H clubs were, per se, a social work
effort. Social workers were only peripherally involved in them.
However, they had ample ramifications for social welfare planning
in rural areas, and as such they served to pave the way for an expanded rural practice.

Probably the most important group organization of the period
in rural areas were the Young Men's and Young Women's Christian
Associations (YMCAs and YWCAs). The development of local leadership was perhaps the prevalent theme of the rural YMCAs and YWCAs
of the first three decades of this century. In a paper presented to the
Forty-Ninth National Conference on Social Work, D. C. Drew, national secretary of the New York YMCA, commented:

> The natural and primary social groups of men, young men,
> and boys . . . have formed the social environment for the
> development of the rural association program in its recre-
> ational and service aspects. The constant changes and un-
> certainties of these primary groups in rural localities have
> necessitated constant expert leadership called supervision.
> . . . The county, through a process of experimentation,
> has been found to be the best unit of administration. [46]

THE JUVENILE COURT ACT AND THE
REGIONALIZATION OF SOCIAL SERVICES

The last seminal development that influenced social work practice in rural communities before the depression years was the organization or regionalization of rural social welfare services into units
larger than the individual villages or small communities. The county
level organization efforts of the 1920s highlighted the role of governmental bodies in the provision of rural social services before they
were to become mandatory as a result of early New Deal legislation.
Furthermore, social work manpower needs in rural areas have always
been intimately connected to the legislation that supports the provision
of services to rural communities. Efforts to train social workers for
rural areas have been, consequently, accelerated or decelerated by
the momentum of government sponsorship.

As has already been noted, the Home Service of the Red Cross
had spearheaded the notion of regionalization during the war years.
After 1919 rural leaders began to refer to it with increased frequency.
Discussions of the county, the region, or even the state as alternative

units for the organization of the interior became commonplace at
meetings and in the literature. Although the dialogue basically had
to do with administrative organization of services, regionalization
and standardization were also themes noted in specialized fields such
as the codification of child welfare legislation. [47]

During the period of 1917 to 1927, social work was characterized
by the introduction of systematic surveys of social conditions. [48] Rural
social research grew in importance stimulated by the activities of the
scientifically oriented rural sociologists. These sociologists, although believers in research, were also committed, much like social
workers, to problem solving.

> Rural social research . . . may take as its purpose or ob-
> jective one of the three following goals, or a combination
> of these: first, to give students first-hand experience of
> social fact finding; second, to ascertain facts on rural so-
> cial conditions as such for the purpose of increasing the
> volume of rural scientific knowledge; and third, to ascer-
> tain scientific facts regarding specific communities for the
> purpose of projecting and executing practical programs of
> local improvement and social progress. [49]

Rural social surveys were utilized both in city and country to
bring about legislative changes and reform. The efforts at standardization and regionalization of rural social services utilized data rendered by those systematic social studies of the country.

The establishment of the most appropriate unit for rural community development was one of the central problems surveyed. Defining the rural community and establishing a workable social unit
with its boundaries were themes that concerned students of rural
life. Herman N. Morse of the Presbyterian Board of Home Missions
of New York, addressing the Forty-Sixth Annual Session of the National Conference on Social Work, suggested:

> Last week, at the meeting of this conference, there was a
> certain amount of discussion as to the unit on which the
> social organization of the country should proceed. . . .
> The question, it seems very clearly now, is not what unit
> we would like to use, but what the unit actually is; that is,
> the unit of territory and population within which people ac-
> tually do work together. [50]

There was one piece of legislation that also brought about extensive reorganization of the social services in the country. In 1899 Illinois had enacted the first juvenile court law, "An Act to Regulate the

Treatment and Control of Dependent, Neglected and Delinquent Children." By 1919 all the states but Connecticut, Maine, and Wyoming had enacted juvenile court laws. In the rural districts, the juvenile court operated on county, bicounty, and even tricounty bases. In many cases the existing court of record functioned also as the juvenile court.

Social workers were involved, from the very beginning, in the work of the juvenile courts. North Carolina emerged in the leadership of rural states. Wiley H. Swift, of the National Child Labor Committee in Greensboro, presented "A Redefining of the Scope and Functions of the Juvenile Court, in Terms of the Rural Communities" to the 1921 National Conference of Social Work. In this paper he summarized existing conditions regarding rural children:

> There are children in these rural counties, thousands of
> them. Some are abused, some are just poor, and some
> are going wild. Unfortunately, there are no private agen-
> cies, such as you have in the city, to cover the field. The
> church does a little, oh, so little, but about all that is done.
> The Red Cross, hard as it may be trying, is touching only
> the high places. I see no prospect of any great improve-
> ment in this respect, and therefore, feel not only free but
> forced by observation to say that whatever is to be done in
> strictly rural communities for the care of children, unfor-
> tunate for any reason, will have to be done by someone em-
> ployed to do it and paid for his work out of public funds.
> Rural social work will have to be paid for just as school
> teaching is paid for—a thing well recognized in well-orga-
> nized cities, a thing that must come to be recognized every-
> where. [51]

Naturally, an expanded view of the services of the juvenile court would result, in Swift's view, in the ensuring of at least one competent social worker per county:

> For the time being, therefore, I am of the opinion that in
> the rural sections of those states about which I know some-
> thing, the juvenile court should have jurisdiction of all de-
> linquent, neglected, and dependent children. In saying this
> I seek not so much to preserve the jurisdiction of the court
> as to insure at least one competent social agent for every
> county. There is no hope of getting two soon; there is no
> great assurance of getting even one in the rural counties
> of some states. [52]

It is important to note that, during and after World War I, North Carolina established a broadly acclaimed statewide social welfare system. By legislative mandate, every county had to set up a welfare board with jurisdiction over various services. The North Carolina plan was in many ways a precursor of obligatory county-based social welfare programs established by the Federal Emergency Relief Administration (FERA) during the New Deal. The North Carolina plan was used as a model of county level organization by many other states, and was amply discussed in the literature.[53] Although these discussions about a system for organizing social services helped expand the administrative horizons in the country and eventually contributed to document the need for social work personnel in rural areas, at their onset those discussions did not dwell on what the essence of the practice was in the rural locale.

Toward the end of the 1920s as the organization theme became more comprehensive, discussions about the sponsorship of services and the nature of social work practice in rural communities began to appear.[54] One of those articles is worth special mention since it introduced a term that was to permeate dialogues about the essence of the practice and the proposals for service delivery and training during the depression and New Deal. The article was Louise Cottrell's "Organization Needed to Support and Free the Local Worker for Undifferentiated Case Work,"[55] and the term, as can be surmised, was "undifferentiated" social work, presently being labeled "generalist approach."

NOTES

1. Clayton S. Ellsworth, "Theodore Roosevelt's Country Life Commission," Agricultural History 34 (October 1960): 155.
2. Ibid.
3. Ibid.
4. It must be noted that historians have pointed out that while Liberty Hyde Bailey, chairman of the commission, eventually made many public appearances to present its findings to the public, in its inception he had disagreed with the commission's proposed purpose of publicity and with the idea of his being its chairman. It was apparently Gifford Pinchot who conceived of the commission's progressive public role. See D. Jerome Tweton, "Progressivism Discovers the Farm: The Country Life Commission of 1908," North Dakota Quarterly 39 (Summer 1971): 58-61.
5. Roy Lubove, The Professional Altruist: The Emergence of Social Work as a Career, 1880-1930 (Cambridge, Mass.: Harvard University Press, 1965), p. 137.

6. Ibid., pp. 137-41.

7. Merwin S. Swanson, "The American Country Life Movement, 1900-1940" (Ph.D. diss., University of Minnesota, 1972), p. 1.

8. L. H. Bailey, "Rural Development in Relation to Social Welfare," Proceedings, National Conference on Charities and Corrections, 35th Annual Session (Richmond, Va., 1908), p. 83.

9. Ibid., p. 91.

10. Theodore Roosevelt, "The Roosevelt Commission Report Special Message, February 9, 1909," reprint from Senate Document no. 705, 60th Cong., 2d sess., 1909, Rural America 7 (January 1929): 3.

11. Ibid., p. 4.

12. Lubove, The Professional Altruist, p. 143.

13. "Civics and Country Life," Survey 24 (September 17, 1910): 867; "Rural Social Workers Meet," Survey 26 (August 19, 1911): 747-49.

14. Swanson, "The American Country Life Movement," p. 172.

15. "Report of the Commission on Country Life—A Summary," Rural America 7 (January 1929): 5-8.

16. John C. Campbell, "Social Betterment in the Southern Mountains," Proceedings, National Conference on Charities and Correction, 36th Annual Session (Buffalo, N.Y., 1909), p. 137.

17. Charles L. Chute, "The Cost of the Cranberry Sauce," Survey 27 (December 2, 1911): 1281-84.

18. Ibid., p. 1284.

19. Ibid.

20. J. J. Kelso, "Children in Rural Districts," Survey 27 (October 21, 1911): 1054.

21. Ibid.

22. Ibid., p. 1055.

23. Katherine Piatt Bottorff, "Tragedies of Village Slums," Survey 28 (September 21, 1912): 767-69.

24. Ibid., p. 767.

25. "Rural Leaders and Their Problems," Survey 30 (August 30, 1913): 655-56.

26. William T. Cross, "Rural Social Work," Proceedings, National Conference on Social Work, 44th Annual Session (Chicago, 1917).

27. Ibid., p. 641.

28. Ibid., pp. 641-42.

29. W. Frank Persons, "Home Service in One Rural County," Survey 40 (June 29, 1918): 370.

30. "Home Service and Civilian Charities," Survey 42 (April 26, 1919): 139-40; "Training for Home Service," Survey 42 (May 10, 1919): 250.

31. Ibid.

32. Merwin S. Swanson, "Professional Rural Social Work in America," Agricultural History 46 (October 1972): 517.

33. Henrietta L. Lund, "Casework in Rural Communities," The Family 2 (March 1921): 13.

34. Ibid.

35. George H. Von Tungeln, "Rural Social Research—Methods and Results," Proceedings, National Conference on Social Work, 54th Annual Session (Des Moines, Iowa, 1927), p. 333.

36. Ibid.

37. Ibid., p. 335.

38. Ibid.

39. Walter Burr, "The Philosophy of Community Organization: The Rural Community Ideal," Proceedings, National Conference on Social Work, 52d Annual Session (Denver, 1925), p. 397.

40. Ibid., p. 399.

41. Josephine Brown, "The Use of Volunteers in Rural Social Work," Proceedings, National Conference on Social Work, 49th Annual Session (Providence, R.I., 1922), p. 267.

42. Jesse Frederick Steiner, "Education for Social Work in Rural Communities: Rural Sociology—Indispensable or Merely Desirable?" Proceedings, National Conference on Social Work, 54th Annual Session (Des Moines, Iowa, 1927), p. 587.

43. Ibid., p. 589.

44. Harold J. Matthews, "Special Problems of Rural Social Work," Social Forces 6 (September 1927): 67; Mary Ellen Richmond, Social Diagnosis (New York: Russell Sage Foundation, 1917).

45. Helen Dwight Fisher, "The Boy, the War and the Harrow," Survey 39 (March 30, 1918): 704-6.

46. D. C. Drew, "The Rural Social Work of the Young Men's Christian Association," Proceedings, National Conference on Social Work, 49th Annual Session (Providence, R.I., 1922), p. 327.

47. "Child Welfare Studied in Oklahoma," Survey 39 (March 30, 1918): 713-14.

48. H. Paul Douglas, How Shall Country Youth Be Served? A Study of the "Rural" Work of Certain National Character-Building Agencies (New York: George H. Doran, 1926).

49. Von Tungeln, "Rural Social Research," p. 331.

50. Hermann N. Morse, "The Underlying Factors of Rural Community Development," Proceedings, National Conference on Social Work, 46th Annual Session (Atlantic City, N.J., 1919), p. 552.

51. Wiley H. Swift, "A Redefining of the Scope and Functions of the Juvenile Court, in Terms of the Rural Community," Proceedings, National Conference on Social Work, 48th Annual Session (Milwaukee, 1921), p. 89.

52. Ibid., p. 90.

53. E. C. Branson, "The North Carolina Scheme of Rural Development," Proceedings, National Conference on Social Work, 46th Annual Session (Atlantic City, N.J., 1919), pp. 546–49; Howard W. Odum, "The County as a Basis of Social Work and Public Welfare in North Carolina," Proceedings, National Conference on Social Work, 53rd Annual Session (Cleveland, 1926), pp. 461–67; Jesse Frederick Steiner, "An Experiment in Rural Social Organization," Social Forces 5 (June 1927): 634–38.

54. Margaret Reeves, "The Indirect Responsibility of a State Department for Children," The Family 8 (July 1927): 168–71.

55. Louise Cottrell, "Organization Needed to Support and Free the Local Worker for Undifferentiated Case Work," Proceedings, National Conference on Social Work, 54th Annual Session (Des Moines, Iowa, 1927), pp. 118–22.

2
THE DEPRESSION, NEW DEAL YEARS, AND SOCIAL WORK PRACTICE IN RURAL COMMUNITIES

THE MAKINGS OF SOCIAL REFORM

The first two decades of the twentieth century were fraught with rural economic problems. During the years of World War I Americans produced bountiful food that saved much of Europe from starvation. Consequently, agricultural regions experienced a boom. Rural interest among the nation's welfare organizations had remained high during the war years, but after the war national attention to rural matters all but disappeared.

Euphoric feelings of peace and plenty captured the life of the cities. June Axinn and Herman Levin described the postwar urban prosperity:

> The years between the close of the war and the depression of the 1930s were a time of peace during which many Americans achieved individual prosperity. They found it through credit and installment buying and through participation in the glittering promises of speculation. They did not concern themselves with the problems of those brushed aside by society's advances, nor with the obvious abuse of power and influence by those who led the way in speculative activity. Despite the recession of 1921, urban standards of living moved up. Booming profits, high levels of employment, and rising real wages meant that Americans felt able to purchase and employ a flood of new products—cars, radios, home electricity, motion pictures, silk stockings.[1]

For the average urban dweller, the immediate postwar years provided a haven from hardships past. Levels of consumption rose and what was good for business appeared, at least on the surface, good for the nation.

But while urban dwellers were prospering and enjoying "new life in the doctrine of laissez-faire"[2] during the frenetic 1920s, rural areas were suffering and experiencing much economic turmoil. Robert Goldston wrote of those years:

> On the far side of Paradise during the golden decade lived the majority of American farmers and workers. Under the stimulus of war and post war demands for food, the American farmer had increased his yearly output by almost 15 percent. . . . But when European agriculture resumed production, the demand for American food products sharply declined. Farm income in the United States fell from $17.7 billion in 1919 to $10.5 billion in 1921. The farm price index fell, from 215 to 124 during the same period. And from this terrific slump American farmers did not recover.[3]

During this same period, miners were experiencing much strife in rural areas. Their efforts at unionization largely defeated, many were obliged to work for less than subsistence wages.

As the 1920s progressed, farm prices continued to fall but mortgages and taxes remained high. Furthermore, "adding social salt to the farmer's economic wounds was his feeling of being unaccountably 'left out' of American life."[4] When farmers sought help from the national government through their senators, Calvin Coolidge observed: "Farmers have never made money. I don't believe we can do much about it."[5]

The reform spirit that had characterized social work activity during the decade of World War I gave way to a new social work mood concerned not with social but with character reform. In the urban areas, social workers turned from political activity to Freudian analysis. In the rural areas, the time and situation did not permit a similar shift.

While the philosophical differences between the psychodynamically oriented urban workers and their socioeconomically concerned rural counterparts continued to grow for decades, the end result of the new 1920s casework emphasis was the long-term decline of community-oriented rural activity. Thanks to the contradictions of the frenetic 1920s (contradictions amply discussed by Chambers[6]), some voices did rise to call national attention to the plight of ruralites who were being left out of this national euphoria. Although the selections of the literature of the late 1920s stressed the difficulties of farmers, during the same years many other rural areas, particularly those that were rural industrial, were put on the map due to labor explosions. The textile mills of Gastonia and Marion, North Carolina, and Danville, Virginia, were scenes of terror and bloodshed.[7] The coal-mining regions of Kentucky and West Virginia saw union disagreements that culminated in the disintegration of the United Mine Workers (UMW) in West Virginia in 1924.[8] Strikes and bloodshed continued in Kentucky throughout the decade. Florence Reece, an eyewitness miner's wife, described the situation as follows while reminiscing with Kathy Kahn about the way in which she conceived the famous song "Which Side Are You On?":

> I was thirty when I wrote "Which Side Are You On?".
> We couldn't get a word out any way. So I just had to do
> something. . . . That's when I wrote the song. We didn't
> have any stationery 'cause we didn't get nothing. . . . So
> I just took the calendar off the wall and wrote . . .
>
> > If you go to Harlan County,
> > There is no neutral there,
> > You'll either be a union man
> > Or a thug for J. A. Blair
> > (Chorus)
> > Which side are you on?
> > Which side are you on?[9]

The situation grew increasingly worse until by early 1931, "Fred Croxton of the President's Emergency Committee called conditions so bad that they were almost unbelievable." During the first months of the Roosevelt administration, "Louis Stark, after a swing through several coal areas, declared that the situation in West Virginia was the worst in the nation."[10]

After 1929, when the depression that had affected rural areas for years spread throughout the nation, rural communities across the country became more angry and vociferous about their quandaries. Angry Iowan farmers blockaded highways and refused "to bring food into Sioux City for thirty days or until the cost of production had been obtained."[11] Farmers' Committees organized demonstrations protesting the foreclosure of mortgages. Frederick Lewis Allen writes of the farmers involved in the activities:

> They threatened judges in bankruptcy cases; in one case
> a mob dragged a judge from his courtroom, beat him,
> hanged him by the neck until he fainted—and all because
> he was carrying out the law.
>
> These farmers were not revolutionists. On the contrary, most of them were by habit conservative men.
> They were simply striking back in rage at the impersonal
> forces which had brought them to their present pass.[12]

It was in the context of these times of turmoil that the widespread social proposals of the New Deal, their accompanying emphasis on social welfare legislation, and consequently on social work activity, were brought about.

In 1927 Henry A. Wallace, editor of Wallace's Farmer and later secretary of Agriculture during the New Deal, presented to the National Conference on Social Work in Des Moines, Iowa, a paper entitled "Economic Problems of the Farmers."[13] This paper analyzed the roots of the financial problems of farmers and anticipated the strong regulatory thrust of many of the economic and social legislative acts of the New Deal, acts that brought about not only a radical shift in the nature and sponsorship of relief but also widespread employment of social workers outside city limits.

Another important anticipatory discussion of what was to come was provided by Grace Abbott, then chief of the Children's Bureau, before the same conference in 1927. In her paper "Developing Standards of Rural Child Welfare," Abbott summarized the economic and social conditions in which children found themselves in rural areas.[14] She condemned the lack of enforcement of much of the existing social legislation and the disparity of standards from county to county across the nation. The need for equalizing and bringing under public control the administration of basic social welfare measures in rural areas was highlighted by Abbott's intelligent comparisons:

> For both, city and country, the development of a well
> thought out program adapted to meet varying local needs
> is of fundamental importance. For both, efficient state
> departments of public welfare and public health are nec-
> essary.
> I hope it is clear that I am not suggesting that there is
> any royal road to a rural social welfare program. . . .
> At the present time there are those who are seeking to
> undermine all social welfare activities, to label as com-
> munistic mothers' pensions, child labor legislation, or
> efforts to save the lives of mothers and babies. . . .
> This would be very discouraging if we did not know some-
> thing of the history of the social reform movement.
> Fifty years ago public schools were attacked as social-
> istic, while thirty-seven years ago (1890) compulsory
> school laws were so described.[15]

Three other articles, precursors of what the New Deal was to bring about, are worth mentioning at this point. "Trends and Problems in Rural Social Work"[16] by Dwight Sanderson and "A Preface to Rural Social Work"[17] by W. W. Weaver were published in Rural

America in 1930 and 1932, respectively. They both emphasized the need for rural health and child welfare services, and strongly advocated the establishment of county social service units across the nation. "The Case for Federal Relief," written by Gifford Pinchot, an old-time country lifer and two-term governor of Pennsylvania (1923 to 1927 and 1931 to 1935), was a call for the most dramatic and influential piece of legislation that was to come and drastically change the delivery pattern of social work services to rural areas.[18] That was, of course, the Federal Emergency Relief Act of 1933:

> Is this nation, as a nation, to reach out a hand to help those of its people who through no fault of their own are in desperation and distress? Shall federal aid be granted in this great national crisis? It is not a question of ability to help. We are the richest nation on earth. If federal aid is needed, it can be granted. Congress has only to say the word. Shall the answer be yes or no?
>
> My answer is yes. To my mind it is the only possible answer. . . .
>
> This is not local crisis, no state crisis. It is nationwide. I can not believe that a national government will stand by while its citizens freeze and starve, without lifting a hand to help. I do not see how it can refuse to grant that relief which it is in honor, in duty and in its own interest bound to supply.[19]

SOCIAL WORKERS AND THE ABCs OF REFORM

One of the major impediments to governmental intervention throughout the years had been the citizenry's attitudes about acceptance of such measures. But the devastating effects of the depression were so obvious and pervasive that "everywhere there was agreement as to the necessity for more governmental action."[20]

What were some of the realities facing rural folk and forcing them to give up their long-held fears about government intervention? A study done by the Federal Emergency Relief Administration (FERA) in 1935 described the rural farm situation of 1933. The following report on the outcomes of that study appeared in Survey:

> In making the study of the depression's effects on rural workers, the FERA obtained data as of October 1933, on the occupations of male heads of rural households, both relief and non-relief, in communities under 2,500 population in forty-seven counties of nineteen states. The

study, it is believed, typifies rural occupational conditions for a large part of the nation. . . .

Of the employed heads of rural households on relief,
29 percent had shifted from the occupations they had usually followed before the depression, and most of these
men had gone one or more steps downward on the occupational ladder. Men who usually had owned farms now
were renting them or working on other men's farms as
laborers. Some were performing unskilled work in non-
agricultural industries. . . . Sharecroppers and tenants
who had given up their farms had dropped to the level of
farmhand or unskilled industrial laborer.[21]

Adding further descriptions of the indignities brought to these men by
the downward shift in the occupational ladder, the report concluded
that in spite of abandoning lifelong vocations, by 1933 it was found that
"these men had been unsuccessful in making an adequate living in their
new occupations and were obliged to accept relief."[22]

By the time Roosevelt came into office, government intervention in the social and economic affairs of the nation was minimal, accepted, and often even welcome in the rural areas that had learned
that the help of kin and neighbor would no longer suffice. Realistic
rural writers recognized this fact. Reminiscing in 1943 about the
earlier days of voluntary help in rural Nebraska, Tom A. Leadley,
editor of the Nebraska Farmer, and Louis W. Horne commented:

Since pioneer days on the midwest prairies, local aid for
victims of sickness, prairie fires, grasshoppers, bliz-
zards, drought and flood has been, for the most part,
just plain old-fashioned neighborliness. It has had its
roots not only in genuine human kindness but also in the
need to subdue a common enemy whose unpredictable ap-
pearance might lay low next year the family which last
year helped out a distressed neighbor.

Those were the days where a neighbor was judged pretty
much by his generosity to the fellow on the other side of
the tracks, to the hailed-out farmer in hill country, or to
any victims of uncontrollable circumstances which took
away loved ones, jobs, or means of livelihood. But outside the field of emergency aid, welfare needs and methods
have outgrown the "pass-the-hat" era, when the individual
looked after the unfortunates in a community.[23]

By 1933 it was clear that by and large the country was ready for
the ABCs of reform. On March 4, Franklin Delano Roosevelt was in-

augurated as president of the United States. His inaugural address stressed the need for immediate action. "There is nothing to do but to meet everyday's troubles as they come," he said to the nation. His actions indeed brought forth broad reforms of the social conditions of rural areas.

On March 16, 1933, Roosevelt sent to Congress the Agricultural Adjustment Act (AAA), which proposed a variety of means for government support of farm prices. William E. Leuchtenburg writes that "in framing a farm bill, Secretary of Agriculture Henry Wallace preferred the 'domestic allotment' plan developed by several economists . . . and advanced most persuasively by Milburn L. Wilson of Montana State College."[24] The domestic allotment plan proposed to pay farmers who restricted production. Their benefits would be based on parity and would allow those farmers to maintain the purchasing power they had before the war. Leuchtenburg further describes the bargaining process that preceded the passage of the AAA. Political mastery was the order of the day, and political mastery was what helped the controversial bill become law.

> Roosevelt had his own ideas about a satisfactory farm program—he disliked dumping, wanted decentralized administration, and stipulated the plan should obtain the consent of a majority of farmers—but above all, he insisted that farm leaders themselves agree on the kind of bill they wanted. In this fashion, he avoided antagonizing farm spokesmen by choosing one device in preference to another, and threw the responsibility for achieving a workable solution on the farm organizations.[25]

Historians of the period make it clear that there was great controversy around the bill. Many groups, including the McNary-Haugenites, were bitterly opposed to reducing acreage, but all groups were willing to bargain and so was the administration. "Wallace, who wanted a farm act before planting time, proposed an omnibus bill which would embody different alternatives."[26] As a result of all this maneuvering, the AAA, though amended by both progressives and conservatives, was passed in May.

Just as colorful is the background of the Civilian Conservation Corps (CCC). The passage of the CCC embodies some of Roosevelt's notions of the beneficial effects of country living and many of the still prevailing myths of earlier times about the character building effects of fresh air. Again, Leuchtenburg writes:

> Roosevelt was not indifferent to the plea of majors and county commissioners for federal assistance, but the

relief proposal closest to his heart had more special aims:
the creation of a civilian forest army to put the "wild boys
of the road" and the unemployed of the cities to work in
the national forests. On March 14, the President asked
four of his cabinet to consider the conservation corps idea,
a project which united his belief in universal service for
youth with his desire to improve the nation's estate. More-
over, Roosevelt thought that the character of city men would
benefit from a furlough in the country. The next day, his
officials reported back with a recommendation not only for
tree-army legislation but for public works and federal
grants to the states for relief. [27]

It is said that although Roosevelt disliked public works spending, the
social work advisers in his cabinet, Frances Perkins in Labor and
Harry Hopkins, as well as Senators La Follette (Wisconsin) and Costigan (Colorado) convinced him. On March 21 the Civilian Conservation Corps was proposed and became law eight days later.

On March 30, 1933, Congress passed a bill creating the Federal
Relief Administration to distribute, through state relief agencies,
$500 million of the federal treasury to help the needy. This historic
measure, which had also been heavily inspired by Perkins, Hopkins,
La Follette, and Costigan, broke the political resistance of those who
had clung to the belief that helping the poor was only a local responsibility. As Harry Hopkins, federal relief administrator, pointed out
to the National Conference on Social Work in 1933, the same social
workers who had carried the burden of relief in the private agencies
prior to the FERA, had "moved into public enterprises and are administering unemployment relief from one end of the country to another."[28] The consequences of the Federal Emergency Relief Administration for the spread of social services to the remotest corners
of the nation were amply documented and exceeded all expectations
of social workers and laymen alike.

Before discussing in depth the initial and long-lasting effects of
the Federal Emergency Relief Administration, it is important to make
reference to the impact of some of the other New Deal agencies that
had been created by the bills previously mentioned (the AAA and the
CCC). In a less forceful manner, these agencies also had repercussions on the social welfare activities of rural areas since they attempted to provide, in various forms, rural relief and/or monies for
farm rehabilitation. In his study of those agencies, Broadus Mitchell
explained:

The AAA was intended to help primarily commercial farmers, those raising sizable cash crops. Many of these were

sufficiently distressed, but generally they were distinguished from the five million families and single persons living on farms near destitution. Among these were owners of exhausted or otherwise submarginal land, often in parcels too small to support a family; part time farmers whose side occupations in lumbering or mining had disappeared; tenants of various grades running down to croppers; agricultural laborers, hundreds of thousands of whom had lost a better status because of debt, through the crop restriction program of the AAA, or from the competition of agricultural machinery, masses of them becoming migrants; and lastly a few million young people backed up on the farms because they could no longer find jobs in the cities. [29]

A similar opinion of the AAA was offered by H. L. Mitchell in Mean Things Happening in This Land. Mitchell described in colorful fashion the plight of the cotton sharecroppers of eastern Arkansas:

The sharecropper of Eastern Arkansas sometimes said that the mules they used had more sense than some men. In 1933 when the cotton was plowed up, the mules balked at walking on the cotton rows. Every mule, from the time he was put on the plow, had been taught that the cotton plant was sacred. If he got too close to the plants, his head was jerked and he was hit with the plow-line. During the plow-up, the mules were reported to have let out vociferous brays of protest. Some people . . . pointed out it didn't make sense to restrict cotton production when children lacked clothes, and families did not have enough sheets and pillow cases. . . . The program wrecked the already desperate lives of nearly a million sharecropper families who were no longer needed on the land; they were evicted and set adrift to roam the countryside, and crowd up with others in the small southern towns and cities. [30]

Mitchell, however, points out that some thought had been given to the protection of the sharecropper through an ambiguous Section 7 in the law. However, most opinions concur that the document was weak and essentially favored the landowner who had complete control over the enforcement of the contract with the government and who, more often than not, had no intention of ensuring reasonable outcomes for the tenants.

Whatever help came to migrants, sharecroppers, and landless rural dwellers came primarily from the Federal Emergency Relief

Administration and the Works Progress Administration (WPA), and not from the Agricultural Adjustment Act. Direct relief from the FERA was often combined with loans to buy seeds and implements, measures that were labeled rehabilitation. The Federal Emergency Relief Administration, which had started these rehabilitation measures in the southern states, broadened the practices in 1925, seeking to restore families to self-support. But because many lived on submarginal lands, the practices were often unsuccessful. Finally, the AAA and the FERA began buying land in these submarginal districts and transferring their dwellers to better soils. Broadus Mitchell summarized the final outcomes of this resettlement activity:

> In April 1935, the several sorts of federal rural social work were combined under the Resettlement Administration, whose main duties were to relocate farmers from 10,000,000 acres of submarginal land, and to rehabilitate other impoverished farmers where they were if the land justified the effort, thus gradually getting them off relief. [31]

The procedures, projects, and outcomes of the rural rehabilitation division of the FERA were reviewed for social workers by Lawrence Westbrook, assistant administrator of that agency, at the 1935 National Conference on Social Work in Montreal. Westbrook reflected the ongoing concern with creating a class of rural people dependent on relief to which Broadus Mitchell alluded.

> The American public is now having to support approximately a million farm families who are unable to make a living at the farm business which once sustained them and their fathers before them. The national government has undertaken what we term an exploratory program to try out various methods of removing these families from relief. The Federal Emergency Relief Administration organized a Rural Rehabilitation Division a year ago to start these destitute farmers on the road to recovery. [32]

According to Westbrook, administrative details were left to the various states, which proceeded to set up rural rehabilitation experiments with the cooperation of community advisory committees. Westbrook reported that at the end of the first year "some 20 percent of the one million families [which had been initially accepted as rehabilitants by the various states had] been started on the road to self-sufficiency." [33]

Whether the figures and improvements suggested by Westbrook and other federal officials who made speeches and presentations to assembled social workers throughout the country accurately reflected the situation is outside the scope of this book. It is not the purpose of this study to write an in-depth critique of the effectiveness of the New Deal legislation in relation to rural areas. What is important at this point is to note that the Federal Emergency Relief Administration involved rural social workers not only in the administration of assistance in the country but also in the determination, study, and support of the various efforts at rehabilitation and resettlement.

In 1934 Mary Irene Atkinson presented to the National Conference on Social Work in Kansas City a paper entitled "The Rural Community Program of Relief."[34] Atkinson's paper provided a detailed analysis of changes in the relief-giving structures and practices of local communities as a result of the advent of public monies. Atkinson provided virtually a state-by-state description of events immediately preceding and following the Federal Emergency Relief Act. She surveyed the states on two questions: the machinery utilized to administer local (and later federal) relief in rural areas and the attitudes of officials, lay citizens, and clients.

In describing the administrative organization of relief prior to 1932, she stated:

> In the majority of the forty-eight states, public money available for poor-relief purposes was administered by local officials, township trustees, county poor-boards, commissioners, over-seers of the poor, selectmen, etc., the official title varying with the geographical area, but the functions remaining practically the same. . . . Upon the basis of available data, it appears that prior to the participation of state and federal agencies in local relief programs, 35 percent of the United States had some form of machinery for carrying on country-wide welfare activities, but that the program was not completely operative even in the seventeen states which had made a beginning.[35]

Referring to the attitudes of officials and citizens prior to 1933, she suggested that:

> there was not a general realization of the fact that millions of local public funds were even then being spent in the country for a variety of poor-relief purposes; that the legislative basis for such relief expenditures was in many particulars almost a replica of the Elizabethan codes regarding the care of paupers; and that these public funds were being administered by untrained elective officials.[36]

As far as social work services in rural relief activities were concerned, Atkinson added:

> In hundreds of rural communities in this country, . . .
> the only exposure public officials and other citizens had to
> organized social work was through the medium of state departments of public welfare. In some of the states, as,
> for example, Mississippi and Arkansas, even this was
> lacking as there was practically nothing in the way of a
> state welfare program prior to the establishment of the
> emergency relief commission. [37]

Atkinson's review of the situation after 1933 helped her ascertain that the most common systems of relief administration were:
distribution of federal relief funds through already organized and developed county child welfare boards (for example, Alabama); or distribution of relief through a State Emergency Relief Administration with a board in each county, or with at least a county committee.
These state administrations often had either a regional or a county social service director and field staff (as in Florida, Pennsylvania, and Ohio). [38]

Some of the plans surveyed by Atkinson were quite ambitious and elaborate. In New Mexico, for example, the situation was as follows:

> In each county the county unit of the State Welfare Bureau
> is also the county administrative unit for federal relief.
> In those counties where permanent units had not been organized prior to the receipt of federal relief, new set-ups
> were instituted. The plan for the new units was the same
> as for the old units, namely, county welfare associations.
> The aim is to have a trained social worker in charge of
> each of the units.
>
> The impracticality of a state relief commission having
> to deal with the township trustees, selectmen, overseers
> of the poor etc., became immediately apparent when we
> were plunged into a large-scale relief-administration
> problem. Sheer necessity, therefore, has 1) pushed us
> toward the goal of county unification of welfare activities,
> 2) made it possible to provide social service in rural communities as a substitute for the haphazard methods of the
> local relief officials, and 3) through the possible participation of committees of lay persons and public officials in
> the emergency program, increased the opportunities

for interpretation of what constitutes a socialized public welfare program. [39]

On the issue of attitudes of officials, laypeople, and clients after 1933, Atkinson reported much ambivalence and an array of responses from resistance to support. In the following conclusions, Atkinson highlights the impact of the Federal Emergency Relief Act measures for the future of social work practice in rural communities. For social work was and has remained inextricably linked to relief administration in rural areas:

> It seems fair to conclude that the attitudes of local officials responsible for finances and for poor-relief administration and of the self-supporting lay public range from firm resistance to all aspects of the relief program to that of acceptance of the policies emanating from Washington and the various state capitals; that in spite of resistance or acceptance, people in rural communities have gained some conception of a new approach toward administration of relief by persons qualified by training and experience for the task; and that even in communities where local officials appear to be living for the day when the curtain can be rung down on the current scene, it will not be so easy to revert to the predepression techniques.
>
> The social worker who goes into a rural community which never before has had any social service except that given by elective officials and volunteers has placed upon her an unusual responsibility. The community's decision as to whether the county relief administration should be kicked out as soon as the subdivision can be freed from state and federal domination or whether it is something to carry forward depends to a large extent upon the way in which the social worker has interpreted the program and the attitudes she has created by her own personality. [40]

Atkinson's comprehensive treatment of relief administration in the rural United States included suggestions for social service planning beyond the New Deal years. Atkinson recognized the necessity of integrating social services into single units and the imperative of training generalist social workers for rural practice. She also expressed the hope that what the New Deal had started would be seminal efforts for the development of rural social services:

> As a result of our emergency administrations there are evidences in our rural areas which indicate the practica-

bility of integrating the various social welfare services in one unit in the locality too small to afford specialized activities. This would seem to indicate more rather than less generalized training for rural workers and a new philosophy regarding social planning.

It is fair to assume that many communities will make the cutover from an emergency relief administration to a long-time welfare program if there is sufficient leadership from the top and proper participation from the local communities.

It seems not too fantastic then, to hope, that under the leadership of the New Deal rural America will become something more than a place from which to move. [41]

LOCALITY SPECIFIC PRACTICE
FOR RURAL COMMUNITIES

The descriptive literature on the social work efforts initiated by the New Deal is extensive. Survey, The Family, Rural America, Social Forces, and Sociology and Social Research published many articles that had to do with the nature of the rural population receiving relief, [42] the migratory movements affecting rural areas during the depression, [43] and the impact of various pieces of legislation passed by an active and welfare-minded Congress. [44] Only a few of the articles then published can be mentioned here. Those selected highlight social work practice issues that have transcended those days.

In July 1934 Survey published a frank discussion by Esther Morris Douty, a case worker for the Chapel Hill County Board of Charities in North Carolina, entitled "FERA and the Rural Negro." Douty suggested that "probably the most fundamental change" in the life of southern blacks had come "from the fact that the FERA has given a measure of independence to a group tied for generations to the white landlord by the urgent need of food and shelter."[45] But should anyone think the move from dependence to independence was easy and unencumbered for southern black farming populations, Douty stressed the role of the social worker in the transitional period:

"Why should I feed my tenants," a landlord asked the other day, "when the Welfare can look after them? After all, I pay taxes. Other farmers are taking advantage of this federal money. Why shouldn't I? I need all the money I can get for myself." Another landlord will say, "Sam you'll have to get your food from the Welfare this year. I can't carry you; besides, if the Welfare furnishes your rations,

maybe you can work off last year's debt to me." Argue as
the case worker will, the landlord stands pat. His tenants
can move, feed themselves, or get help from the Welfare
office. Since a landlord who will "carry" his tenant is difficult to find, moving rarely helps the situation and as the
tenant cannot feed himself, the burden falls on the local relief agency. Although this attitude of the landlords is socially irresponsible and economically warped, it serves,
nevertheless, to weaken further the chain binding tenant to
landowner. [46]

The role of the rural social worker was beginning to shift from
mere dispenser of benefits to interpreter of policies, advocate and
supporter of social reform. Furthermore, Douty's discussion began
to make it clear that the social worker in a rural area required
greater familiarity with the environmental conditions of the particular
locale than did her urban counterpart. A worker unfamiliar with the
norms and unwritten codes of southern landlords and tenants would
have found it extremely difficult to intervene effectively as an interpreter of social legislation.

There were other articles that also highlighted the theme of locality specific practice for social work in rural areas. In "Rural Relief Administration in the Northwest," Raymond Thompson deals with
the problems of relief administration given the unique characteristics
of a topographically rough Idaho county where only a third was tillable
soil, a county where help was needed for people who had depended on
the lumbering industry, either by logging off their lands or securing
employment in sawmills or logging camps. The social workers had
to be tuned to the needs and idiosyncrasies of those people. As Thompson suggested, referring to those early rural relief workers, "Yes,
we're pioneering in a country where they [the clients] pioneered before." [47]

Paul H. Landis also stressed the relationship between rural
social work and community mores. In stressing local mores he not
only underscored the locality specific aspects of the practice but also
other basic social work principles that are easy to forget in relief
work (such as respect for the dignity and integrity of the client):

If I were going into a run-of-the-mill county as director,
my first act, after I got the lay of the land, would be to
call the social work staff, case-work supervisors and investigators into counsel to try to impress on them my own
firm belief, that about the most important job in the United
States these days is to maintain the self respect of our people who are on relief through no fault of their own. [48]

From all corners of the nation poured the discussions of locality-specific knowledge, whether it be cultural patterns of the people, topography of the terrain, means of rural subsistence, and so forth. From the Missouri hills, Elizabeth E. A. Gissal reported what a student had observed:

My memory of rural life was colored by what I knew of northern Ohio, where the commercial and truck farms are very different from the small, poverty-stricken, and forlorn patches of planting up and down the lopsided hills and valleys of Missouri. . . .

Not only is the country-side poverty stricken but each community has a certain isolation and aloofness which the case worker must understand.[49]

From the Northwest wrote Samuel and Jeanette Gerson:

There is one more set of false assumptions that should be mentioned before we go on to describe some experiments in orienting the rural worker. They may be summed up in the belief that, having a knowledge of rural life in one section of the country, a worker is thereby qualified to undertake social service in any rural area. With all their variations, cities are standardized in comparison with rural areas. The conditions facing the farmer of diversified crops in Ohio, the truck farmer of New Jersey, the corn farmer of Iowa and the wheat farmer of the Dakotas are different in important ways. . . . Climate plays a leading role in this drama. . . . The social worker needs to know what it means to say that the mean annual rain fall at Bismarck, North Dakota has been about 16 inches, whereas in Illinois it runs about 37.[50]

All these articles stressed directly or indirectly the relationship between rural sociology and social work practice in rural communities.[51] Gertrude Vaile wrote "The Contributions of Rural Sociology to Family Social Work" in June 1933.[52] Whether rural sociology courses did cover all the content that Vaile deemed necessary background for rural practice might have been questioned. She did, however, provide suggestions of topics that constituted, in her view, essential knowledge to be covered:

Perhaps the greatest contribution of sociology lies in that detailed, many sided analysis of the rural culture within which the family life is set and which the social worker needs to know if she is to be intelligent in working with rural families. Any rural social worker who has not had good courses in rural sociology needs to do considerable reading covering the following subjects: the economic foundations of the rural community life, based as it is on the single occupation of farming and services to farmers; the way the family farm system brings the entire family into participation in the occupation . . .; the relations between the open country and the little town and what they may mean to the life of each of the two parts of the rural community; the major rural institutions, the church, the school, the agricultural and civic organizations, the local government. [53]

Although owing to the period in which she was writing Vaile concentrated only on farming as a means of rural subsistence, she did recognize the importance of understanding not only the open country but also the rural town:

Rural life includes not only life in the open country but also in the country town. On the whole, there seems to be a larger number of families who need the help of social work in the village than in the open country. [54]

RURAL SOCIAL WORK OR SOCIAL WORK IN RURAL COMMUNITIES? CHARACTERISTICS OF THE RURAL WORKER

The increased social work activity in rural areas resulting from the depression problems and the New Deal legislation served to intensify among practitioners a discussion that although of long standing had not had the same impact before. At its core was the question of whether the application of the basic principles and processes of social work in urban and rural settings was different or the same. There were essentially two opposing camps in this debate.

One point of view, perhaps best represented by Josephine C. Brown and Josephine Strode, argued that rural social work was unique, if not in essence, certainly in form. In 1933 Brown wrote The Rural Community and Social Casework. In this book, which became a classic, Brown stated that although the basic casework method was universal, it required adaptations when applied to the rural locale:

The social case worker in the rural community will find that, while the fundamental principles of case work are

the same whether she works in city, town, village, or open
country, there are certain modifications in method which
may be advisable in making an adjustment to rural conditions. [55]

The question of what those adjustments were, however, was addressed
by Brown in a pragmatic manner rather than a theoretical way. She
listed specific characteristics of rural populations and communities,
as well as specific pieces of information regarding the rural environment (for example, county maps, existence or nonexistence of social
service exchanges, farm bureaus, and so on) with which the social
worker should be familiar.

Brown also discussed the specific locality-relevant referents
of rural practice and the personal and professional characteristics of
a good rural worker:

> The rural worker . . . should have initiative, ingenuity
> in developing resources . . . she should be willing to ef-
> face herself and to let others take credit for accomplish-
> ments in which she has had a share. . . . Executive ability
> of a high order, good judgment and vision are essential. . . .
>
> Experience with rural life is of undoubted value. This
> background, however, has been found unnecessary by
> workers of special adaptability and imaginative powers
> who have made up for the lack by study, reading and ob-
> servation. [56]

On the issue of whether a rural social worker needed to have
been born in a rural area, Brown stated:

> It is not desirable, even if it were possible, to limit the
> contribution of social workers with rural background to
> rural communities, nor that of city-bred workers to
> cities. Each group has an important contribution to make
> to the other, and this fact should be taken into account if
> a social worker with city background is being considered
> for the position. [57]

On this point, however, there was some disagreement between Brown
and authors such as Herman M. Pekarsky who suggested:

> To Miss Brown's foundation qualities for the rural social
> worker I would add a further stone: a native philosophy
> indigenous to the soil. In other words I would recruit
> rural social workers from rural people, from those born

on the soil, with an innate respect for the man who lives by it.[58]

Another advocate of the uniqueness of form of social work in rural areas was Josephine Strode of Kansas. Strode's pieces of professional grass-roots wisdom are still well remembered by those who worked in rural areas during the Depression and New Deal years.[59] Strode's folksy and plainspoken articles were published in Survey from October 1938 onward.[60] Strode was not engrossed in method but in rurality, and in contrast to Brown, whose training showed in her writing, Strode was able to remain "one of the group" in spite of her training. Strode's articles, cast as letters to Miss Bailey, Survey's itinerant observer of social work in the country, were a treasure of humor and reality.[61] On the matter of differences between rural and urban practice, she wrote:

> Rural social workers, too, must go at their problems realistically in terms of the situation, resources available, and their own abilities. Because rural work is different—and it really is, . . .—I was glad to know this past summer of a job analysis being made of the duties of county social workers in rural areas.[62]

But when it came to naming what those real differences were, Strode, like Brown, listed adaptations of the method to the rural locale rather than differences in the essence of the practice. She stressed: 1) The generalist or undifferentiated nature of rural practice:

> The rural social worker has no segments in her job. She must be administrator, community interpreter and organizer as well as case worker for a multiplicity of social services.[63]

2) The importance of knowing about the specific region, its people and idiosyncrasies, that is, the importance of locality specific knowledge:

> An important consideration in any program of rural publicity is the tempo of rural life. Things can't be done in a hurry. Farmers are accustomed to waiting six months or longer for a crop. In western Kansas, we've been waiting six years![64]

3) The value of peerlike rather than authoritylike professional relationships:

> Because of their roots in our democratic pioneer life, our
> rural people dislike class distinctions and anything that
> makes for differences. [65]

4) The importance of active community participation in any decision-making process:

> A rural social worker who was unable to get the interest
> of his community group told me how he finally figured out
> the reason for his failure. He knew all about the value of
> cooperation, and the necessity of carrying the community
> and county commissioners with him, but his most ingrati-
> ating efforts fell flat. It was only as he thought through his
> failure that he realized he had been trying to carry the
> group in his way, instead of facilitating the group thinking
> from which—and only from which—could come true group
> decisions. [66]

On the debate of whether social work practice in rural areas
was different or the same, the point of view opposite that of Brown
and Strode was argumentatively and strongly represented by people
like Carol L. Shafer of Wisconsin, who opposed the need to "categorize
workers into an urban and rural species."[67] Shafer denied that geographic locale was a determinant of uniqueness of method. Problems
for the likes of Shafer were universal:

> Rural and urban, between which the border is never cer-
> tain, are only two determinants among many others of
> greater strength. The uniqueness of the individual and dif-
> ferentiated treatment are principles of case work which
> need no redefining for the rural field. [68]

As to the notion of adaptation of the basic method for the rural
field that Brown had so strongly advocated, Shafer responded:

> It has been said that the rural field requires re-adaptation
> of fundamental social work philosophy and techniques, a
> new application of accumulated experience, principles and
> practice is under way, but does not that process occur
> everywhere and constantly? Is it not one of social work's
> middle names? To maintain that the rural field is unique
> in its needs and treatment requirements seems to me an
> unworthy position needlessly dissipating our efforts. [69]

Although the controversy of whether social work in rural areas
was the same as in urban areas continued, a close adaptation or an

altogether different field was never settled. It appears that after 1935 the issue subsided, and that the view of Brown, who had by then acquired national notoriety as undersecretary to Harry Hopkins, prevailed. Yet by 1935 it had been firmly established that social work required important adaptations for the rural locale.

DIFFERENTIATED OR UNDIFFERENTIATED PRACTICE FOR RURAL COMMUNITIES

Another issue also discussed by practitioners during the Depression and New Deal years was that of undifferentiated or generalist versus differentiated or specialist practice. Brown and Strode had taken clear stands in favor of undifferentiated practice for rural areas. There were others, however, who disagreed. They were principally practitioners ingrained in the specialized traditions of East Coast practice, where the voluntary agencies with their highly specialized areas of endeavor had been the prevailing model.

The opposers of undifferentiated practice ranged from the rather mild ones, who wanted to caution against too much "undifferentiation,"[70] to the very adamant[71] and poetic ones, who expressed their opposition firmly or even in poetry:

> dear boss
> i just finished miss brown's book
> and i dont wanna be
> a rural case worker
> on account of i dont claim
> to be a superwoman. . . .
> moreover
> boss what worker
> could possibly have
> all those qualifications
> laid down by miss brown. . . .
> by the time she learned
> how to be a bookkeeper
> treasurer stenographer
> file clerk statistician
> case record writer . . .
> amateur farmer psychologist
> fund collector and interpreter . . .
> and has six years in college
> with courses in agriculture
> and farm management . . .
> what i mean is boss she would be
> very aged no less. [72]

However, Brown's and Strode's statements for undifferentiated practice were so well founded on the study and observation of the elements of rural life, that by the end of the New Deal years no one was arguing any longer about the appropriateness of undifferentiated rural practice.

TRAINING RURAL WORKERS

The training required for practice in the rural field was a question of concern from the times of the first Country Life Commission. The American Country Life Association held meetings and institutes for rural workers as early as 1910, when a summer session was offered at the Massachusetts Agricultural College in Amherst. In 1922 Josephine Brown discussed the personal traits and technical expertise required of rural workers, hinting at the need for special preparation for the rural field. [73] Surveys on the place and importance of rural sociology and rural economics in the curriculum were carried out in the 1920s and early 1930s, [74] but it was not until the Federal Emergency Relief Act began to be implemented that questions of special training for rural workers were seriously raised.

The administration of relief in remote counties necessitated the employment of local personnel. More often than not, these indigenous workers, who came from all walks of life, had little formal education. How could they be prepared for the stresses of those demanding positions? Local relief administrators were baffled with a variety of questions: What kind of training should be provided to relief workers? Were they, in the fashion of the day, doing "casework," and if so, how should their natural abilities be enhanced? What should be the duration of training? Where should it take place? Who should be selected for it?, and many more. Through its division of training and research, the Federal Emergency Relief Administration made available sums of money for the training of its workers. Short-term institutes and seminars were held in rural localities. Supervision was intensely used as a teaching tool and workers were sent, often out of their rural states, to the schools of social work that generally were located in large cities.

Out of this frenetic training activity came a number of descriptions and conclusions. The remedies were as varied as the problems, but at least the idea that rural workers required "something special" was firmly established. A lot was argued about the validity of training away from the rural locale. Generally, research showed that any training was better than no training at all. Much was said about offering training in the land-grant colleges and universities, which were, after all, naturals for the task. There was much argument about the level of training (graduate or undergraduate) and the content of it (general or job related). Descriptions of experiments for the training of relief and Federal Emergency Relief Administration workers were abundant. Many articles and pamphlets were published by the Federal Emergency Relief Administration's division of research. They described various ways in which schools of social work and local Federal Emergency Relief Administration training departments attempted to tackle the development of rural workers.

In "An Experiment in Training for Rural Social Work," Lucille Cairns discussed the short course offered by the University of Missouri beginning in 1934, designed "to attract native rural young people of university training."[75] The training project had been sponsored by the division of women's work of the Missouri Civil Works Administration, worked out by the rural sociology department of the university, and financed by the State Relief Commission. For this course, students were selected by each county through a committee formed by the chairman of the relief committee, a physician, the county superintendent of schools, the home demonstration and agricultural agents, a prominent farmer, and a prominent farm woman. The students had degrees ranging from a B.S. to a Ph.D. and many had been teachers. Courses were arranged for a period of ten weeks, to cover about ten graduate credit hours and concentrated on casework and relief administration rather than on rural content. Cairn's description leads one to infer that the short course was job related.

A similar example of training was described by Mary Lois Pyles in "Learning with our FERA's."[76] It had taken place at Washington University in St. Louis and involved 100 selected Federal Emergency Relief Administration workers from nine states. Pyles's statements point out that at least initially many rural workers experienced discomfort upon encountering an urban training environment:

> The fears of difference between rural and urban work and
> case work and relief decreased during the semester. As
> the students found familiar material in class discussion
> and field experience they realized that here was oppor-
> tunity for help with problems faced back home. . . . Some
> felt discouraged about returning to work in communities
> without . . . resources. [77]

Some of the important points mentioned by Pyles continue to plague present-day practitioners. This is true especially in rural areas where, as has already been stated, public social welfare provisions, particularly relief, often constitute the crux of the social services offered by the community:

Relief practices were of paramount importance because of
the student's past experience and expectation to return to
the public relief field. There seemed to be inconsistencies
between case work and relief policies. . . . An understanding of case work philosophy helped work out some of
the questions about clients who lie, conceal resources,
and stir up trouble in the community. . . .
  Then doesn't that take us into other fields of responsibility? Suppose meeting the need of the family means getting the community to understand the need and the family
a little better? Suppose the community needs to understand the agency better. [78]

Besides Pyles's, there were many other articles that stressed
in-service training efforts, [79] the accomplishments of short courses,
or the importance of supervision as a training tool. [80] Perhaps worth
singling out as descriptive of an innovative approach was an article
by Mary F. Bogue and Magdalen Peters entitled "Two Experiments in
Training for Supervisory Personnel in New York. "[81] This article described a project in which the New Jersey division of the Federal
Emergency Relief Administration joined forces with the New York
School of Social Work to develop a training unit in which enrolled students were mixed with employed FERA personnel from rural counties.
The experiment attempted to underscore the contribution that indigenous
rural workers who possessed a great deal of locality specific knowledge
could make to the training of workers in an academic setting. Although
the experiment was a commendable attempt to remedy the underutili-
zation of rural workers with less than broadly recognized academic
certification in the training of new rural personnel, the idea, for the
most part, did not catch on rapidly.
  Toward the end of the New Deal years, the literature began to
reflect, even if in a sporadic or scanty fashion, the concerns of educators who were asking broader questions about training for the rural
field. Those educators wondered about what was to become of rural
training once the Federal Emergency Relief Administration efforts
subsided, and wanted to make recommendations about content for
future, less job-related training programs. Once again Pekarsky offered his comments:

The weakness of rural social work is one of the several
disturbing realities of the American scene exposed by the
operations of the FERA. . . . For two years in the face of
local lethargy and sometimes open opposition, the FERA
pushed steadily. . . .

Now the federal pressure for standards is gone, but the
real job remains, requiring not only the best technical
skills of social workers but the capacity to interpret and
develop pressures from within the community, without
which the job cannot be done. [82]

Pekarsky wanted to plot a "training cycle for rural workers." He felt
the FERA had accomplished a first set of goals. Beyond those, he
could see some general aims with a less "clearly plotted" course:

The subject matter of this part of the training course would
differ with different sections of the country, but there are,
it seems to me, certain essentials which can be outlined.
There should be, first of all, study of the history of the
particular region, its economic development in relation
to its natural resources and the influence of both on the
influx of certain ethnic groups in its population. With this
should go detailed study of the social institutions of the region and the small communities—the grange, rural school
and church, women's organizations and so on. [83]

A. A. Smick added to Pekarsky's recommendations in "Training for Rural Social Work." [84] Smick departed from the premise that
the adaptations of the social work method for the rural locale were so
great and essential that it was imperative to develop schools of "rural
social work":

It is rather presumptuous to suppose that a student trained
in an urban environment, with its specialized social agencies, will learn to recognize and make use of the different
types of social forces and resources available in a rural
area. . . . How often a social work program in a rural
area has met with violent opposition because the worker,
trained in an urban environment, has lacked this knowledge
and understanding! [85]

Smick recommended that given the position of leadership that the
land-grant colleges had established in the rural field, schools for
rural social work would be well advised to grow from them:

It would seem little short of tragic if we should now fail
to take advantage of the opportunity of providing leadership in this field of social work through the establishment
of graduate schools of rural social work in our land-grant
colleges. [86]

Smick's advice was to become the center of bitter controversies in the 1940s.

As far as content for the programs of these proposed schools, Smick urged that there should be, first, "courses in the principles, methods and techniques of rural social work, designed to give the worker a technical background and a professional approach to his work."[87] Second, he proposed a series of supplementary "courses in rural sociology, home economics, farm management and related subjects" designed to give the student a thorough understanding of rural areas. Third, Smick called for "supervised field work in a rural area"[88] designed to help students apply their theoretical training to rural conditions.

Smick's ambitious recommendations ended with the charge that the proposed graduate school of rural social work "assume the role of leadership in developing social service agencies and resources" for the rural areas they would serve. He was convinced that if those schools did not evolve by the end of the depression emergency, they would not develop for years to come, and anticipated that it would take another emergency to accomplish the task.

NOTES

1. June Axinn and Herman Levin, Social Welfare: A History of the American Response to Need (New York: Harper & Row, 1975), pp. 136-37.

2. Ibid., p. 137.

3. Robert Goldston, The Great Depression (Greenwich, Conn.: Fawcett, 1968), pp. 18-19.

4. Ibid., p. 19.

5. Ibid.

6. Clarke A. Chambers has discussed the contradictions of the 1920s: "It was a Jazz Age and an Age of Sobriety; a Golden Decade when two thirds of the families of the land lived below a margin of health and decency." Seedtime of Reform: American Social Service and Social Action, 1918-1933 (St. Paul: University of Minnesota Press, 1963), p. 235.

7. Ibid., pp. 238-39. A description of the role of social workers in this and other rural-industrial disputes was provided in a strongly prolabor and feminist article by Florence Kelley, "Our Newest South," Survey 62 (June 15, 1929): 342-44.

8. Irving Bernstein, The Lean Years: A History of the American Worker 1920-1933 (Cambridge, Mass.: Riverside, 1960), p. 382.

9. Kathy Kahn, Hillbilly Women (New York: Avon, 1973), p. 9. Lyrics of "Which Side Are You On" courtesy of Florence Reece, Knoxville, Tenn.

10. Bernstein, The Lean Years, p. 382.

11. Frederick Lewis Allen, Since Yesterday (New York: Harper & Row, 1968), p. 382.

12. Ibid., p. 69.

13. Henry A. Wallace, "Economic Problems of the Farm," Proceedings, National Conference on Social Work, 54th Annual Session (Des Moines, Iowa, 1927), pp. 19-26.

14. Grace Abbott, "Developing Standards of Rural Child Welfare," Proceedings, National Conference on Social Work, 54th Annual Session (Des Moines, Iowa, 1927), pp. 26-37.

15. Ibid., p. 37.

16. Dwight Sanderson, "Trends and Problems in Rural Social Work," Rural America 8 (January 1930): 3-6.

17. W. W. Weaver, "A Preface to Rural Social Work," Rural America 10 (January 1932): 5-6.

18. Gifford Pinchot, "The Case for Federal Relief," Survey 67 (January 1, 1932): 347-49, 390.

19. Ibid., pp. 347, 390.

20. Axinn and Levin, Special Welfare, p. 165.

21. Joanna C. Colcord and Russell H. Kurtz, "Dislocated Farm Folk," Survey 71 (August 1935): 246.

22. Ibid.

23. Tom A. Leadley and Louis W. Horne, "Riding the Range Again," Survey 79 (September 1943): 241.

24. William E. Leuchtenburg, Franklin D. Roosevelt and the New Deal, 1932-1940 (New York: Harper Torchbooks, 1963), p. 48.

25. Ibid.

26. Ibid., p. 49.

27. Ibid., p. 52.

28. Harry L. Hopkins, "The Developing National Program of Relief," Proceedings, National Conference on Social Work, 60th Annual Session (Detroit, 1933), p. 65.

29. Broadus Mitchell, Economic History of the United States Depression Decade (New York: Rinehart, 1947), p. 208.

30. H. L. Mitchell, Mean Things Happening in This Land (Montclair, N.J.: Allanheld, Osmun, 1979), pp. 41-42.

31. Broadus Mitchell, Economic History of the United States, p. 210.

32. Lawrence Westbrook, "Getting Them Off Relief," Proceedings, National Conference on Social Work, 62nd Annual Session (Montreal, 1935), p. 618.

33. Ibid., p. 621.

34. Mary Irene Atkinson, "The Rural Community Program of Relief," Proceedings, National Conference on Social Work, 61st Annual Session (Kansas City, 1934), pp. 166-77.

35. Ibid., p. 166.

36. Ibid.

37. Ibid., p. 169.

38. Ibid., p. 170.

39. Ibid., p. 171.

40. Ibid., p. 177.

41. Ibid.

42. See, for example, Henry A. Wallace, "The Farmer and Social Discipline," Rural America 12 (January 1934): 3-7; Irving Lorge, "Farmers on Relief," Survey 73 (November 1938): 348-49, with extensive references to monographs of the Federal Emergency Relief Administration and the Works Progress Administration.

43. T. J. Woofter, Jr., "Rural Relief and the Back to the Farm Movement," Social Forces 14 (March 1936): 381-88.

44. To interpret the New Deal government machinery, Survey set up a department of emergency information edited by Johanna C. Colcord and Russell H. Kurtz of the Russell Sage Foundation. See Survey 10 (1934), nos. 1 through 12.

45. Esther Morris Douty, "FERA and the Rural Negro," Survey 70 (July 1934): 215.

46. Ibid., p. 216.

47. Raymond Thompson, "Rural Relief Administration in the Northwest," The Family 16 (June 1935): 117-18.

48. Paul H. Landis, "If I Were A County Relief Director," Survey 71 (July 1935): 209.

49. Elizabeth E. A. Gissal, "Truly Rural," The Family 14 (July 1933): 156.

50. Samuel and Jeanette Gerson, "The Social Worker in the Rural Community," The Family 16 (January 1936): 263.

51. See also Vocille M. Pratt, "The Significance for the Caseworker of Rural Cultural Patterns," The Family 19 (March 1938): 14-19.

52. Gertrude Vaile, "The Contributions of Rural Sociology to Family Social Work," The Family 14 (June 1933): 106-10.

53. Ibid., p. 106.

54. Ibid., p. 108.

55. Josephine C. Brown, The Rural Community and Social Casework (New York: Family Welfare Association of America, 1933), p. 91.

56. Ibid., pp. 70-71.

57. Ibid., p. 68.

58. Herman H. Pekarsky, "Rural Training for Rural Workers," Survey 72 (April 1936): 104.

59. Mattie Cal Maxted, a former Oklahoma Federal Emergency Relief Administration supervisor and Arkansas educator of long-standing, first directed me to Strode's writing as having been some of the most helpful and down-to-earth articles she had encountered in her rural career. (Taped interviews with Mattie Cal Maxted by the writer, Fayetteville, Arkansas, December 1977).

60. Josephine Strode, "Social Work at the Grass Roots" and "An Open Letter to Miss Bailey: Rural Social Workers Do Everything," Survey 74 (October 1938): 307-9; "Publicity by Way of the Barn Door," 74 (November 1938): 345-47; "Learning from the Job," 74 (December 1938): 380-81; "Getting Along with the Bosses," 75 (January 1939): 13-14; "Old Folks Are Like That," 75 (February 1939): 41-42; "Beef Prunes and Ink Blots and Other Aspects of Aid to Dependent Children," 75 (March 1939): 76-77; "Swinging the Depression with the Killer-Dillers, Hot-Shots, and Alligators," 75 (April 1939): 108-10; and "Tighten the Corner Where You Are," 75 (May 1939): 138-39.

61. Beginning in March 1933, Gertrude Springer wrote a feature column of social work observations that Survey published as "Miss Bailey's" commentaries until June 1944. One of Miss Bailey's originals appears in the Appendix.

62. Strode, "An Open Letter to Miss Bailey: Rural Social Workers Do Everything," p. 307.

63. Strode, "Learning from the Job," p. 380.

64. Strode, "Publicity by Way of the Barn Door," p. 345.

65. Ibid., p. 346.

66. Strode, "Learning from the Job," p. 380.

67. Carol L. Shafer, "This Rural Social Work," Survey 75 (May 1939): 136.

68. Ibid., p. 137.

69. Ibid., p. 136.

70. See, for example, L. Josephine Webster, "Undifferentiated Casework for a Rural Community," The Family 10 (November 1929): 216-17.

71. E. Kathryn Pennypacker, "No One Can Do Everything," Survey 75 (December 1939): 369-71.

72. Marilla Rettig, "why i do not think i would make a good rural case worker," Survey 72 (January 1936): 15.

73. Josephine C. Brown, "A City Case Worker in the Country," The Family 3 (December 1922): 187.

74. See, for example, Edmund de S. Brunner, "The Teaching of Rural Sociology and Rural Economics and the Conduct of Rural Social Research in Teachers' Colleges, Schools of Religion and Non-State Colleges," Social Forces 9 (October 1930): 54-57.

75. Lucille Cairns, "An Experiment in Training for Rural Social Work," The Family 16 (June 1935): 114-17.

76. Mary Lois Pyles, "Learning with our FERA's," The Family 16 (January 1936): 281-84.

77. Ibid., p. 281.

78. Ibid., p. 283.

79. Josephine C. Brown, "In Service Training for Public Welfare, the Whys and Whats," Survey 74 (October 1938): 210; and "In Service Training for Public Welfare, the Hows," 74 (November 1938): 347-48.

80. Minnie Alper, "Supervision in A Rural Setting," Proceedings, National Conference on Social Work, 66th Annual Session (Buffalo, N.Y., 1939), pp. 295-303.

81. Mary F. Bogue and Magdalen Peters, "Two Experiments in Training for Supervisory Personnel in New Jersey," The Family 16 (February 1936): 295-301.

82. Pekarsky, "Rural Training for Rural Workers," p. 104.

83. Ibid.

84. A. A. Smick, "Training for Rural Social Work," Sociology and Social Research 22 (July 22, 1938): 538-44.

85. Ibid., p. 539.

86. Ibid., p. 540.

87. Ibid.

88. Ibid., p. 543.

3

THE DEFENSE YEARS, THE WAR, AND POSTWAR PROGRAMS: SOCIAL AND ECONOMIC CHANGES OF RURAL LIFE

SOCIAL SECURITY, THE CHILDREN'S BUREAU, AND RURAL SERVICES

The end of the Federal Emergency Relief Administration in 1935 coincided with the beginning of the Social Security Administration, which further and more permanently established social work in rural areas. The county social security offices took over the provision of services for the aged, the unemployed, and children, and continued to stress the professional standards that the Federal Emergency Relief Administration had initiated. Although neither farmers nor farm workers were covered by the Old-Age and Survivors Insurance (OASI) provisions of the Social Security Act as initially passed in 1935, the Social Security Act public assistance programs for children, the needy, and aged, and the blind were open to farm workers on the same basis as to any other person. *

The administration of the public assistance provisions of the Social Security Act meant careful overseeing of county practices by state offices (home offices) and visiting workers.[1] The law itself and the bulletins for its interpretation continued to stress improvements in the practices of relief administration throughout the nation. In an article entitled "General Welfare and Social Security Legislation," Helen I. Clarke stressed some of those improvements:

> By provision for fair hearings Congress ensured that certain designated groups of persons should have a right to assistance if needed. Local prejudice should not be the final

---

*Amendments in 1950, 1954, 1956, and 1958 made several million farmers and farm workers eligible for OASI.

arbiter of need. In fact, then, the public assistance provisions of the Social Security Act do assume [that] individuals coming under the designated categories [have] a
right to a minimum standard of living. The provisions
of the act concerning the confidential nature of the relationships of agency and client further put into effect our
democratic theory that each man's home is his castle and
safe from intrusion.[2]

The Social Security Act not only extended relief benefits but
also vastly improved and increased child welfare services. E. Kathryn Pennypacker wrote in Survey:

It seems to me that the provisions of the Social Security
Act applying to child welfare, were the crystallization of
the "best thinking" of the country in regard to the unmet
needs of children in rural areas.[3]

Although the Social Security Act was criticized for dividing services to children between two administrative bodies, with aid to dependent children assigned to the Social Security Board and the development of special services assigned to the Children's Bureau, the
fact was that the Children's Bureau took up the task of "developing
child welfare services in predominantly rural areas,"[4] and by 1940
"federal funds, administered by the Bureau, were providing a major
part of the cost of child welfare services in 512 rural counties and in
ten New England areas composed of some sixty-nine 'towns.'"[5]

County Social Security offices and Children's Bureau offices
continued to require trained personnel for the rural areas. The Children's Bureau was often indicted for having developed an "aristocracy
of personnel and services."[6] On this matter, Gertrude Springer commented:

The Children's Bureau is fully aware of this criticism
but is not greatly disturbed by it. Its franchise, it main-
tains, is to demonstrate the efficiency of modern case
work in terms of actual rural community development no
less than of actual service. The values of qualified personnel, adequate salaries, controlled case loads, and
freedom for the exercise of initiative are all part of that
demonstration.[7]

Springer emphasized the role of the bureau in making the highest standard of social work its norm and the best of qualified workers its standard practice:

It is too early to attempt any precise measure of the effect of the child welfare services on the slowly changing pattern of rural social organization. But that the steady effort has penetrated into rural life and has been fruitful seems clearly established by the record of the past five years. From this record the services emerge today as the hero—or should it be the heroine?—of the story, as far as it has gone, of the long struggle to develop modern social work programs and practice in rural America. [8]

RURAL TRAINING AND THE ACCREDITATION DILEMMA

By the time of World War II, and because of the continuity of demand for trained personnel presented by the Social Security law, the professional schools of social work were aware of the need for rural training and a few were offering it in their programs. Committed rural observers such as William E. Cole of the University of Tennessee thought that this move on the part of the schools had been reluctant rather than spontaneous:

This regime [rural training] was, as a practical necessity, forced upon the schools, because until the depression and the passage of the Social Security Act, and the attendant state and local welfare organizations set up or approved to administer categorical assistance, there was little firm demand for trained social workers in the rural field. By 1940, however, there were 70,000 social and welfare workers in urban areas and 12,000 in rural areas and by this time rural social work had become an important segment of the profession. [9]

The University of Chicago, for example, integrated rural material into its curriculum, established a rural field work center, [10] and served as the motivating force for the publication of Grace Browning's book, [11] Rural Public Welfare: Selected Records, in 1941. The University of Minnesota continued to offer its rural work short-courses with great success, and other schools exhibited similar efforts.

However, to the dismay of many observers and in spite of the profession's interest in rural training, the connection between the agricultural and mechanical colleges and the preparation of rural practitioners that Smick called for in 1938 (and that was discussed in Chapter 2) never materialized. [12] In many ways, the failure to connect with the agricultural and mechanical colleges and their well-established rural connections spelled, at worst, the demise, and at best, the retreat of rural training into a 30-year limbo. [13] It also entered into a controversy of great significance that was to last a decade. Although this controversy revolved primarily around the issue of levels of training for rural workers (graduate versus undergraduate), it also had to do with the question of appropriate training institutions (private or land-grant), and the relationship between social work and sociology.

It is not the purpose of this volume to discuss in great detail the history of accreditation in social work education. In the context of this narrative, it will suffice to say that between the years of 1942 and 1952, there existed two national accrediting organizations in social work education. One, the American Association of Schools of Social Work (AASSW), encompassed primarily the traditional schools of the East Coast and supported from its inception two-year graduate education for social workers. The other, the National Association of Schools of Social Administration (NASSA), grew out of a meeting of the South Western Committee for the Social Sciences and was formed primarily by large public universities of the South and Southwest to support the continuation of undergraduate social work education as the most appropriate solution for the training of social workers for public rural agencies. Ernest B. Harper, longtime chairman of the National Association of Schools of Social Administration, spoke of the historical forces leading to its formation:

> Dissatisfaction on the part of local colleges and tax supported Universities with the accrediting policies of the American Association of Schools of Social Work, which was founded under another name shortly after the close of World War I, began as early as 1935. During the depression and emergency relief period, numerous training courses for welfare workers were established in both state and private institutions. Some of these were graduate, but the majority were undergraduate curricula. In 1937 the AASSW voted to become purely a graduate association, effective 1939. This action placed the departments offering undergraduate instruction in the arms of a dilemma. Undergraduate training was obviously needed to staff the 3,000 or more county relief agencies, but the possibility of professional recognition even for the better schools offering such instruction was threatened—in fact, such recognition was impossible after 1939. [14]

Although the AASSW eventually made some concessions to schools offering one-year graduate programs (they were accepted to

membership as Type I schools, offering "certificate" programs),
Harper suggested that those concessions were not felt to be sufficient.
In the following paragraph, he highlights the problems of the AASSW
with the land-grant colleges and the departments of sociology mentioned before:

> Three interest groups may be noted as outstanding in stimu-
> lating the forces that led shortly to the founding of the new
> association. First, as indicated above, was the concern of
> the state universities and land-grant college administrators
> with the problem of training personnel of all types for state
> service, and their impatience with the specialized accredit-
> ing agencies in general. Second, the departments of so-
> ciology were also involved as more and more courses in
> applied fields were introduced in the curriculum. Depart-
> ment heads reacted against what they conceived to be un-
> necessarily high professional standards, and a too limited
> definition of the scope of social welfare. Finally, many
> social workers, particularly in rural areas and sparsely
> settled sections of the country, were greatly concerned
> with the dearth of workers with even generic training and
> turned to the undergraduate departments of their state in-
> stitutions to supply the need. [15]

Naturally, the National Association of Schools of Social Administration received from the start the blessings of the Association
of Land-Grant Colleges and Universities and of the National Association of State Universities. By 1944 the NASSA's membership included
28 institutions located in 27 states and was formally recognized as an
accrediting agency in social work by the National Association of Land-
Grant Colleges and the National Association of State Universities. [16]

Thus, what had been a rather theoretical suggestion at the time
Smick wrote his training plan recommending that the agricultural and
mechanical colleges be made training centers for rural social work
ended up as a major revolt in the accrediting system of social work
education, a revolt that continued until the beginning of the Council
on Social Work Education in 1952, and is still vividly remembered by
many old-timers.

The picture of the involvement of the accrediting organizations
in rural training would not be complete without referring to the fact
that both the AASSW and the NASSA maintained ongoing curriculum
committees to study and develop rural training. The files of the rural
subcommittee of the curriculum committee of the American Association of Schools of Social Work boast of names like Helen Clarke,
Marion Hathaway, and Gertrude Vaile. The subcommittee conducted

a survey of agencies involved in rural practice about content required
for the training of rural social workers. It received many responses,
such as the following from Eleanor Slater of the American Friends
Service Committee:

> I believe that it is probably true that most existing types
> of rural social work, centering largely in the administra-
> tion of relief through county agencies, are not very funda-
> mentally different from urban case work, and require
> only a somewhat modified social case work training.
>
> But it is my profound conviction that in very depressed
> rural areas, especially in the South, a new and pioneering
> kind of social work is needed which requires not only spe-
> cial training, but a rather special kind of person as well. [17]

Slater suggested that the rural worker should have knowledge
of rural sanitation, rural community leadership, and rural education
since the school was the focus of so many social and religious activities in rural areas. However, most of those suggestions had been
previously made during the New Deal years, and it was obvious that
novel thinking on the nature of rural social work was reaching a plateau in the early 1940s.

The rural subcommittee was very concerned with the development of rural materials. It was also obviously concerned with the
threatening relationship with the land-grant colleges. It was apparent
by 1941 that the relationship was tense and delicate and that the members of the American Association of Schools of Social Work, particularly its rural subcommittee, were straining to avoid a crisis. In
a letter from Gertrude Vaile of Minnesota to Elizabeth Wisner of Tulane, Vaile stated in relation to some additions she had made to a
rural subcommittee report:

> I was trying to point out the close relationship between the
> Public Welfare Administration and the Department of Agri-
> culture programs, while cryptically suggesting—but side-
> stepping—the issue of training for Social Work in the Col-
> leges of Agriculture. [18]

The files of the American Association of Schools of Social Work
rural subcommittee reveal that there were many studies being carried
out by schools and agencies in an effort to determine what constituted
basic knowledge for rural workers. It was apparent that the schools
had accepted the fact that basic social work method required many
adaptations for the rural locale, and that during the early 1940s it
was their aim to determine what those adaptations were.

Among those studies, one carried out at the University of Minnesota under the direction of Anne I. Fenlason was often referred to. [19] That study of the training needs in Minnesota revealed that 27.6 percent of the workers in that state were employed in rural public agencies. The study also highlighted important "differences in urban and rural areas in respect to the <u>social structure</u> of the community and the community <u>structure</u> and <u>functions</u> and <u>administrative problems</u> of the agencies."[20]

Other studies suggested as useful by the rural subcommittee were those from the U.S. Department of Agriculture that "provide significant material bearing on problems of relationship between the public welfare program and other rural social programs."[21] The subcommittee felt that rural trainees needed to examine the special services to individuals under the Department of Agriculture since they affected the daily work of social workers in rural communities.[22]

> Has social work, for example, any contribution to make to the handling of the agricultural migrant with whose problem the Department of Agriculture is trying to grapple constructively? Care of the transient has traditionally been our job. Has social work any contribution to make to the problems of removal and resettlement of rural people stranded in isolated areas, a problem with which county officials and the local planning committees on Land Use are now struggling . . .?
>
> Are we prepared to discuss community organization in rural counties and make a real contribution towards social thinking in that field if we have never considered such problems of social structure and functioning . . .? Has social work any contribution to make to the health and medical care plans now being developed?[23]

In summary, the subcommittee on rural social work discussed again, in the context of the 1940s and within the framework of training, many of the questions that had been debated by the New Deal workers in their efforts to determine and firmly establish the essence of rural social work practice.

The NASSA archives reveal the writings of Mattie Cal Maxted of Arkansas, secretary of the association, and William E. Cole, head of the department of sociology of the University of Tennessee. Maxted, who had grown up in Oklahoma and had worked extensively in rural communities in Arkansas, was convinced that the only way to secure professionally trained workers for rural communities and to ensure community understanding of the role of social workers was to train local people in the undergraduate programs of the state universities.

Maxted was a witty pragmatist who made her points without reservations. Arguing that basic undergraduate training for rural workers was better than no training at all, she stated:

> Although the salaries in social work are low, many of the social workers are actually overpaid in view of their training and the quality of their work. . . . Applicants for social work positions emphasize their need for work, not their qualifications for the job. We are reminded of a quotation from Mary Richmond written in 1897 in which she said, "You ask me," wrote the clergyman, "what qualifications Miss Blank has for the position of Agent of the Charity Organization Society. She is a most estimable lady and the sole support of a widowed mother. It would be a real charity to give her a job."[24]

Maxted emphasized the feeling of impotence that most rural workers experienced in relation to graduate training outside their states and even outside their own localities. She believed that accessible undergraduate teaching in the state colleges would help remedy the situation. In "Don't Forget Your Country Cousin," published in Survey in 1946, Maxted drove home the point that graduates of schools of social work outside rural states seldom returned to their own regions to practice:

> City pastures are greener than this. The postwar prospects are for even more lush browsing grounds. Graduate trained social workers would be less than human if they turned instead to the dry stubble of many rural areas.[25]

Maxted believed that undergraduate training in the state universities not only played a community relations role for the social work profession but also accomplished that "locality specific" tone about which rural workers were so concerned:

> Even though it is "undergraduate" rather than "graduate," training within the state has certain practical advantages. The student learns about state conditions, problems, personnel, laws, and resources, with a detail that could not be the case in a school located elsewhere.[26]

William E. Cole presented a paper at the National Conference on Social Work in 1949 entitled "Training of Social Workers for Rural Areas."[27] In this paper, Cole stated further recommendations about the necessary content of rural training, highlighting the role of the

National Association of Schools of Social Administration in the growth of rural training efforts:

> With the growth of social work activities in rural areas, and with the growth of NASSA, increased attention has been given to the wisdom of differentiated training for social workers. This differentiation is based on two hypotheses: first, that the functions and activities of the rural social worker are different and, secondly, that the physical facilities with which the social worker works are different.
>
> On the basis of the jobs they have to do, I would like to indicate the following areas in which training is needed beyond the customary preprofessional and professional courses in psychology, sociology, the history of social work, interviewing, case recording, research statistics, casework, procedure, law and social welfare, welfare administration, current problems in welfare administration, etc.
>   1. Basic Training in State and Local Government
>   2. Basic Training in Rural Sociology
>   3. Community Organization
>   4. Group Work
>   5. Social Work Reporting and Interpretation.[28]

What becomes obvious to the reviewer of the historical records of rural social work training is that although the subject apparently remained open and continued to be discussed at the professional meetings till 1949, the basic ideas as to what should constitute core training for rural workers were no longer new but had become repetitious. Educators were no longer drawing new thoughts from the needs of practitioners. They had said what had to be said about the essence of the practice, and discussions in the literature became scanty.

In February 1941 Survey devoted a whole issue to "Social Work at the Grass Roots." By this they meant the rural grass roots of the nation. That particular publication constitutes one of the last journal issues devoted to the writings on rural social work practice to be found in the literature for decades to come. After 1944 the index to Survey stopped classifying rural social work articles, and those few that appeared were classified under the other practice issues to which they related, even if peripherally or fundamentally they were rural.[29]

The National Conference on Social Work included rural papers in its 1940, 1943, and 1946 meetings, but references to rural subjects were nonexistent in all other annual sessions until 1969. The two 1940 papers had to do with problems of administration of social welfare programs rather than with issues relating to the nature of practice in rural settings. [30] The 1943 papers, [31] written at the height of Children's Bureau activity, related to specific problems of child welfare in nonmetropolitan areas, and the 1946 paper had to do with forms of recreational activities for the elderly. [32] They were all, in short, how-to papers rather than philosophic positions on the controversial essence of rural social work.

The pattern just described for Survey and the Proceedings was similar in other professional publications. [33] Rural social work practice had somehow established its identity, and in doing so had begun to decline as a subject of debate. There were, of course, other factors that contributed to the demise of the topic and gave birth to other areas of dispute and worry to which rural people in general, and rural social workers in particular, would turn their attention. Among those factors were World War II and its impact on equality and civil rights.

THE DEFENSE PROGRAM:
RURAL SOCIAL AND ECONOMIC CHANGES

Karl L. Schaupp, in a paper entitled "Medical Care Experience of the Farm Security Administration in California," described for the assembled members of the National Conference on Social Work an economic and human problem that was to cause concern beyond the southwestern states at the start of the national defense program in 1941: the displacement of farm people and the national flood of agricultural migrants.

In 1937, the flow of migrant farm workers from the middle Southern states to California became a flood which reached the estimated total of two hundred and fifty thousand in the following winter. The supply of workers far exceeded the demand, and hundreds of families, all of whom had come with small reserves, were soon destitute. They had left their former homes because drought, soil erosion by dust storms, and the mechanization of farming had left them without the necessities of life. They turned westward because some of these people had for years been accustomed to follow certain crop harvests. It was the mass movement that was unusual—a mass so large that it completely flooded the labor market. [34]

With a view to the future and an awareness of the magnitude of the farm labor problem, Senator Robert M. La Follette, Jr., addressed the same conference to discuss the issue of agricultural migration in view of the emerging national defense program. La Follette explained that during the years preceding 1941, the number of farm laborers had so far exceeded the number of workers needed to produce the country's crops that the desperate competition for work caused farm wages to lag far behind farm prices as the latter recovered from the depression lows:

> It has been reliably estimated that in 1940, there was a reserve of 5,000,000 unused or ineffectively used workers pressing upon the agricultural labor market. . . . There is, in some quarters, a detestable exploitation of these workers, who, generally, have been unable to offer effective resistance. Their numbers, their racial and social heterogeneity, and their exclusion from protective social legislation have made them easy prey to vicious recruitment and employment practices. . . .
>
> Haphazard and disordered migration is the result of a completely disorganized labor market. Inadequate housing, insufficient public health and educational opportunities, and a lack of opportunity to participate fully in the benefits of community life are common. [35]

But it was not only the migrant segment of the rural population that was suffering or that was, as La Follette pointed out, being abandoned by policy makers and social amelioration alike:

> Also, there are the large number of additional rural residents who may encounter destitution, but have not yet suffered. Approximately two hundred thousand farm boys, annually, must find jobs in urban industry. . . . The same is true of the 350,000 to 500,000 agricultural workers who will be displaced as a result of technological changes during the next decade. [36]

La Follette eloquently suggested to the conference that the magnitude of the problem should not cause the nation to abandon it. La Follette believed that it would take a concerted national plan to bring the problem of rural destitution (migrant and nonmigrant) under control. A firm believer in national, federally sponsored regulatory policies for social problems, La Follette advised that any national defense effort that did not seriously tackle the problem of rural destitution would be in error. With seeming clairvoyance, he warned the nation that urban and nonurban problems would be, in the long run, seriously aggravated by failure to "protect and render effective" the organization of manpower as the defense effort was initiated:

But, now, in the year 1941, this great giant, and sometimes,
sleeping, America of ours, is throwing off its lethargy and
mobilizing its mighty resources in a huge effort to make our
national defense secure. We will commit a grievous error
in judgment if we fail to consider fully agricultural migration and its by-product problems in the context of this mighty
national defense program and the eventual transition which
must come when the crisis is past. For our program of
national defense is activating forces that are beginning to
answer in some fashion on a temporary emergency basis
the broad issues I have described. If we can bring an understanding of the problems of agricultural migration to
those who are in charge of formulating and administering
our national defense program, we will do a great service
to both, national defense and the victims of underlying
economic problems. . . . Indeed, the way in which our
defense program is shaped may have much to do with the
ultimate destiny of uncounted millions of our rural population who face destitution. [37]

Whatever national efforts were made for rational social planning during the defense years did not amount to much, and rural agricultural problems began to be compounded by the social and medical
problems of the proliferating defense towns. "There is no one truly
typical defense town," wrote Jonathan Daniels, a journalist. [38] "Defense towns include the semirural construction settlements around the
new army cantonments and camps, the new flying fields, the new navy
posts." [39] For Daniels, it included the "war-crowded wilderness,
where amoebic dysentery might be more dangerous than a wildcat" [40]
and all other places where workers, soldiers, women, and children
were. Many of those defense towns rose where the corn had risen the
year before, and for every crowded defense conglomerate there was
a sad counterpart: the deserted village or small town abandoned by
those mobile rural people who could go in search of the age's boom
town. "Much fun has been made of cotton choppers who turned up as
carpenters, and of welders who until they were on the jobs did not
know a blowtorch from a popgun," Daniels wrote again. [41] However,
the efforts of those untrained rural people were more thrilling than
amusing, as they rose not only to the challenge of displacement, new
jobs, and a foreign way of life but also to the challenge of their country. Matched against the odds of health dangers and poor housing,
those rural workers did an amazing job:

There has never been in America any worse housing than
that which sheltered a great many men who built the bar-

racks for the soldiers. Anything that anyone has ever heard about bad housing could be duplicated in some of the towns which the army created overnight around its camps and factories. You cannot bring 14,000 workmen into a town of 500 people and hope to house them. Yet that was the expectation at Childersburg, Alabama. Such military planning sometimes seemed, indeed, to be a scheme against housing. That happened not only in towns but in the open country too. Indeed, through its land acquisitions before the first year of defense was ended, the government had taken away the homes of almost as many farmers as the Farm Security Administration, in three years, had helped to acquire under the Tenant Purchase Act. [42]

The words of La Follette had not been heeded. The efforts at rational defense planning touched only the surface of the rural problem. The consequences of the displacement of agricultural populations were to be felt for decades after the war. On occasions, the displacement helped rural people to earn a living in an increasingly technological and industrial world. At other times, it significantly detracted from the quality of their lives and the lives of the communities they left behind.

THE WAR YEARS AND THE
MYTH OF RURAL AFFLUENCE

Joanne Mermelstein and Paul Sundet have written that "in popular American mythology, the War Years [1940 to 1945] ended the 'farm problem' and started rural America on the way to economic security and progress."[43] Mermelstein and Sundet's qualification of this situation as mythological is corroborated by many descriptions of observers of the occupational, social, and family disruptions suffered by the rural dweller due to the war turmoil. But the myth of rural wartime prosperity had, like many myths, sufficient grounds for emergence: "public assistance declined dramatically in almost all states, farm income increased, and farming took on new status as a defense-necessary industry."[44]

Margaret M. Brooks wrote a "Rural Worker's Diary" from a typical farming community in an unnamed state:

The statisticians of the University Farm say farm prices for September 1942 were 38 percent above September 1935–1939—meaning, I suppose, an average of those five years. The increase in farm prices in this particular county seems to be above that amount. [45]

This illustrates the rising prosperity of those dwellers left on the farm. She also wrote:

> The public assistance case load is static in some respects, but in certain phases there is a marked change. . . .
>
> Relief in September 1940 cost about $2,500 and in September 1942 this had gone down to $1,200. In the only city of the county, relief in May 1940 cost about $1,800 as compared with $1,650 for September 1942. When I counted through the persons on direct relief in September 1942 in this city, I wasn't able to find a single person who was ablebodied. Two years ago medical services were only a small part of the relief cost. Today they account for over half the general relief expenditures. [46]

This last statement was significant in indicating that the exodus of young men toward war-related industries and the war itself was leaving behind those who could not afford, physically or emotionally, to go.

In spite of these signs of ambivalent prosperity, the improved financial rewards that the war brought to many rural areas caused some social observers to skew their statements and predictions because they looked more toward the apparent rise in wages than toward the many accompanying social disruptions of displacement and employment in war-related industries. But not all observers ignored these conditions. In 1942, for example, Catherine Groves Peele of the Family Service Association of Durham, North Carolina, wrote for The Family an article describing the evacuation of 350 families from a rural area taken over by the War Department for Camp Butner in North Carolina. [47] Peele explained that following months of uncertainty over the discussion of camp boundaries, many farmers who thought they were inside the camp found themselves outside its boundaries, and vice versa. Such uncertainty caused anxiety and labor losses to the farmers in the area whose main crop, tobacco, had to be planted early. Peele gave many case illustrations and concluded that "the most serious result of the evacuation, both for the individual families and the communities in the neighborhood of the camp, would appear to be the net loss in farming population."[48] The following case record was transcribed, among many others, as an example:

> Mrs. D was referred by a public health nurse for help in getting a prescription filled for one of her children. She has three children of school age, two younger. Her husband, helped by his son by a previous marriage, had earned an adequate living for the family as a tenant farmer

in the camp area until they were evacuated last April. Discouraged at having to move after they had started their crop and finding that the few landlords that they knew had already secured tenants, the family sold what farm equipment they had and moved to town. Mr. D, who is partially disabled, gets irregular work as an unskilled laborer and his son has enlisted in the army. The man's earnings are small but the family hopes to get along with the help of an allotment from the boy's army pay. They are living in the section of the city which had the highest white delinquency rate and since coming to town they have become known to four social agencies because of their financial difficulties. [49]

Peele showed that the evacuation of a rural area resulted in the same problems that were found in urban clearance projects. An unanticipated additional problem for the rural areas had been the emergence of temporary well-paid jobs in camp construction, due to which many farmers gave up their lifelong occupation:

Thousands of men were needed to construct the army camp and men from surrounding farms have gone to work there at wages higher than those paid by local concerns. Social workers have found that in general the money so earned is being spent each week, largely because the families are finding their living expenses higher than they had expected . . . the camp is due to be completed this fall and so those farmers who have not raised a crop are in many cases faced with the need of earning a living as laborers during the winter months. Some plan to go to other parts of the state where federal construction jobs are just beginning, leaving their families behind when housing facilities are inadequate. Others will work in local communities as unskilled laborers with greatly reduced income. [50]

Rural communities were being shattered at their very fiber. Although the amount of cash money received by its dwellers did increase due to the war boom, many other traumatic disruptions accompanied this tenuous and questionable economic security. The expanded kinship relationships that had characterized rural families broke down; traditional patterns of life and support became insufficient; and the small towns saw their styles of survival altered by more impersonal relationships. When external support was required to continue coping with daily stresses, old-time friendships, churches, and communities were no longer there; "new responses, including day care and supportive family counseling, become part of the major formal service delivery system—the public welfare agency. "[51]

The rural United States also saw the emergence of another phenomenon that, although initially associated with work in defense areas, was to remain an important feature of the country till present days: the trailer campsite. In 1943 Louise Olson and Ruth Schrader published in Sociology and Social Research a study of trailerites conducted at camps around the defense area of St. Charles, Missouri.[52] Although the study viewed the new phenomenon in a positive fashion— in fact, it may have been biased in favor of trailer life by a former study of trailer vacationists and retired people reported by Cowgill in 1941[53]—the Olson and Schrader study reported some interesting conclusions about those already described changing patterns of rural life. The population studied by Olson and Schrader in over 15 camps in the St. Charles area was young (average age of family head 32.8 years) and came from over 17 states to find employment in the defense area. Under the heading of "Institutional and Community Contacts," the authors reported:

> Out of 70 cases analyzed, 41 families had attended church regularly before they began to live in trailer camps; but only 8 families regularly attended church under trailer camp conditions. Moreover, 36 out of the 70 families never attend church now, whereas formerly only 9 families did not attend church at all. Eighteen of these families that never attend church now used to be regular church goers.
>
> That the transition from stable home life to mobile rather than the mobile life itself is a factor in this reduction of church attendance is evidenced by the fact that of those families that had lived in a trailer less than a year almost two-thirds (64 percent) did not attend church.[54]

Under "Social Relationships and Attitudes," the same study reported:

> Most social contacts of the trailer population were with other members of camps. Seventy percent of the women stated that they had no friends among the town people.[55]

In spite of these findings, the authors of this research did not assess the life of the group of rural trailerites studied to be in any way indicative of social disruption. They did, however, stress the importance of integrative community efforts that social workers, had there been any practicing as community organizers, should have pursued:

Since trailerites live in a form of social isolation, their contacts with town people are limited. Perhaps a greater effort might be made by both town people and trailerites to integrate the latter into stable community life. Churches in particular might help in the transition from a fixed to a mobile home.[56]

But facts indicate that social work practitioners and social and religious ministers were unsuccessful, even if they tried, in arresting the mobile phenomenon represented by the trailerite rural community that emerged during the war. As late as 1963 Roy C. Buck, writing in the Yearbook of Agriculture, condemned the social ameliorators for not adjusting to the reality of transiency that, to him, represented a new and significant cultural and economic shift:

Trailer parks, a new form of community life, dot the rural landscape and ring centers of rapid expansion. They house a new category of migrant worker. They gather heavy-construction workers, military personnel, young couples, retired people, and a motley assortment of persons who enjoy the freedom and autonomy of temporary residence. Established community institutions, which assume permanency of residence as a criterion for participation and service, are frustrated by the trailer community. . . .

The trailer resident symbolizes the growing mobility of our population. Movement, a characteristic traditionally reserved for city "ne'er-do-wells" and country "no accounts," is becoming an accepted life norm. . . .

Local institutions must find ways of vitally serving mobile and potentially mobile people. Here is a high priority problem, for if our institutions fail to meet the demands of an economy that places increasing value and reward on willingness to move, what happens to the notion of the responsible man voicing his concern through the traditional channels of democracy?[57]

There were other issues in the rapid metamorphosis of rural communities that came to the attention of social workers. The labor shortage had great impact on agricultural activities. With all available manpower gone to war, many counties reported that farmers were auctioning off land they could not afford to cultivate without help. Child labor became a general concern. Survey reported the discussions on this matter that ensued at the National Conference on Social Work:

Child labor, already more than a bogey man in many a defense and agricultural district, came under discussion through the National Committee on Child Labor. Myron Falk of Baton Rouge, La. and Paul L. Benjamin of Buffalo, N.Y., spoke out against the tendency to loosen legal restrictions under the cloak of "patriotism." Pointing out the many ways in which employers evade child labor laws, particularly those employing young girls as waitresses and "carhops," Mr. Falk called for federal funds to "come to the rescue" of states not able to finance enforcement. Mr. Benjamin urged an expanded training program calculated to bring in "Negroes who are clamoring for work," young people over sixteen or eighteen, older men, and a larger number of women. Said he:

The floodtide of child labor breakdown bills in state legislatures must be resisted. Continuous and prolonged work crushes the child's personality and destroys his initiative. If new hands are to pick up the torch of freedom, children must still dream dreams.

Congressman Sparkman of Alabama challenged any distinction between an industrial labor force and an industrialized farm, saying that work on the latter teaches children nothing and robs them of the education they need for adult life. [58]

There were many other issues. Rural sociologists and social workers spoke about the health rejectees, [59] the neuropsychiatric rejections and casualties of the war, [60] and the need for consolidated collection of war funds. [61] But all in all, compared with the output of action and accomplishment of the New Deal years, their words were more stirring than their actions. The defense and war years, while causing radical and substantial shifts in the nature of rural communities, were not years of very productive social work activity. Apparently, the metamorphosis of the country occurred while planners and ameliorators slumbered.

THE MOVE TOWARD EQUALITY: CIVIL RIGHTS AND THE RURAL AREAS

Referring to what occurred after World War II, Mermelstein and Sundet ably describe:

When Johnny came marching to his rural home, both Johnny and home had changed. Between World War II and the Ko-

rean conflict, substantial portions of the rural population
continued to prosper economically. The ex-serviceman
or defense worker had tasted a different life and often
either sought to bring another environment home with him,
or saw the rural style too provincial and soon moved, if
able, to the city. [62]

But these authors point out that "largely excluded from the post-war
boom were rural minorities, including white sub-cultural groups as
well as racial minorities."[63]

In an article entitled "Wartime Changes in Arizona Farm Labor,"
E. D. Tetreau reported in 1944 that the proportions of Mexicans, Mexican nationals, Indians, and Negroes in the cotton fields had increased
significantly. This was due to active recruitment of these minorities
by individual operators, farmer organizations, and governmental
agencies. [64] It must also be pointed out that the Immigration and Nationality Act of 1917 contained a provision permitting foreign workers
to enter the United States for farm work under temporary conditions.
Congress and the Nation states that during World War II larger groups
of Mexican workers began entering the United States:

The Mexican workers made up by far the largest group of
foreign workers. Called "braceros," the Mexicans were
employed chiefly in cotton, vegetable and fruit work in
Texas and California and, to a lesser extent, on the same
type of work and also on sugar beet cultivation, in Arizona,
Arkansas, New Mexico, Colorado and Michigan. [65]

It must also be remembered that other foreign groups were per-
mitted entry under the Nationality Act of 1917 to man temporarily agricultural activities. Basque shepherds, for example, settled in
many of the western states (Nevada, Oregon). They were allowed by
succeeding immigration bills to become permanent residents. Their
problems, apparently, did not become the object of social scientists'
investigations. Basque shepherds still roam the sparsely populated
hills of many western sheep-raising states.

Tetreau concluded that in spite of the higher hourly wages received by the minority farm workers, they did not achieve corresponding increases in weekly and monthly earnings (poor working habits
were, at the time, given as the cause). [66] Tetreau further stated that
although without minority help irrigation systems would have choked
and cotton crops would have been a total loss, "social conditions in
family and community are not keeping pace with money earnings.
These shortcomings and depletions strike hardest at the community's
childhood."[67]

In spite of similar problems that also plagued rural areas outside the western states, the public's consciousness of civil rights and equal treatment was growing fast. It was during the war years that liberal observers began to relate to the developing field of race relations as a bona fide area of endeavor that did not seem, any longer, completely hopeless:

> And against the previous stubborn attitude of majority white opinion, the thrust of liberal leadership has begun to show results. There is a gradual, if grudging, realization that one tenth of our manpower is too important to be ignored and that our international relations are being affected by our present state of race relations. That present state in this country is bad, as only the blindest optimist would deny. Yet it would be rank pessimism to deny that, in spite of the disgraceful outbreaks of recent months, the past two war years have produced heartening signs of new interracial leadership and vision. If we can hold these gains and keep from suffering new losses, we can be sure not only of winning our war abroad but also of beginning to win our fight for true democracy at home. [68]

In the midst of a national mood of greater acceptance, and aided by some of the slowly developing integrated practices of the armed forces, rural areas and small towns could not continue to hold fast to many of the provincial and discriminatory practices that had existed before the war, particularly toward blacks. There were many instances when rural patriotism overshadowed bigotry (which had never been solely a rural characteristic):

> Wherever these experiences of common effort, common hardships, and common sacrifice take place, men inevitably progress in mutual respect and understanding. Unfortunately, practices in the armed services which have resulted in racially segregated units and assignment of duties on a racial basis have limited the number of such experiences. In the forward areas, however, distinctions tend to break down, and on all the fighting fronts white soldiers and Negro soldiers are learning to work and fight together. Such a distinguished Southerner as the Governor of North Carolina has stated publicly that letters he has received from southern white soldiers indicate that they will return from the war with a new realization of the demands of justice and fair play toward their Negro fellow-citizens. [69]

Many training schools for officers in the army were located in small
towns in the heart of the rural South. Yet, reports indicated that:

> Negro officer candidates in the army are sent to training
> schools where they study, eat and live with other officers
> without segregation or discrimination. One of these
> schools was at Fort Monroe, Virginia, and one at Fort
> Benning, Georgia and relationships were excellent in
> both. [70]

But the road to enhanced civil rights and liberties for rural and
nonrural minorities was paved with difficulties. For every forward
step there were often backward ones:

> When every day brings forth some new instance of dis-
> criminatory practices, by which equal sacrifice is repaid
> with unequal treatment and honorable service rewarded
> with humiliation, it is difficult to realize that progress is
> being made. Yet slowly and haltingly those responsible
> for the armed services seem to be moving toward thinking
> as Americans, rather than as racists, and toward the rec-
> ognition that men who are called to arms to defend democ-
> racy need to know that democracy exists for them. [71]

In the 1940s and 1950s social workers became cognizant of and
open to, even if haltingly, the advocacy of civil rights and liberties.
Rural workers attempted their share and the literature is sprinkled
with examples of some of their efforts. In January 1946 Survey published an article by Paul Jans, a church social worker in St. Louis,
Missouri, describing his efforts at "Race Relations at the Grass
Roots." His work, although humble and process oriented, illustrated
the nature and style of the social work advocacy of the period:

> There was plenty of experience which showed the unwisdom
> of trying to convince, all at once, the majority of any pop-
> ulation segment that both races could and should work to-
> gether in harmony. Such a mass educational effort merely
> gives reactionary groups advance warning to organize
> against it. The appeal to democratic rights, the Consti-
> tution, Christian ethics, is effective only when a majority
> of the group to which the appeal is made have reached a
> stage of social conscience where these concepts have inti-
> mate and personal meaning. Certainly, they had little
> meaning to one typical white youngster in the center. He
> objected strenuously to the introduction of Negroes to the

building on the ground that this meant "the center would
welcome Hitler if he came to St. Louis. There is no difference between Nazis and Negroes." The neighborhood
as a whole, we felt, was hardly better conditioned to accept them. [72]

Efforts such as this of the Fellowship Center in St. Louis, though un-
able to cause broad societal changes, were not worthless:

For a church-trained social worker to find boys who had
never been inside a church saying "What kind of Christians
are we if we can't get along with colored people?" was both
interesting and revealing. These youngsters, troublesome
to society, were not ashamed when taunted by others for
their attitudes. [73]

In October 1948 the Social Work Journal, then the official publication of the National Association of Social Workers (NASW), published a whole issue devoted to civil rights controversies. [74] In one
of the articles, Louis E. Hosch, executive assistant of the American
Council on Race Relations, states:

Since its early beginnings, the profession of social work
has been aware of the problems of our minorities. Social
workers and laymen have developed specialized services,
programs, and even agencies to cope with the special
problems of racial, religious and national minorities. On
the one hand, these developments have been successful in
alleviating some problems; on the other hand, they have
often, unfortunately, emphasized differences which served
no functional purpose. [75]

In relation to conditions in rural areas, Hosch reviewed the states
application of social insurance legislation, as an indicator of how
practices were affecting rural minorities:

While race, religion, or national origin are not considera-
tions for determination of eligibility for old age and survivors insurance and unemployment insurance, differences
in the application of these insurance systems to the population as a whole does result in differentials which affect
minorities adversely. These differentials stem from the
legislation creating the programs rather than from their
administration. The predominantly rural and agricultural
states have relatively fewer persons eligible to receive re-

tirement or survivor benefits. This situation works a severe hardship on the Negro population of rural and agricultural areas. . . .

Social workers and others who are familiar with wage records maintained by some employers, for instance, Negroes in the South and Mexicans in the Southwest, are concerned with the effective preservation of insurance rights by those employers. Similarly, in those communities where discriminatory practices and segregation are formal, public, and direct, it is inevitable that administrative interpretation of the "involuntary" character of unemployment would also be biased. [76]

Benjamin E. Youngdahl addressed the National Conference on Social Work in Cleveland in 1949 with a critical statement of the conference's hesitant stance on civil rights:

As a representative of the profession of social work, I was embarrassed when I learned that the American Sociological Society several years ago decided that it would hold its sessions only in cities that gave full privileges to all its members.

My final case, therefore, involves the National Conference on Social Work itself, and our decision as a Conference to hold our meetings, under certain circumstances, in places that do not discriminate on the basis of color. It is recognized that a Conference vote has been taken, but I submit that that this entire matter needs re-evaluation by the Conference. Has the time come when we can add our weight to the forces that would once and for all give equal accommodation of food and lodging to our members who come to Conference meetings? Has not the time arrived when the chances for success of such a move are good? Quite possibly, this might mean holding our meetings in two or three cities for several years, but this is a small cost to pay for an eventual victory. If other conferences follow our leadership and that of the American Sociological Society and other organizations, the commercial interests will be quick to see what is happening to their income account.

How can social work be helpful in the present conflict around civil rights? First, we must put our own house in order and show by example to our fellow citizens that we mean what we say, and that we do what we think. This means that we must review our practices continuously and bear down to effectuate the necessary changes. [77]

On the theme of putting one's own house in order, Lester B. Granger wrote of some of the biased practices of agencies that impinged upon the development not only of clients but of social workers themselves:

In dealing especially with Negro, Jewish, and Latin-American staff workers, the differential is expressed in severe restriction of the worker's assignment on a racial or cultural basis, extreme reluctance to increase the number of "minority" group workers on the staff, and in some rare cases hostility manifested by other staff members towards this "different" group. [78]

But just as all social workers were being admonished by Youngdahl for their hesitant position on civil rights and minority commitment, for it is true that the worst in the practice mirrored discrimination and inequality, "the best in rural social work began to extend both individual and programmatic help, a decade before it became fashionable within the profession."[79]

The efforts of many of those early rural social work pioneers have been accurately described by Lewis W. Jones. In an article entitled "Social Centers in the Rural South," Jones enumerated many of the service centers that emerged "in response to the needs of rural people in a period of drastic social change."[80] Jones highlighted the leadership of various churches in the building and running of such centers that exemplified the fact that "the rural South has changed in community organization and in the attitudes and thinking of people."[81] Many of those centers served interracial populations and, as such, pioneered more open attitudes in small communities. They were also an expression of another social phenomenon: the formalization and consolidation of service delivery in an economy where the primary kinship group was no longer prevalent. As Paul Landis put it, "Social work is a technique for seeking a solution to the individual's need in an anonymous world."[82] Changes in the structure of the communities, the closing of local stores, and the removal of the local schools were causing more formal responses to problems that had been informally solved before.

The Rural Life Council of Tuskegee Institute and the Highlander Folk School at Monteagle, Tennessee, were instrumental in organizing in 1949 the Conference of Rural Community Centers. Most of the organizations participating in the conference were sponsored by churches and they all worked with rural minorities, sometimes at great risk. Their programs were as varied as their locations: from the improvement of the economic condition of the people served (Liberty County, Georgia and Bricks, North Carolina), to the provision of basic education for a Negro-Indian population (Mobile County, Alabama), to the standard settlement house program for disadvantaged coal miners (Scott's Run Settlement House, West Virginia, and Highlander Folk School).[83] So "the best of rural social work" was beginning to ally itself with the people of the communities served. Those people had begun to realize the predicament of their particular locales. For "all of these areas belong in the category of diminished resources. Crops, trees and minerals have been exploited, and in the wake of exploitation there are stranded people."[84]

In 1950 Survey published another landmark article by O. C. Dawkins entitled "Kentucky Outgrows Segregation."[85] The article reported on the breaking down of the traditional southern segregationist policies in higher education. Five institutions in Kentucky, in an unprecedented action, opened their doors to Negroes. It was interesting, but perhaps not surprising, that Berea College, with its traditional commitment to Appalachian people, was the first institution to welcome Negroes. The article states that:

> Meeting shortly after the bill was signed by Governor
> Earle Clements, the trustees announced that they had
> "empowered our administration to admit such Negro
> students from the Appalachian Mountain region whom
> we find qualified."[86]

But the movement did not stop at Berea. "Three Catholic colleges in Louisville immediately followed suit."[87] Statements were issued by the heads of those colleges expressing "thorough satisfaction that legal barriers against the full application of the principles of Christianity and democracy in the field of higher education" had been removed.[88]

What was important about the repeal of the Day Law in Kentucky was that it represented a trend that was bound to influence other southern states. Furthermore, unprecedented from a rural perspective, the changes were being attributed to the local population, largely mountaineer in origin, rather than to immigrants from the North:

> The growth of industry in the state has had much to do with
> the change, undoubtedly. But Kentucky's new industrial
> population is native, largely mountaineer, and not immi-
> grated from the North. Those who came in across the river
> from Indiana were in large part Kentucky people to begin
> with. Control of the Courier Journal is not in Kentucky
> hands, but Barry Bingham, the president, is from a North
> Carolina family, and Mark Ethridge, the publisher, is a
> native of Mississippi.[89]

Change had truly begun to occur in the rural United States. In the late 1950s and 1960s, there was further awakening of the nation's social conscience, even if such awakening was in many ways hard to explain when the country had been concerned with communism and plots of foreign and domestic intrigue. But it was a fact, a fact that once again exemplified the triumph and strengths of democracy in the midst of confusion. Strong beliefs had persisted even among the persecuted. The Social Work Journal had illustrated those beliefs for social workers when it quoted David E. Lilienthal's statement before the Congressional Committee on Atomic Energy:

> I deeply believe in the capacity of democracy to surmount
> any trials that may lie ahead, provided only we practice
> it in our daily lives. And among the things we must prac-
> tice, while we seek fervently to ferret out the subversive
> and antidemocratic forces in the country, we do not at the
> same time, by hysteria, by resort to innuendo and smears,
> and other unfortunate tactics, besmirch the very cause
> that we believe in, and cause a separation among our people,
> cause one group and one individual to hate another based on
> mere attacks, mere unsubstantiated attacks upon their
> loyalty.[90]

The rest of the civil rights story is now public record. Harry Truman was the first president to seek full entry of the federal government into civil rights legislation. His clear and strong stand cost him the electoral votes of four southern states due to the Dixiecrat rebellion. Legislative action on civil rights was slow, but Eisenhower, Kennedy, and Johnson all continued the work Truman had begun. The first Civil Rights Act of the century was passed in 1957, followed by another one in 1960. These bills were not very broad and had to do mainly with voting rights.

Aided by a number of Supreme Court decisions (many of which emerged from a rural context) and by the work of black leaders in the South, the stage was being prepared for more comprehensive legislative proposals. In 1954 Brown v. Board of Education of Topeka, Kansas, initiated a chain of events when it held that "in the field of public education the doctrine of 'separate but equal' has no place. Separate educational facilities are inherently unequal."[91] In December 1955 blacks in Montgomery, Alabama, stood behind Rosa Parks, and began a year-long boycott of buses; sit-ins were organized in Greensboro; freedom riders went into Mississippi in 1961; by 1965 Martin Luther King and Reverend L. Shuttlesworth had staged protest marches in Selma, Birmingham, and Montgomery.

In his first address to Congress following the assassination of John F. Kennedy, President Johnson, a southerner, "called for 'earliest possible passage of the civil rights bill for which he [Kennedy] fought so long.' "[92] Finally, on July 2, 1964, after long congressional debate, Johnson signed a broad bill into law, asking the nation for peaceful compliance so as to "close the springs of racial poison."[93]

But as in most movements toward equality, greater access to information brought forth further discovery of inequality. Specific to rural areas, in a February 27, 1965 document entitled "Equal Opportunity in Farm Progress," the Civil Rights Commission reported "pervasive patterns of discrimination against Southern Negroes in the administration of United States Agricultural Department programs."[94] The document further stated that Negroes had been consistently denied access to many services, "provided with inferior services when served, and segregated in federally financed agricultural programs whose very task was to raise their standard of living."[95] The report indicted the department for double standards of staffing in all its divisions, which resulted in "failure to recruit, employ or upgrade Negroes, or to permit them to serve white farmers [and in the] isolation of Negroes in separate offices or at segregated meetings."[96]

So in spite of radical changes, progress, and reform, the 1960s did not bring forth complete solutions to any of the old problems. Social researchers and social workers alike learned, if they did not already know, that the problems of the rural United States would continue to exist: some of them had been alleviated, some had worsened, and many had remained to be rediscovered. There was enough time in that turbulent decade of the 1960s for social scientists to rediscover, as did Michael Harrington in The Other America, rural poverty and rural deterioration. The Johnson years of antipoverty action and domestic peace corps were yet to come.

NOTES

1. See, for example, D. G. Springer and N. Springer, "Counties are Different" and "The Education of Mr. Wyat," Survey 77 (February 1941): 41-48.

2. Helen I. Clarke, "General Welfare and Social Security Legislation," Sociology and Social Research 29 (January-February 1945): 173. Clarke was anticipating one of the major themes that developments during the war years would bring to the attention of rural communities: that equality of opportunity and services extended to all racial and ethnic groups, and that the central government was prepared to stand behind this constitutional right.

3. E. Kathryn Pennypacker, "They Do Care," Letter to the Editor, Survey 76 (March 1940): 115.

4. Gertrude Springer, "In Predominantly Rural Areas," Survey 77 (February 1941): 39.

5. Ibid.

6. Ibid., p. 40.

7. Ibid.

8. Ibid.

9. William E. Cole, "Training of Social Workers for Rural Areas," paper originally presented at the NASSA meeting of the National Conference on Social Work, National Conference on Social Work, 76th Annual Session, Cleveland, 1949. Courtesy of NCSW, this article appears in full in Appendix 3.

10. Merwin S. Swanson, "Rural Social Work in America," Agricultural History 46 (October 1972): 534.

11. Grace A. Browning, Rural Public Welfare: Selected Records (Chicago: University of Chicago Press, 1941).

12. A. A. Smick, "Training for Rural Social Work," Sociology and Social Research 22 (July 22, 1938): 538-44.

13. Some students and critics of the land-grant college movement in the United States might perceive this situation differently, for while it is true that the land-grant colleges had well-established rural connections, it is also true that those connections have tended to reflect the wealthier groups of rural America. Recently, a number of organizations and publications have pointed out the ties between the land-grant and agribusiness (see, for example, Jim Hightower, Hard Tomatoes, Hard Times, the preliminary report of the Task Force on the Land-Grant Complex [Washington, D.C.: Agribusiness Accountability Project, 1972], and the article by Peter H. Schuck in the Appendix, which additionally points to the failure of the black land-grant legislation to provide significant help to rural universities, since the black land-grants have been traditionally underfunded when compared with their white counterparts). Yet the point made by Smick in 1938 referred to the fact that at least in terms of established legitimacy, the land-grant colleges could have enhanced rural social work's ability to disseminate as a force in rural areas.

14. Ernest B. Harper, "Accomplishments and Aims of NASSA," paper presented at the National Conference on Social Work, 75th Annual Session, Atlantic City, April 19, 1948, mimeographed (New York: Council on Social Work Education Archives, National Association of Schools of Social Administration File), p. 2.

15. Ibid., p. 4.

16. Ibid.

17. Eleanor Slater, letter to Marion Hathaway, secretary of the rural subcommittee of the American Association of Schools of Social Work, July 10, 1939 (New York: Council on Social Work Education Archives, American Association of Schools of Social Work, Curriculum Committee Files).

18. Gertrude Vaile, Letter to Elizabeth Wisner of Tulane, February 3, 1941 (New York: Council on Social Work Education Archives, American Association of Schools of Social Work, Curriculum Committee Files).

19. See Gertrude Vaile, memorandum "Materials from and about Rural Social Work, January 30, 1941," mimeographed (New York: Council on Social Work Education Archives, American Association of Schools of Social Work, Curriculum Committee Files), pp. 1, 2.

20. Ibid., p. 2.

21. Ibid., p. 3.

22. For an excellent summary of resources provided through the Department of Agriculture that social workers could utilize, see Raymond C. Smith, "Rural Resources," Proceedings, National Conference on Social Work, 67th Annual Session (Grand Rapids, Mich., 1940), pp. 271-79.

23. Vaile, Memorandum "Materials from and about Rural Social Work," p. 3.

24. Mattie Cal Maxted, "The Need for Undergraduate Trained Social Workers in Arkansas" (New York: Council on Social Work Education Archives, National Association of Schools of Social Administration file no. 630k), pp. 49-50. This paper of Mattie Cal Maxted appears in full in the Appendix by courtesy of the author. Mattie Cal Maxted is now a retired professor from the University of Arkansas, Fayetteville.

25. Mattie Cal Maxted, "Don't Forget Your Country Cousin," Survey 82 (September 1946): 219.

26. Ibid., p. 220. See also editorial notes, "Undergraduate Training and Social Work," and "Further Comments on Undergraduate Training," The Family 24 (May and June 1943): 112-15 and 153-56, respectively.

27. Cole, "Training of Social Workers."

28. Ibid., pp. 45, 46-49. For a full explanation of the categories listed by Cole, see the Appendix, where this important paper has been transcribed in full.

29. See, for example, Margaret M. Brooks, "Rural Worker's Diary," Survey 79 (May 1943): 143-45; Tom Leadly and Louis W. Home, "Riding the Range Again," Survey 79 (September 1943): 241-42; A. R. Mangus, "Spotlight on Rural Needs," Survey 83 (July 1947): 203-4. A. R. Mangus's paper appears in full in the Appendix.

30. Benjamin E. Youngdahl, "The Effect of Administrative Procedures on Casework in a Rural Setting," Proceedings, National Conference on Social Work, 67th Annual Session (Grand Rapids, Mich., 1940), pp. 280-88; Smith, "Rural Resources."

31. Benjamin E. Youngdahl, "Community Organization in Rural Child Welfare Services," and Ruth Corey Aleshire, "Problems of

Adoption in Rural Areas," Proceedings, National Conference on Social Work, 70th Annual Session, War Regional Conferences (New York, St. Louis, Cleveland, 1943), pp. 171-79 and 417-25, respectively.

32. Theresa S. Brungardt, "Fun for the Older Person in the Country," Proceedings, National Conference on Social Work, 73rd Annual Session (Buffalo, N.Y., 1946), pp. 221-27.

33. The Social Service Review included rural articles till 1943; then only one other historical essay appeared in 1964. The Social Work Yearbook changed its rural social work entry to rural social problems in 1939. The index for the Proceedings of the National Conference on Social Work included no rural social work entries between 1944 and 1955.

34. Karl L. Schaupp, "Medical Care Experience of the Farm Security Administration in California," Proceedings, National Conference on Social Work, 68th Annual Session (Atlantic City, N.J., 1941), p. 494.

35. Robert M. La Follette, Jr., "Agricultural Migration—Past, Present and Future," Proceedings, National Conference on Social Work, 68th Annual Session (Atlantic City, N.J., 1941), pp. 148-49.

36. Ibid., p. 149.

37. Ibid., pp. 150-51.

38. Jonathan Daniels, "National Defense and the Health and Welfare Services in the United States, I: From the Viewpoint of the Local Community," Proceedings, National Conference on Social Work, 68th Annual Session (Atlantic City, N.J., 1941), p. 89.

39. Ibid.

40. Ibid., p. 90.

41. Ibid., p. 91.

42. Ibid., pp. 91, 92.

43. Joanne Mermelstein and Paul Sundet, "Epilogue," in Pioneer Efforts in Rural Social Welfare: First Hand Views since 1908, ed. Emilia E. Martinez-Brawley (University Park: Pennsylvania State University Press, 1980), p. 457.

44. Ibid.

45. Brooks, "Rural Worker's Diary," p. 144.

46. Ibid.

47. Catherine Groves Peele, "In Times Like These: Evacuation of Farm Families," The Family 23 (March 1942): 274-76.

48. Ibid., p. 274.

49. Ibid., p. 275.

50. Ibid.

51. Mermelstein and Sundet, "Epilogue."

52. Louise Olson and Ruth Schrader, "The Trailer Population in a Defense Area," Sociology and Social Research 27 (March-April 1943): 294-302.

53. Ibid., p. 300.

54. Ibid.

55. Ibid., p. 301.

56. Ibid., p. 302.

57. Roy C. Buck, "An Interpretation of Rural Values," A Place to Live, the Yearbook of Agriculture, 1963 (Washington, D.C.: U.S. Department of Agriculture, 1963), p. 5.

58. Kathryn Close, "Social Workers along Three Fronts: Report from the National Conference of Social Work, N. O., 1942," Survey 78 (June 1942): 166-67.

59. Samuel J. Kopetzky, "Health for Rejectees," Survey 78 (January 1941): 9-10.

60. Leadley and Home, "Riding the Range Again," pp. 241-42.

61. "State War Chests," Survey 78 (September 1943): 212.

62. Mermelstein and Sundet, "Epilogue," p. xvi.

63. Ibid.

64. E. D. Tetreau, "Wartime Changes in Arizona Farm Labor," Sociology and Social Research 28 (May-June 1944): 385-96.

65. Ibid., p. 396.

66. "Labor Relations Laws," Congress and the Nation, 1945-1964, I (Washington, D.C.: Congressional Quarterly Service, 1965), pp. 761-62.

67. Ibid.

68. Lester B. Granger, "Techniques in Race Relations," Survey 79 (December 1943): 325.

69. Charles S. Johnson, Into the Main Stream: A Survey of Best Practices in Race Relations in the South (Chapel Hill: University of North Carolina Press, 1947), p. 76.

70. Ibid., p. 74.

71. Ibid.

72. Paul Jans, "Race Relations at the Grass Roots," Survey 82 (January 1946): 12.

73. Ibid., p. 13.

74. "Civil Rights in Social Work," Social Work Journal 29 (October 1948).

75. Louis E. Hosch, "The Rights of People Served," Social Work Journal 29 (October 1948): 141-49.

76. Ibid., p. 143.

77. Benjamin E. Youngdahl, "Civil Rights versus Civil Strife," Proceedings, National Conference on Social Work, 76th Annual Session (Cleveland, 1949), p. 35-36.

78. Lester B. Granger, "The Rights of Social Workers," Social Work Journal 29 (October 1948): 146-47.

79. Mermelstein and Sundet, "Epilogue."

80. Lewis W. Jones, "Social Centers in the Rural South," Phylon 12 (1951): 279-84. This article appears in full in the Appendix.

81. Ibid.

82. Paul H. Landis, Rural Life in Process (New York: McGraw-Hill, 1940), p. 463.

83. Jones, "Social Centers in the Rural South," pp. 281-83.

84. Ibid., p. 283.

85. O. C. Dawkins, "Kentucky Outgrows Segregation," Survey 86 (July 1950): 358-59.

86. Ibid., p. 358.

87. Ibid.

88. Ibid.

89. Ibid.

90. David E. Lilienthal, "Statement before the Congressional Committee on Atomic Energy," Social Work Journal 29 (October 1948): 140.

91. "The Federal Role in Civil Rights," Congress and the Nation, 1945-1964, vol. 1 (Washington, D.C.: Congressional Quarterly Service, 1965), p. 1597.

92. Ibid., p. 1598.

93. Ibid.

94. "Civil Rights Commission Reports, 1959 to 1965," Congress and the Nation, 1945-1964, vol. 1 (Washington, D.C.: Congressional Quarterly Service, 1965), p. 1614.

95. Ibid., pp. 1609-14.

96. Ibid. Peter H. Schuck has discussed the unequal treatment received by the black land-grant colleges at the hands of USDA in his article "Black Land Grant Colleges—Discrimination as Public Policy," Saturday Review 55 (June 24, 1972), which appears in full in the Appendix.

4

RURAL PRACTICE
DURING THE 1960s AND 1970s:
REFORMS AND DEVELOPMENTS

GREAT SOCIETY PROGRAMS AND THE NATIONAL
ADVISORY COMMISSION ON RURAL POVERTY

The broad directions of U.S. farm policy changed very little
during the 1960s. Farm production, which was by then highly mech-
anized, continued to yield steady increases although the agricultural
population experienced steady decreases. Scares of farm overproduction that would cause prices to drop precipitously, driving more
rural dwellers into the welfare-burdened cities, continued to be
heard. President Johnson helped put through Congress a revision of
the old Democratic system of production limitations and price supports. Agricultural overproduction did worry the nation, but the central rural problem that occupied social scientists and policy makers
alike was that of poverty.

In 1964 Congress enacted the Economic Opportunity Act (EOA),
a major legislative victory for Johnson. The bill authorized ten
separate programs under the supervision of the Office of Economic
Opportunity (OEO). These programs were designed

> to make a coordinated attack on the multiple causes of
> poverty; together [they] were to alleviate the combined
> problems of illiteracy, unemployment and the lack of
> public services which, according to Administration sta-
> tistics, left one fifth of the nation's population impov-
> erished. [1]

The Economic Opportunity Act of 1964, as signed by Johnson,
established the Job Corps to "be located in conservation camps and
training centers in rural and urban residential centers."[2] It was the
purpose of the corps to provide enrollees "with education, vocational

84

training, and useful work experience, including natural resources conservation."[3] The EOA also initiated work training, work study, and adult education programs.

Most specifically related to rural needs, the EOA established the Urban and Rural Community Action Programs (Title II of the act). Title II "authorized federal grants to community action programs conducted by state or local public and private nonprofit agencies with maximum participation of local residents, in order to eliminate poverty by developing employment opportunities, improving human performance and motivation, and by bettering the conditions under which people live, learn and work."[4] Title II of EOA provided a formula for allocating community action funds among the states and directed that funds be "distributed equitably within a state between urban and rural areas."[5]

Title III of the same bill authorized programs to raise the income and living standards of low-income rural families and migrant workers. Title IV established Volunteers in Service to America (VISTA), empowering the director of the Office of Economic Opportunity to recruit and train volunteers to work at the local level and help Indians, migratory workers, and other groups who were not necessarily rural dwellers.

In the books, the Economic Opportunity Act of 1964 had a fair commitment to the rural poor. But in real life, the situation was much more problematic. In a symposium on antipoverty programs held at Duke University in 1965, Governor Terry Sanford of North Carolina highlighted the role of the states in securing the funds and operationalizing the programs that the federal government was making available through the Office of Economic Opportunity. Local and small community participation was often hard to obtain without a motivating force between those small communities and the federal bureaucracy. Sanford pointed out that state agencies had a crucial role to play in aiding local communities to understand the programs and apply for aid. He believed that because small communities were often mystified and discouraged by federal procedures, the state agency could make the difference as to whether they participated in a poverty program at all.[6]

But while several states, notably New Jersey and California, were active and aggressive in their role in rural antipoverty programs, Sanford feared that the examples were too few. The record shows that Office of Economic Opportunity funds were heavily allocated in the cities:

> Office of Economic Opportunity funds have been drawn
> heavily to the cities. Urban poverty woes obviously are
> more visible, and city politicians have greater leverage

in Washington while rural areas have often been slow to
organize for OEO programs or simply lack the talent.
"It's tough to recruit professional staff people for Mississippi or Alabama when there are good jobs in Cleveland."[7]

The problems of recruiting competent personnel for rural areas
were not new. The securing of Great Society funds required the utilization of specialized talent as well as the intervention and support of
key local and national political figures. Rural areas were often un-
able to meet Washington's deadlines and thus suffered in the allocation
of resources.

Last year a good many requests from rural communities
for summer Head Start . . . arrived in Washington only a
few days before the starting date. The cities, by comparison, had their requests in two and three months in
advance. In a situation like this, there's no question
about who gets the available funds.

Office of Economic Opportunity figures illustrate the
inequality. Of the 680,000 youngsters in Head Start classes
last summer, only 169,000 lived in rural areas. Similarly,
Office of Economic Opportunity job programs have trained
243,000 individuals to date, but only 48,000 were from rural
communities; its legal assistance program has reached
225,000 poor clients, but only 41,000 of them were rural.[8]

It was evident that few rural residents were aware of the existence of programs that could help them. Many federal agencies attempted to remedy this problem and the problem of analysis of need
by establishing cooperative approaches with the local communities.
In relation to Manpower Program Development, for example, an in-
teragency task force was set up by the cabinet-level Rural Development
Committee in 1964. The task force included representatives from the
Departments of Agriculture, Commerce, Health, Education and Welfare, Housing and Urban Development, Labor, and the Small Business
Administration. The task force reviewed the problems involved in
developing educational and training programs in rural areas and established pilot projects in Arkansas, New Mexico, and Minnesota.[9]

The task force emphasized the employment of local people
thoroughly familiar with the areas as coordinators of the pilot projects. Local figures were employed as liaison between the federal
agency and the communities. "Arrangements for employing the county
coordinator in Arkansas were handled by the Federal-State employment security system; in Minnesota, by the Agricultural Extension Division; and in New Mexico, by the Vocational Education system."[10]

Because of cooperative arrangements, some of those projects were able to go beyond the mere assessing of manpower needs of specific areas. In carrying out their surveys, they inventoried a variety of other local social needs and made their figures available to the appropriate agencies. For example, in the Arkansas project

> the names and addresses of 700 heads of households which lacked indoor water or sewage facilities were given to the local Farmers Home Administration. The local Farmers Home Administration home economist contacted 126 of these persons whose net family income fell below the $3,000 poverty level to inform them of low interest FHA loans.[11]

That the War on Poverty efforts brought forth a more concentrated and global approach in dealing with rural poverty was clear even to its most embittered critics. The situation was not utopian, but at least it appeared that the words of Michael Harrington had not passed unnoticed:

> In case after case, it has been documented that one cannot deal with the various components of poverty in isolation, changing this or that condition but leaving the basic structure intact. Consequently, a campaign against the misery of the poor should be comprehensive.[12]

Yet critics of Great Society programs did not perceive the coordinated national effort as altogether commendable. They charged mismanagement, unclear plans and goals, programs in confusion, politicos using the War on Poverty for their own purposes, the ever-present problem of discrimination of minorities, and governmental investment in the socioeconomic status quo of a nonegalitarian society.

In his study of rural poverty and politics, which was constructed as a case report of the activities of the Organization for a Better Rice County (OBRC) in Minnesota, Paul David Wellstone stated:

> It was not until the late 1960s that poverty was officially recognized in Rice County. In 1967 an official "anti-poverty" program, the Rice-Goodhive-Wabasha Citizens Action Council was established to "serve the poor." My first introduction to rural poverty and politics was through the Citizens Action Council (CAC). Observing the agency "serve the poor" was quite an experience. This local OED program was a case study of what the late Saul Alinsky called "political pornography." The agency was controlled

by conservative labor and veteran interests, along with the
public officials who sat on the policy-making board. There
was little meaningful participation by the poor. . . . When-
ever poor people spoke out at meetings, they were put
down. Once humiliated at a meeting, they rarely came
back.[13]

In an article in the Progressive, John Rogers, a San Antonio
newspaperman, indicted Johnson's attempts to help those who lived in
his own backyard:

The Administration's progressive programs which offer a
measure of relief to the poor in most areas of the country
have no more chance of early success in South Texas than
they do in the farm regions of Mississippi. The reason is
the same: the local system of economic and political power
which seeks to keep Great Society benefits from reaching
the poor. The "anglo" power structure of South Texas par-
allels closely the white structure of the Deep South, with
similar stifling results. As in Dixie, the few Texans who
hold the economic, political, social and religious reins
are not about to let them go. They protect their hold primarily by keeping the Mexican-Americans politically and
economically submerged.[14]

Even Volunteers in Service to America, which to most observers
was the least politically influenced of all Great Society programs,
came under similar criticism. Just as the Peace Corps did not go into
any country without an invitation for its members to work on one specific project, so Volunteers in Service to America was subjected to
the approval of the state governor, and thus, according to the critics,
vulnerable to all sorts of political maneuvers. Referring to the governor's veto powers and in the case of south Texas, Rogers commented:

The local veto is only one obstacle which the citizens concerned with poverty in South Texas have to clear. The governor's veto is even more potent. . . .
    Governor John Connally received national attention last
spring when he vetoed a war on poverty project. So did
Governor George Wallace of Alabama. Connally's veto
was slapped on a $381,000 Neighborhood Youth Corps
project proposed by the Texas Farmers Union. It would
have provided summer employment for high school students
from thirty-three school districts in eight counties of South
Texas. In his veto message, Connally charged that the

Farmers Union was "quasi-political." . . . His veto undoubtedly discouraged other possible sponsors that could
expect to be looked upon with disfavor by the governor.[15]

Eventually, in fall 1965, Congress took some of the sting out of the
controversial veto question by including a provision that allowed the
director of the Office of Economic Opportunity to override governors'
vetoes.

Political criticisms, though potent in relation to all antipoverty
programs, were probably milder in relation to VISTA since its administrators were more likely to come from welfare agencies and
labor organizations than from the State Department, and since the
program attracted so many undergraduate students and elderly people
who, as a group, were viewed as apolitical.

An issue of the Economist, a British publication, reported of
VISTA in 1965:

> For the most part the VISTA volunteers are neither radicals
> nor intellectuals out to attack the entrenched powers that be.
> They are curiously apolitical. Their approach, in a general
> sense, is Christian, but without the faith or the militancy of
> the worker-priest; reformist, but without the command of
> the facts or the conviction of the effective reformer; intense,
> but without the revolutionary's willingness to use any means
> to gain his ends.[16]

Yet Wellstone points out in his study of the OBRC the often controversial reports associated with VISTA volunteers, whose commitment to advocacy depended more on their personal orientations than
on any directives given to the volunteers. Wellstone points out the
case of two well-liked VISTAs who worked for the OBRC,[17] against
the case of another whose identification with the local welfare agency
was so detrimental to the OBRC that it caused her final expulsion.

> The first action taken by the volunteer staff was to oust
> the VISTA from the organization. They pressed the is-
> sue by walking out of the office and refusing to do any or-
> ganizing until the VISTA was removed.[18]

Escalation of the war in Vietnam brought forth other criticisms
of the War on Poverty. Laymen maintained that no country had ever
waged two wars successfully and that the competition for resources
would become too steep. Economists sympathetic to the War on Poverty but too worried of losing most national resources to the military
establishment were hasty to point out that poverty programs did not

compete for resources only with military programs but with all other possible ways of allocating tax monies. "Military spending and poverty programs compete with private consumption and private investment, as well as all other objects of public expenditures."[19] The dilemma was, as usual, a matter of making choices in the allocation of the federal dollar.

Although military expenditures for the Vietnam War did affect antipoverty expenditures in general, the effect was probably least felt in the rural areas. In a study of regional impact of federal spending conducted by Murray L. Weidenbaum, an economist at Washington University in St. Louis, it was disclosed that while defense and space spending flowed most strongly to the high-income regions of the Far West, Mideast, and New England, nondefense federal spending tended to favor the low-income regions of the Southeast and Southwest.[20]

On December 9, 1967, the National Advisory Commission on Rural Poverty, which had been appointed by Johnson in 1966 to undertake a year-long study of the problem, released its report, entitled The People Left Behind.[21] The report of the commission, which had been chaired by Kentucky's democratic governor Edward T. Breathitt, discussed the problems of rural poverty in relation to agricultural aid programs and problems of urban misery and unrest:

> The report . . . said that the urban riots of 1967 had their roots in considerable part in rural poverty because a high proportion of the people crowded into city slums came there from rural slums. Unemployment, which was as high as 37 percent among farm workers, compared to a national average of about 4 percent and a rate of about 18 percent in rural areas generally, was seen as a major problem. . . . The report said that instead of raising the incomes of rural people, some rural programs helped create wealthy landowners. It noted that changes in technology increased farm output by 45 percent between 1950 and 1965, while reducing farm employment by the same amount, causing a great exodus to the cities.[22]

The recommendations of the Commission on Rural Poverty were in keeping with the tone of all antipoverty programs: heavy emphasis on access to jobs, manpower development, health, housing, and education of the rural poor. As a result of the commission's recommendations, Congress enacted PL 90-488 in August 1968, authorizing the Farmers Home Administration (FHA or FmHA) to make loans to farmers for projects that would supplement family income. The same bill made available to rural districts funds for the planning and subsidizing of rural housing.[23] But it was becoming progressively

clearer that the rural United States required further boosters to be
set on the road to economic and industrial recovery. Such boosters
were hoped to come from the rural development commissions.

FURTHER EFFORTS AT ECONOMIC RECOVERY: THE RURAL DEVELOPMENT COMMISSIONS

In March 1965 another landmark measure of the decade, the
Appalachian Redevelopment Act, was enacted into law. This law was
the culmination of two years of serious efforts of the Appalachian Regional Commission, which had been established by President Kennedy
with representation of the Appalachian states and the federal agencies
concerned with the region. The commission had described Appalachia
as "a region apart—geographically and statistically,"[24] and had set
out to find a regional plan of action within 12 states to combat the poverty that lurked in the mountains, valleys, and hollows.

The Appalachian Redevelopment Act was described as "purpose
oriented rather than need oriented"[25] by Sales Management in August
1965. But that did not mean that the need was not there. The article
stated that the program hoped to "pull the region out of a decade and
a half of economic doldrums brought about . . . by poor planning and
marketing ineptitude on the part of industries that once formed the
economic base of the 11-state area."[26]

Once a powerful mining and agricultural region, Appalachia's
strength had become its weakness. Coal had been uncrowned as king
and the engine that had driven the tractor had also driven the farmhand
off the rural areas. In the decade between 1950 and 1960, unemployment in Appalachia rose 40 percent compared with a nationwide average of 21 percent. Furthermore, contrary to national trends, unemployment in Appalachia was higher among men than women.

The Appalachian Redevelopment Commission, although attempting to take measures on a regional basis, was confronted with the fact
that in attracting new industry to the area, the experts were often
identifying some of the few already prosperous Appalachian sites as
the areas of prime growth potential. Governors from heavily rural
states were reported to have been greatly distressed by such identi-
fications:

Far from reasoning together, governors of heavily rural
states are looking with distrust on what they consider to be
over-emphasis on urbanization. The outcry had a particularly loud ring when it was learned that Litton's [Litton
Industries Economic Development Division] confidential
preliminary report to the Commission pointed out that the

areas of greatest growth potential were in already relatively prosperous urban areas. The backwoods areas of
Eastern Kentucky and West Virginia, where the pockets
of poverty were so severe as to spur support for the legislation, feared receiving the short end of funds.[27]

However, regardless of its problems, the Appalachian programs
were viewed as a new concept of regional development favored by local
government and private industry. Even initially, $842 million was
earmarked for highway development, without which no industries
would have been able to carry products to market.

Although the economic side of Appalachian redevelopment was
fundamental to the region, there was another side of equal or greater
import for social welfare planners and workers. Abraham S. Levine
suggested in Welfare in Review that "to establish viable programs to
relieve the distress of the region, it is necessary to understand the
people who suffer from this condition."[28] The case of Appalachia,
which will be used here as an illustration, could be, to a lesser degree, extended to all rural areas upon which federal antipoverty and
regional development funds were bestowed.

It must be remembered that in addition to the Appalachian Redevelopment Commission created by the Appalachian Redevelopment
Act of 1965 (PL 89-4), the first of the Great Society programs to clear
the 89th Congress, there were five other commissions established by
Title V of the Public Works and Economic Development Act of 1965
(PL 89-136): the Ozarks, New England, Upper Great Lakes, Four
Corners, and Coastal Plains. Alaska was added in the senate bill
only. There were, however, fundamental differences in scope and
funding levels between the Title V commissions and the Appalachian
one. While the former five remained primarily planning bodies, the
Appalachian Commission was heavily involved in operationalizing services for those rural states.

LEARNING ABOUT THE RURAL POOR:
A SOCIAL SCIENCE COROLLARY OF REDEVELOPMENT

During the late 1960s, writings about Appalachian people became frequent. Writers and researchers frequently offered contra-
dictory analyses of the characteristics of the rural poor in the mountains and diverse solutions for poverty in the hollows and rolling hills.
In Yesterday's People, Jack Weller described the Kentucky mountaineer as individualistic, self-centered, fatalistic, and traditional.[29]
Because Weller felt the mountaineer was detached from work, job
security, and satisfaction, Weller anticipated that escalation to the

middle class with its object orientation was "scarcely even a remote goal for this people."[30] Thus hasty generalizers might have assumed that the work-oriented programs of the Great Society would have little effect among those people.

John Fetterman, in a book entitled Stinking Creek, painted an equally dismal picture of poverty in the Cumberland Plateau region of Kentucky.[31] Although compared with the smells of crowded elevators full of ladies who "reek of oils and perfumes and powders" in the cities, he found the smells of poverty of the hollows less nauseating. He had to agree with the Council of the Southern Mountains "that of the 8,000,000 people in the nine-state Appalachian area, possibly as many as 4,000,000 [would] someday join the sickened ranks of the migration."[32]

A more positive note was offered by John B. Stephenson in Shiloh.[33] Having studied a number of families in a changing Appalachian community in North Carolina over a period of months, Stephenson concluded that there were various types of families in southern Appalachia, from the very traditional to the ones who accepted modern ways of life. Although he implied it would take 20 years of better education, vocational training, and guided migration, the condition of the poor could be amended in rural Appalachia. Harry M. Caudill reached the same conclusions in Night Comes to the Cumberlands.[34] His ending, in fact, was rather optimistic if certain programs could be adopted.

As far as the remediators were concerned, some suggested that migration was one of the major answers to the poverty problems of Appalachian people. Sar A. Levitan, for example, stated:

> Many will oppose placing emphasis upon relocation and mobility as a means to combat rural poverty.
>
> But considering the realistic commitments and competing priorities, it is quite clear that in the immediate future existing programs will provide only limited help to the rural poor. Migration assistance in a high employment economy is possibly the most effective program in the short run.[35]

In an article entitled "Regional Development and the Rural Poor," Niles M. Hansen, a professor of economics at the University of Texas, severely criticized the stance the President's National Advisory Commission on Rural Poverty had assumed in relation to the issue of population migration, calling it an approach oriented more toward places than people.[36] The commission's position was based on the assumption that there was plenty of work that needed to be done in rural areas, and that the rural poor wanted jobs in their communities within reasonable distances from their homes. Recognizing that industries that are generally attracted to rural communities are not rapid growth enterprises—typically textiles, food, apparel, lumber, and furniture favor rural areas—the commission believed that subsidies by the federal government should encourage industrial development of the smaller towns of the country. The commission answered that such an approach would remediate the problems of the rural poor, who by migrating often exchanged rural slums for urban slums. The commission preferred to see rural industries subsidized by the nation as a whole than by the sweat and further deterioration of the rural poor.[37]

Yet Hansen, utilizing comparative analyses from France, Italy, and Canada, where federal subsidies had failed to activate real development of lagging areas, reported that there was no convincing evidence that central government programs could attract enough industry to the countryside to provide people everywhere with jobs in proximity to their places of residence. He suggested that money often would be better spent for relocation subsidies and information to facilitate rational migration.[38]

Rational migration was also sometimes held as a very desirable alternative by social workers who often felt the chances of success of relocation programs were related to the availability of social work and vocational training for the participants. Harvey A. Abrams, for example, wrote of a successful relocation program for unemployed small community dwellers of northeastern Minnesota in which "social workers had a major role in planning and operation."[39]

But there were those who argued against migration as a solution to the economic problems of depressed areas. Eva Mueller and Jane Lean argued that migrants in southern Appalachia, for example, were better educated than the population as a whole. Since out-migration had always exceeded in-migration, "the net result has been to retard the rise in the educational level of the population"[40] as a whole.

Furthermore, there were also those pragmatic social scientists, more concerned with the positive utilization of manpower than with the negative implications of migration, who, like Mary Wylie, a social planner from the University of Wisconsin, reinterpreted "creaming" in positive terms for the rural community:

> I think perhaps at this point it might serve us well to reinterpret the "creaming phenomenon" into something less than absolute terms and remind ourselves that skimmed milk is quite healthy. . . . The point I want to make is this—when demographers tell us we are left with less talent they are not saying we are left with no talent. What we do have in nonmetropolitan America is a relatively stable population which has had the time to know and understand its community, its institutions, and its people.[41]

In fact, the creaming of the rural United States, when interpreted from the service perspective of the 1970s, much enlightened by gerontological research, became less of a tragic economic event and more of a challenge to innovative social planners.

SOCIAL WORKERS IN RURAL WAR ON POVERTY PROGRAMS

The antipoverty programs of the 1960s and the national rural commissions organized during that decade for the redevelopment of lagging areas had far-reaching consequences for the delivery of social work and other human services to the nonmetropolitan United States. The Office of Economic Opportunity's Head Start and Job Corps programs created delivery centers of unique importance. Every rural community interpreted such programs according to its own special needs and idiosyncrasies within the broad framework of the federal guidelines. Head Start was often viewed not just as an opportunity for poor children but also as an opportunity for preschool education for all children; anecdotal information corroborates that centers were often run that way. Practitioners in the social welfare fields became, perforce, if not by choice, heavily involved in the communities in which they worked. Advisory boards became cognizant once again of their own powers of decision making. Intracommunity relations often became more coherent as citizens tried to organize in quest of the federal dollar. Intercommunity relationships solidified on regional bases to meet often existing population requirements of matching funds demands for certain service centers.

Although the literature indicates that the effect of antipoverty and rural development programs was far-reaching, documenting the involvement of social workers in those programs is an altogether different matter. There were no analyses made of the jobs held by social workers in rural antipoverty programs, and whatever information exists of their involvement is anecdotal rather than documented. Barry Morrisroe, former director of the Office of Rural Development of the Department of Health, Education and Welfare and presently special assistant to Undersecretary Arabella Martinez, confirmed in conversation some of the statements heard from other rural practitioners.[42] In spite of the federal dollar, social workers were not primarily attracted to rural antipoverty programs during the 1960s. Better salaries and greater sophistication made urban areas the target of their interest and efforts. Trained master's level social workers were too expensive to employ and were seldom recruited by local authorities as social workers in rural areas. Those who became involved in rural practice gravitated to administrative positions in Head

Start, Job Corps, or agencies that subcontracted Community Action Programs.

The involvement of social workers in the various redevelopment commissions was marginal. In the Appalachian Commission, by far the best known and most service oriented of them all, there might have been some social workers involved indirectly in the various health outreach programs sponsored by the commission throughout the Appalachian states.

But the economic implications of those programs and the national attention they called to rural areas served to reawaken the dormant interest of rurally oriented practitioners. As shall be seen, the 1970s brought forth a national movement of identity redevelopment of rural practice in the form of the National Rural Social Work Caucus.

THE COMMUNITY MENTAL HEALTH MOVEMENT
IN NONMETROPOLITAN AREAS

In October 1963 Congress enacted PL 88-164 in response to President Kennedy's request for a "bold new approach" to the problems of mental illness and retardation. The Community Mental Health Centers Act and subsequent amendments made it possible for communities throughout the nation to develop comprehensive mental health programs. Grants from the National Institute of Mental Health (NIMH) encouraged the development of community mental health centers serving defined "catchment areas." In order to receive those grants, each center had to provide five basic services: 24-hour emergency care, short-term hospitalization, partial hospitalization, outpatient care, and programs of consultation and education.

Community mental health centers began to emerge rapidly in the cities. The National Advisory Commission on Rural Poverty further emphasized the need to encourage similar developments in rural areas when it stated in 1967:

> In each of the four most urbanized states, the ratio of
> mental hospital beds "acceptable" to the State supervis-
> ing agency exceeds 30 per 1,000 population. In the four
> most rural states, this ratio is lower than 3 per 1,000.
> The staffing problems in these hospitals are even more
> acute. The result is that senile and other psychotic pa-
> tients from rural areas usually end up in seriously sub-
> standard facilities. Often patients remain in mental hos-
> pitals because of a lack of extended care facilities in the
> community. . . . Outpatient psychiatric clinics for rural
> children and youth are often the only mental health re-

sources available in rural areas. In 1961, only 4 percent
of clinics serving children and youth in the nation were located in rural areas. The 35 states without any rural clinics had around 65 percent of the rural children. Rural
clinics provided only 1.5 percent of the total clinic man
hours of service per week. [43]

A heavy concentration of manpower development monies to be
generally utilized for the training of health practitioners for rural
areas apparently brought forth some positive results. Rural communities began to apply for grants to construct health and mental facilities and to expand the community-based services of the latter. By
1973 a report by the NIMH indicated that of the 500 community mental
health centers funded since 1965

> more than 200, or 40 percent, of the total are rural cen-
> ters. That is, they were funded to serve one or more pre-
> dominantly rural counties—those outside of the Standard
> Metropolitan Statistical Areas. [44]

A similar description of the sequence of events was offered by
Richard L. Fink in a paper entitled "The Role of Mental Health Programs in Rural Areas":

> The latter part of the 1960s and on into the 1970s, we have
> witnessed the discovery of rural mental health needs and a
> commitment to establish comprehensive mental health ser-
> vices in all rural areas. [45]

In 1975 Gertz, Meider, and Pluckman published "A Survey of
Rural Community Mental Health Needs and Resources" in Hospitals
and Community Psychiatry. From the 92 responses they received in
their survey of 215 rural community mental health centers across the
country, these authors formulated a composite description of the rural
mental health scene. Although this description included evaluative
statements, let us first look at those that portrayed the type of programs that had developed in the less than a decade gone by after the
passage of PL 88-164:

> In answer to a question about what programs the various
> agencies offered, the majority of respondents identified
> the five required activities of community mental health
> centers. . . . Drug and alcoholism programs were most
> frequently mentioned as special services offered. . . .
> A few of the more novel programs listed were prenatal
> services, learning-community workshops, training ses-

sions in mental health for new police officers, training
programs for Native Americans that included the use of
medicine men as consultants. . . .

Outpatients programs were mentioned frequently as the
ones that reached the greatest number of clients. The
preference for outpatient care was exemplified by one
Wisconsin respondent who reported that he derived great
pleasure from keeping people out of hospitals. In ten
years his agency had gone from using 250 hospital beds
to using 20 beds, and he anticipated eliminating the last
20 beds within the next few years.[46]

Much more difficult than describing the initial events of the
Community Health Movement in rural areas has been the attempt to
assess the results of its efforts after the first ten years of its existence. Very few documents exist that specifically purport to assess
the community mental health movement in rural areas. Most of the
assessments have come from urban-suburban centers and caution
must be exercised in generalizations.

Fink indicted rural community mental health services in the
same fashion in which Ralph Nader indicted the urban centers. Fink's
position was that the community mental health center had been oversold and underutilized. "We have witnessed, and in fact participated
in, . . . 'the growth of a mental health bureaucracy paralleling, not
supplanting, the state hospital bureaucracy.' "[47] Fink further suggested that the primary thrust of the services had remained one-to-
one psychotherapeutic. In spite of recognizing that "we lack extensive
data on rural mental health" and that "all of us are trapped by our experiences with specific programs," he concluded that due to the pressures on rural areas to develop functioning programs where none had
existed before, "we relied on existing models" and committed the
same errors that had cost urban centers severe criticisms.[48]

On the other hand, an examination of the sparse but rather
solidly data-based literature provided by the NIMH reveals that the
institute supported numerous research demonstration projects aimed
at closing the gap between the state mental hospital and the community, and at mobilizing and strengthening whatever mental health resources already existed in rural areas.[49] The NIMH cited, among
others, the following innovative projects as illustrations: the projects
administered by the Department of Mental Health of Oklahoma for patients returning from state hospital facilities; the Prairie View Mental
Health Center at Newton, Kansas, for patients discharged from Topeka State Hospital; a project sponsored by the state hospital at Little
Rock, Arkansas, to provide educational services to families of discharged patients in seven rural areas of Arkansas; a project carried

out in the mountains of eastern Kentucky that aimed at reaching isolated areas through a team from Eastern State Hospital; and the Ver-
mont Northeast Kingdom Mental Health Service, Inc., which served
three counties isolated from the rest of the state by mountains and
rivers with a population of over 50,000 people, many of French-Ca-
nadian descent. [50] What appeared particularly important was the fact
that many of these projects remained an integral part of the community mental health center services after the initial period of demonstration.

From Prairie View Mental Health Center a report indicates:

> The service delivery activities developed during the course
> of the project have been integrated into the clinical service
> functions at Prairie View Mental Health Center. Mental
> health center boards have assumed responsibility for the
> expenses of the visiting nurse and the minimal contact
> clinics, and are also financing community resource coun-
> cils throughout the tri-county area. [51]

From the Arkansas project it is revealed:

> The payoff has not only been the improvement in the at-
> titudes of the family and community but also the estab-
> lishment of aftercare or other types of mental health
> services in many of the communities. The number of
> Arkansas counties having aftercare services increased
> in two years from 5 to 53, in many cases because the
> program workers helped community leaders to see and
> meet the need for new services. [52]

In relation to aftercare, Gertz et al. seem to agree with the
reports of the NIMH. Their study indicated that by 1975, "outreach
or satellite programs for aftercare in outlying areas were acknowledged as effective means of reducing readmissions to inpatient facilities." In reference to family and community integration of the mental health patient, the report of Gertz et al. varies slightly from the
National Institute's perceptions:

> The third most frequently identified problem was entry of
> the mental health system into the community. The re-
> spondents indicated that community acceptance was in-
> hibited by general public attitudes towards mental illness,
> superstitions, labeling, and the stigma associated with
> being a patient. [53]

A report by Bentz, Edgerton, and Hollister, however, offered results that were similar to those of the National Institute's case studies on the matter of changing community attitudes toward mental illness. Bentz et al. surveyed rural leaders' perceptions of mental illness in two North Carolina counties. Although it was acknowledged that the community leaders identified to participate in the survey had above-average education for the particular areas, the respondents were able to identify and label, with a high degree of accuracy, the existence of a number of symptoms as indicative of mental illness, rather than, for example, deviance, irreverence, irreligiosity, or other such conditions. In fact, the leaders interviewed showed greater acceptance toward mental illness and the utilization of mental health resources than ever before. [54]

Other criticisms uncovered by the study conducted by Gertz and his associates were: lack of adequate resources (manpower and money); geography (distance and population dispersal); and staff resistance to agency changes (including priority setting and conflicting expectations of state and local agencies). [55]

It must be stated that the staff of the National Institute of Mental Health itself is not blind to the complex problems of delivering mental health services to the rural United States. In a recent study focusing on differences in the distribution of mental health resources between the urban and rural segments of the nation's population, the researchers of the National Institute reported that in many cases rural people are seriously underserved:

> The fact that mental health teams are developing a variety
> of innovative techniques to meet existing needs in rural
> areas does not alter the fact that needed resources fre-
> quently have not been at hand. [56]

The study, conducted on behalf of the NIMH by the division of agricultural and life sciences of the University of Maryland, identified three reasons for the marked differences between availability of in-patient and out-patient services in urban and rural centers: first, the basic ecological organization of society itself—metropolitan areas historically have had a greater abundance of human services; second, nonmetropolitan (rural or semirural) areas lack a viable political organization with the power to draw attention to their needs and to obtain essential services; and third, the rural areas cannot attract and sustain an adequate resource base.

In spite of many shortcomings, rural mental health facilities were undoubtedly established in areas where before 1965 there had been none. As early as 1969, Leon Ginsberg cited the community mental health movement as one of the answers in developing comprehensive services for the rural United States. The community mental health movement was indeed a milestone in the development of services to rural populations. The question left for researchers seems to be that of assessing the extent of its impact rather than determining whether it had any impact at all.

SOCIAL WORKERS AND RURAL COMMUNITY MENTAL HEALTH PRACTICE

There is, curiously enough, one point upon which critics and praisers of the movement agreed. That point is the crucial role played by social work practitioners in the staffing of rural mental health facilities since 1965. In "The Role of Mental Health Programs in Rural Areas," Fink stated:

> To raise questions about the role of mental health services in rural areas is to raise questions about social work practice, since social work is the major source of manpower in both the design and delivery of these services.[57]

Rural case histories in the publication of the National Institute of Mental Health point to the fact that social workers were always members of the psychiatric teams, and that in many remote areas, social workers were used as the key practitioners. A report from the National Institute of Mental Health-funded eastern Kentucky project states:

> The hospital, Eastern State, serves a large area that includes four Appalachian counties, those farthest from the hospital. Before the program started, patients from those counties stayed longer in the State hospital and were readmitted more frequently than patients from the rest of the service area. The only local psychiatric resource was a clinic for former patients that was held for two or three days a month in the region's largest community, Pikeville. The clinic team comprised a psychiatrist, a social worker, and sometimes a psychologist, all from the hospital. Three years after its opening the clinic was trying to cope with a case load of 200. At this point the hospital undertook its Institute financed project to test the idea that admissions from the mountain counties would be significantly reduced if a two-man clinical team—a psychiatric social worker and a psychiatric nurse—were stationed in the area fulltime to give help to former patients and to other people who might need it.[58]

A report from Aroostook Mental Health Services, Inc. in Maine indicated that the director was a social worker with training in community organization. Other members of the staff included a psychiatrist, two Ph.D. clinical psychologists, three M.A. psychologists, seven social workers with master's degrees, a psychiatric nurse, and a speech therapist.[59] While the rich diversity and high degree of training of the staff of the Maine center was rather atypical of rural areas, the fact that the administrator and the bulk of the clinical personnel had social work training was not at all uncommon.

As has already been mentioned, these notions were confirmed by Barry Morrisroe of the Department of Health, Education and Welfare, one of the most informed persons about rural services of the last two decades. Morrisroe's subjective but well-informed assessment was that in both antipoverty and rural mental health programs, master's level social workers were generally found in the top level administrative positions, while baccalaureate or preprofessional social work sympathizers were the primary service givers.[60]

Another study of staffing patterns of community mental health centers (CMHCs) conducted by Morton O. Wagenfeld and Stanley Robin suggested:

> Underscoring the health resources imbalance mentioned
> earlier, rural CMHCs have less than half the proportion
> of psychiatrists than the nonrural centers. However, pro-
> portions of social workers, psychologists, and nurses
> are virtually the same across CMHCs in different demo-
> graphic settings.[61]

But as most mental health practitioners would underscore, there were many other people employed in rural community mental health centers who were not social workers:

> One of the most innovative characteristics of the CMHC
> movement has been the training and employment of vari-
> ous kinds of paraprofessionals. . . . Rural CMHCs are
> staffed by greater proportions of these persons than their
> part-rural or nonrural counterparts. In one sense rural
> CMHCs are an innovative vanguard; on the other hand,
> their heavy reliance on nonprofessional staff may be an-
> other index of the professional resources deficit that
> characterizes so many rural human services programs.[62]

It was to these paraprofessionals that many of the social service and mental health training programs were addressed in the 1960s and 1970s. In fact, many of them formed the professional social work ranks as BSW level practitioners after 1974. For it was only then that the National Association of Social Workers accepted into its ranks as full-fledged and bona fide those practitioners who possessed baccalaureate level social work degrees.

Rural mental health practitioners in general, and social workers in particular, seemed to have agreed that a community-oriented practice heavily tuned to the consultation and education components of the mental health programs was of the essence in rural areas. Ginsberg warned in 1969:

> It is important that they [the CMHCs] succeed. Of course, they cannot succeed by trying to provide professionally educated people to give direct services to each person in need. They can succeed, however, by helping educators, ministers, volunteers, and other persons to become astute in evaluating human needs and offering services to meet those needs. [63]

In his critique of rural mental health practice, Fink exhorted social workers to develop closer relationships to their constituents. He viewed a more consumer-oriented practice as the solution to the dilemma of rural mental health care:

> We need to take with us into this new area of practice some truths we learned through many painful lessons while developing services in urban areas. As a result of these experiences, we should have accepted the need for changes in our bureaucratic patterns. We need to move towards collaborative boards, to regard customers as active, not passive, and to respect consumers as knowing their priorities, even though they may not have the expertise to implement programs. [64]

The record shows that apparently rural practitioners were, more so than their urban mental health counterparts, eager to learn the lessons of greater community attunement.

In a paper presented at the Rural Sociological Society Annual Meeting in 1975, Wagenfeld and Robin reported the results of a study in which they had compared urban and rural social workers on a number of variables. Perhaps the ones that best illustrate the greater constituency-oriented practice of rural social workers is that of activism. Activism was measured in a number of ways (organizational activism, personal-professional activism, role discrepancy between the two, and so on), and was defined as "the willingness to change the communities or social structures as a solution to the mental health problem presented in a given vignette."[65] On the issue of organizational activism, Wagenfeld and Robin's conclusions indicated:

> By a significant margin, staff at rural CMHC's perceived that their organizations expected the highest level of community role activism. In addition to perceiving high levels of organizational expectation for activism, rural CMHC staff had the highest level of agreement among themselves about these expectations.[66]

Furthermore, Wagenfeld and Robin also reported that "the fact that they [rural community health centers' workers] are organizationally most activist and relatively activist on the personal plane leads to a high degree of role convergence."[67] Rural workers viewed fewer areas of community life as off-limits to their interventions than did their urban counterparts, and they tended to view their centers as more of a social agency when queried on their perceptions on a "medical facility—social agency continuum."[68]

Care must be exercised in reaching any conclusions in view of the paucity of information about social workers in rural mental health services and the recent date of many of the studies. However, it seems fair to state that the community-minded attitudes that have characterized rural social workers throughout their history become once again manifest when one examines recent data from the antipoverty and mental health movements.

The implications of these apparently desirable personal-professional characteristics of rural workers for the development of educational programs in social work have begun to be mentioned in the recent literature and should be addressed by future researchers. Let this broad sweep narrative provide a basic organizing framework of past rural human service developments from which other more specific studies might depart.

RECENT TRENDS AND THE RURAL IDENTITY

In concluding a review of historical landmarks in the development of rural social work from 1908 to 1978, one cannot ignore, even in passing, a number of other events that greatly enhanced the development of a rural social work identity.

In 1973 a small group of rural congressmen formed the Congressional Rural Caucus. Their goal was the improvement of the quality of life of the countryside. Their impetus had come not only from the structure of the congressional committees but also from the 1967 report of the National Advisory Commission on Rural Poverty, the 1968 Rural Housing Alliance, and a 1971 report from "a small but noble band of civil servants in USDA's Economic Research Service (Helen Johnson, Lynn Daft, Bill Motes, Calvin Beale and Lindley Juers),"[69] which had further shown, with elaborate statistics, that those who lived beyond the suburbs were not sharing proportionately the federal tax dollar or the improved social conditions of the times.

Through hearings, meetings, seminars, and so on, this bipartisan committee helped focus national attention on rural health, housing, transportation, and other rural problems. It further legitimized the existence of a rural identity and provided a national body for the expression of its political concerns.

In April 1975 Washington, D.C. was the scene of the First National Conference on Rural America. The conference called for "the creation of a national advocacy group that would be broadly based and democratically controlled."[70] In October 1975 Rural America was started in response to that call, and Rural America: A Voice for Small Town and Rural People began publication "to provide the facts and ideas which will enable rural (non-metropolitan) people to obtain equity in the goods and services which are essential to the good life."[71] Rural America viewed social services as one of those essential features that were to be shared equally between the cities and the countryside:

> We do not seek an advantage over the people of the great cities. We do not seek to plunder them as rural resources have been plundered. We do not wish to see any of them deprived of any social service or opportunity they now enjoy. We hope to join with them in a common endeavor—to make the good life a little more accessible to all.[72]

In March 1976 the National Rural Center, an independent, nonprofit organization, was established in Washington, D.C. on the premise that the "nation as a whole has an important stake in rural people and communities."[73] The center's concerns are many and include policy recommendations relating to rural needs, evaluation of federal programs, monitoring the writing of legislation, and conducting basic research. The National Rural Center also offers a newsletter and an information service regarding rural issues, including a toll-free telephone number.

There are other more specialized organizations that developed as a result of this national momentum affecting rural people. Not all can be listed here. The following, however, appear to have the most relevancy for social work.

Rural American Women (RAW) was incorporated in the District of Columbia in 1977. RAW states that its objective is "to organize the rural women of America to work together through legislative and voluntary action to develop their individual capabilities, to contribute to the welfare of their families and to the improvement of their communities."[74] RAW provides an advocacy body for rural women in relation to national legislative issues, as well as technical assistance and useful information for rural women to meet their own needs within their communities.

The Association for Rural Mental Health, which like the National Rural Social Work Caucus had close ties to the University of Wisconsin-Extension, was also started in 1977. The association "represents the interests of rural mental health programs in dealing with federal agencies and national mental health associations."[75] The association develops continuing education programs for rural mental health practitioners and publishes a newsletter.

Finally, the year 1977 also witnessed the start of the American Rural Health Association, which promulgates research and education on topics related to rural health.

With these national political and organizational events came other important social work events of national scope. In January 1975 the Council on Social Work Education sponsored a Seminar on Social Work in the Rural and Small Community. The seminar was held in Harrisburg, Pennsylvania, and was coordinated by a handful of practitioners who were working to rekindle rural fires. They were Leon Ginsberg, then at West Virginia University, Hortense Cochrane from Syracuse University, and Joanne Mermelstein from the University of Missouri.[76] A symposium organized by the Center for Continuing Education and Community Action for Social Service of the University of Wisconsin-Eau Claire, held in May 1977, had preceded the Council on Social Work Education gathering. The Eau Claire symposium had also brought together figures who held rural interests; once again, Ginsberg had been a participant and so had Edward Buxton and Mary Wylie from Wisconsin.[77]

Finally, in 1976 the Council on Social Work Education published a book by Ginsberg entitled Social Work in Rural Communities. Ginsberg's volume brought under a single cover and under the umbrella of the national accrediting organization for social work education the dispersed efforts of rural social welfare practitioners. Many of them published articles as a response to Ginsberg's 1969 call for action before the National Conference on Social Welfare in San Francisco.[78] The 1976 volume was designed to draw together some of those articles and "to improve the education of both undergraduate and graduate social workers for service in rural and small communities."[79]

Rural workers had rediscovered their buried identity and were once again ready to perpetuate and improve it through the process of professional education. From that point on, the practice of social work in rural communities, which, though not without precedent, had not been strong since the Depression years, gained momentum.

In July 1976 on the occasion of the First National Institute on Social Work in Rural Areas, the Rural Social Work Caucus was formed in Knoxville, Tennessee. Rallying behind the banners of its then Tennessee promoter, Stephen Webster, the caucus petitioned the Council on Social Work Education to reserve a preannounced slot for it to convene at the Annual Program Meeting in 1977. The caucus was behind the inclusion of a national policy statement on social work in rural areas, which was passed by the delegate assembly of the NASW in July 1977, and the formation of the National Rural Task Force by NASW in 1979. The caucus continued actively to invoke the support of rurally oriented universities to make the national institutes that had created it a yearly event. After Knoxville, institute participants met in Madison, Wisconsin, in 1977; Morgantown, West Virginia, in 1978; and in Laramie, Wyoming, in 1979.

Following Ginsberg's book in 1976, the national social work literature began to include many titles about rural practice and education. Of particular interest are the publications of the University of Wisconsin-Extension (UWEX), which includes a journal, Human Services in the Rural Environment,[80] as well as a number of anthologies edited by David Bast (Wisconsin), Ronald Green and Stephen Webster (Tennessee), and Judy and Joseph Davenport (Wyoming). Researchers such as Mary Osgood of Pennsylvania State University,[81] Carlton E. Munson of the University of Houston,[82] Betty Vinson and Kate Jesberg of the National Rural Center,[83] John Horejsi of the American Public Welfare Association,[84] and many others began offering their findings to social workers in an effort to contribute further to the data base of rural practice. Finally, many rural social work educators began to write and make public their proposals for the preparation of rural workers through national professional panels and publications.

THE PRESENT STATUS OF
SOCIAL WORK IN RURAL COMMUNITIES

In summary, it appears that the present status of social work practice in rural communities is best described by three features. First, contemporary rural social work is characterized by the presence of a number of national advocacy bodies, some solely staffed by social workers, others by a variety of professionals whose roles as advocates for rural populations have much in common with that of social work practitioners. The most prominent group to include primarily social workers is the National Rural Social Work Caucus.

Although promising fuller social work involvement, the National Rural Task Force of the NASW is still only in its infancy stages and has not yet had much impact on national issues. [85] Among the advocacy groups that include a variety of other rurally oriented professional practitioners are the Congressional Rural Caucus, the national and local chapters of Rural America, the National Rural Center, Rural American Women, and so on.

A second feature of current social work practice in rural communities is the commendable but often disjointed effort of hardworking practitioners scattered in a variety of settings: from county departments of public and child welfare, [86] to surviving antipoverty and rural health delivery centers, to publicly funded mental health centers representing, perhaps, the most active employers of trained professional social work personnel in rural areas. Although many of these practitioners do belong to the National Rural Caucus, which is constantly growing, the caucus does not yet include the majority of them and cannot be said to represent a concerted and coherent national voice in rural practice issues.

A third feature characteristic of the present status of rural social work practice is the efforts of social work educators in a variety of university and continuing education settings across the country. Some graduate and undergraduate social work programs have identified themselves as having primarily a rural focus; others have minimally included occasional rural content in their otherwise nonrural curricula. The content and thrust of these 39 programs across the country have been aptly reviewed by Peter Hookey, who emphasized the incipient stage of development of most rurally oriented programs. [87]

Perhaps the present diffusion and scatter in rural social work practice and education are only a reflection of a more pervasive state of affairs that affects all facets of rural life. Speaking at the Western Roundup Regional Conference on Rural Human Services in Missoula, Montana, Henry Hyde, associate director of Rural America, stated that "the current overlap and fragmentation in rural development programs is intolerable." He exhorted his social work audience to convey the needs of its rural clientele to the policy makers in Washington:

> We have no meaning or influence if we are isolated in Washington. As social workers you have to deal with the personal tragedies that are largely the result of the non-response in Washington. If we do not hear from you and what you are up against, we are lost. [88]

Recognizing that the momentum and events of the past ten years, important as they might be, were only the launching pad of future, more coordinated developments in which social workers should be involved, Hyde concluded: "We made a good beginning. If we are successful in our efforts, we must continue to strengthen our network in the field. I hope you'll give us a hand."[89]

This volume began by recognizing the fact that a historical outlook was missing in the present efforts of rural social workers. It ends trusting that the historical perspective provided by this broadstroke narrative of events of the past seven decades will aid practitioners and researchers in moving toward stronger and better coordinated rural social service policies. It is to be hoped that this volume has illustrated the interdisciplinary nature of rural welfare efforts. If we are to continue, our national and local fronts should build coalitions and allegiances. Our efforts should be interdisciplinary, coordinated, political as well as ameliorative. They should involve educators as well as practitioners and should make room for the highly educated master's level practitioner as well as for the baccalaureate, the associate, and the nondegree or indigenous helper. Only the future can tell if the lessons of the past have given us a hand.

NOTES

1. "Johnson's Anti-Poverty Bill Coordinated Several Programs," Congress and the Nation, 1945-1964, vol. 1 (Washington, D.C.: Congressional Quarterly Service, 1965), p. 1326.

2. Ibid., p. 1327.

3. Ibid.

4. Ibid., p. 1328.

5. Ibid.

6. Terry Sanford, "Poverty Challenges to the States," Law and Contemporary Problems 30 (Winter 1966): 82.

7. Burt Schorr, "Suicidal Rural Gap in the Poverty War," Wall Street Journal, February 20, 1968, p. 16.

8. Ibid.

9. John S. McCauley, "Manpower Development in Rural Areas," Employment Service Review 5 (March-April 1968): 11, 12.

10. Ibid., p. 12.

11. Ibid., p. 14.

12. Michael Harrington, The Other America: Poverty in the United States (New York: Macmillan, 1963), p. 168.

13. Paul David Wellstone, How the Rural Poor Got Power: Narrative of a Grass-Roots Organizer (Amherst: University of Massachusetts Press, 1978), p. 4.

14. John Rogers, "Poverty behind the Cactus Curtain," Progressive 30 (March 1966): 23.

15. Ibid.

16. "How Goes the War on Poverty," Economist 216 (September 4, 1965): 883.

17. Wellstone, How the Rural Poor Got Power, p. 82.

18. Ibid., p. 98.

19. John O. Blackburn, "The War in Viet Nam and the War on Poverty," Law and Contemporary Problems 31 (Winter 1966): 40.

20. "Bigger Slice Goes to Poorer Areas," Business Week, November 27, 1967, pp. 54-55.

21. National Advisory Commission on Rural Poverty, The People Left Behind (Washington, D.C.: U.S. Government Printing Office, 1967).

22. "Advisory Commission Criticizes Aid Programs for Rural Poor." Congress and the Nation, 1965-1968, vol. 2 (Washington, D.C.: Congressional Quarterly Service, 1968), p. 578.

23. "Rural Development Act," Congress and the Nation, 1969-1972, vol. 3 (Washington, D.C.: Congressional Quarterly Service, 1972), pp. 347-48.

24. "Appalachian Development Bill Fails in 1964," Congress and the Nation, 1945-1964, vol. 1 (Washington, D.C.: Congressional Quarterly Service, 1964), p. 1331.

25. Steve Blickstein, "Appalachia: The Road Back," Sales Management 95 (August 20, 1965): 23-25.

26. Ibid., p. 23.

27. Ibid., p. 25.

28. Abraham S. Levine, "'Yesterday's People' and Tomorrow's Programs," Welfare in Review 7 (July-August 1969): 8.

29. Jack E. Weller, Yesterday's People (Lexington: University of Kentucky Press, 1965).

30. Ibid., p. 155.

31. John Fetterman, Stinking Creek (New York: Dutton, 1967).

32. Ibid., pp. 32, 155.

33. John B. Stephenson, Shiloh: A Mountain Community (Lexington: University of Kentucky Press, 1968).

34. Harry M. Caudill, Night Comes to the Cumberlands (Boston: Little, Brown, 1962).

35. Sar A. Levitan, "The Steps for Right Now," New Generation, Summer 1968, p. 17.

36. Niles M. Hansen, "Regional Development and the Rural Poor," Social Welfare in Appalachia 2 (1970): 41-49.

37. National Advisory Commission on Rural Poverty, The People Left Behind, pp. 19, 23, ix, 119.

38. Hansen, "Regional Development and the Rural Poor," p. 48.

39. Harvey A. Abrams, "The Role of Social Work in Relocation for Employment," Social Casework 49 (October 1968): 475.

40. Eva Mueller and Jane Lean, "The Case against Migration," New Generation, Summer 1968, p. 7.

41. Mary Wylie, "Social Planning in Non-Metropolitan America," in A Symposium: Planning and Delivery of Social Services in Rural America: Three Papers, ed. William H. Koch (Madison: University of Wisconsin, 1973), p. 23.

42. Telephone conversation between the writer and Barry Morrisroe of the Department of Health, Education and Welfare (Pennsylvania State University—Washington, D.C.), September 6, 1978.

43. National Advisory Commission on Rural Poverty, The People Left Behind, p. 66.

44. Bertram S. Brown, "Community Mental Health Centers in Rural America," in The Mental Health of Rural America: The Rural Programs of the National Institute of Mental Health, ed. Julius Segal, DHEW publication no. ADM76-349 (Washington, D.C.: U.S. Department of Health, Education and Welfare, 1973), pp. 50-51.

45. Richard L. Fink, "The Role of Mental Health Programs in Rural Areas," in Social Work in Rural Areas: Preparation and Practice, ed. Ronald K. Green and Stephen A. Webster (Knoxville: University of Tennessee School of Social Work, 1977), p. 328.

46. Boris Gertz, Jill Meider, and Margaret L. Pluckman, "A Survey of Rural Community Mental Health Needs and Resources," Hospitals and Community Psychiatry 26 (December 1975): 816.

47. Fink, "The Role of Mental Health Programs in Rural Areas," p. 330.

48. Ibid., p. 331.

49. Julius Segal, ed., The Mental Health of Rural America: The Rural Programs of the National Institute of Mental Health, DHEW publication no. ADM76-349 (Washington, D.C.: U.S. Department of Health, Education and Welfare, 1973), pp. 35-48.

50. Ibid., pp. 35-101. See also Mental Health Reports, no. 6 (Bethesda, Md.: National Institute of Mental Health, 1973).

51. Segal, The Mental Health of Rural America, p. 37.

52. Ibid., p. 38.

53. Gertz et al., "Survey of Rural Community Mental Health Needs," p. 817.

54. W. Kenneth Bentz, J. Wilbert Edgerton, and William G. Hollister, "Rural Leaders' Perceptions of Mental Illness," Hospital and Community Psychiatry 22 (May 1971): 143-45.

55. Gertz et al., "Survey of Rural Community Mental Health Needs," pp. 817-18.

56. U.S., Department of Health, Education and Welfare, A New Day in Rural Mental Health, DHEW publication no. ADM78-690 (Washington, D.C., 1978), p. 1.

57. Fink, "Role of Mental Health Programs in Rural Areas," p. 334.

58. Segal, Mental Health of Rural America, pp. 38-39.

59. Ibid., p. 80.

60. Morrisroe, telephone conversation.

61. Morton O. Wagenfeld and Stanley S. Robin, "The Social Worker in the Rural Community Mental Health Center," in Social Work in Rural Communities: A Book of Readings, ed. Leon Ginsberg (New York: Council for Social Work Education, 1976), p. 71.

62. Ibid.

63. Leon Ginsberg, "Social Problems in Rural America," Social Welfare Practice 1969, Selected Papers, National Conference on Social Welfare, 76th Annual Session, New York, May 1969 (New York: Columbia University Press, 1969), p. 179.

64. Fink, "Role of Mental Health Programs in Rural Areas," p. 334.

65. Wagenfeld and Robin, "The Social Worker," p. 6.

66. Ibid., p. 7.

67. Ibid.

68. Ibid., p. 8.

69. "Congressional Rural Caucus," Rural America 1 (March 1976): 1.

70. "Good Life for Rural People Is Goal of New Organization," Rural America 1 (October 1975): 1.

71. Ibid.

72. Ibid.

73. National Rural Center, A Concept and a Program, NRC brochure.

74. Rural American Women, Stepping Out of Obscurity into Involvement (Washington, D.C.: RAW).

75. National Rural Center, A Directory of Rural Organizations (Washington, D.C.: NRC, 1977), p. 9.

76. Council on Social Work Education, memorandum no. 74-310-17 dated December 16, 1974, regarding Seminar on Social Work in the Rural and Small Community.

77. Koch, A Symposium, p. 38.

78. Ginsberg, "Social Problems in Rural America," p. 185.

79. Leon Ginsberg, ed., Social Work in Rural Communities (New York: Council on Social Work Education, 1976), p. iii.

80. At the time this manuscript was being prepared, Human Services in the Rural Environment was being published as an informal newsletter by UWEX. Presently, this journal is refereed under the editorship of Joanne Jankovic and Richard Edwards and is being published by the University of Tennessee School of Social Work.

81. Mary H. Osgood, "Rural and Urban Attitudes toward Welfare," Social Work 22 (January 1977): 41-47.

82. Carlton E. Munson, "Social Work Manpower and Social Indicators: Rural and Urban Differences," mimeographed (Paper pre-

sented at the 1978 Council on Social Work Education, Annual Program Meeting, New Orleans); Carlton E. Munson and Catherine S. Hull, "A Study of Rural Health Services Utilization and Advocacy Social Work Practice," ARETE 5 (Spring 1978): 11-21.

83. Elizabeth A. Vinson and Kate M. Jesberg, "The Rural Stake in Public Assistance," (Washington, D.C.: National Rural Center, 1978). When this manuscript was originally being prepared, "The Rural State in Public Assistance" was only a working paper. It has since been completed. A summary of its findings and recommendations has been included in the Appendix.

84. John Horejsi, Working in Welfare: Survival through Positive Action (Iowa City: University of Iowa School of Social Work, 1977).

85. "Report from the Rural Social Work Caucus," Human Services in the Rural Environment 3 (October 1978): 20.

86. One such practitioner who has recently come to the attention of this author is Naomi Griffith, a supervisor with the Department of Pensions and Security in Alabama. A response to one of the early Survey articles written by Griffith from the perspective of the 1980s and at the request of this author has been included in the Appendix.

87. Peter Hookey, "Rurally Oriented Components of the Social Work Education Curricula: The Report of the 1977 HSITRE Readership Survey," Human Services in the Rural Environment 3 (October 1978): 1-19.

88. Henry Hyde, "Rural Development: What's Coming—What's Needed," Human Services in the Rural Environment 3 (October 1978): 26.

89. Ibid., p. 31.

APPENDIX

1/ Public Work or Social Work in the Front Lines

INTRODUCTION

During the preparation of this book and in attempting to make the Appendix selections as appealing to contemporary practitioners as possible, I asked a friend presently employed in public assistance to read a few selections that appeared in the Survey Midmonthly between March 1933 and the end of the decade. These selections, written by Gertrude Springer, were probably the most popular pieces of advice to busy social workers during the depression years, when the advent of public relief brought to the newly established county offices a host of trained and untrained workers who were faced with many challenging situations as they went about the business of operationalizing the mandates of the law, the desires of the community, and the often conflicting norms the developing social casework method was handing down from its academic circles. Springer's selections were cast in the form of observations by a popular Survey character, Miss Bailey, supposed to be an itinerant public assistance supervisor. Miss Bailey's pieces are historically intriguing because they represent practical and yet deeply humane advice, and because they inspired a number of responses from another popular rural worker of the depression period, Josephine Strode of Kansas. Strode's articles were cast in the form of letters to Miss Bailey and have appeared in full in Pioneer Efforts in Rural Social Welfare: Firsthand Views since 1908.

While Miss Bailey's articles were not intended to be rural some of them were, and the question still remained as to whether they would interest my rural colleagues of the 1980s.

My friend's response, to my surprise, was not one of admiration for Miss Bailey's foresight but rather one of anger for her sporadically paternalistic sounding statements. It thus became apparent that it was worth illustrating the language of the period by inserting at least one of Miss Bailey's articles and somewhat purging Miss Bailey's contemporary image by further explaining what scholars have reported about her intentions in the 1930s and 1940s.

"Some Scars Remain" was written by Gertrude Springer, Miss Bailey, after the advent of World War II. Miss Bailey's theme is one that is not new to public workers nowadays. Federal and/or state special programs for the relief of the poor often have unforeseen consequences for those very people they are designed to help. In Miss Bailey's article, the matter of agricultural economics is wisely brought to the fore and then quickly left aside for the reader to ponder.

This was a common tactic of Springer who, in her characteristic folksy way, would raise issues to intrigue the reader and then set them aside with but a hint of her opinion for the very same reader to mull over, investigate, and resolve. Who could help but be intrigued by the policies of the AAA after reading that "the land that they [farm people] left has been gathered in, usually for delinquent taxes, by a new kind of speculator who works it at the absolute minimum to get the maximum benefits under the Agricultural Adjustment Administration"?

"Some Scars Remain" provides further commentary on the tenacity of public assistance policies that often require from clients the very behavior they are designed to eradicate. If one of the intentions of Aid to Families with Dependent Children (AFDC) is the conservation and preservation of the family, is it not incredible that some states still retain the man-in-the-house rule in public assistance? "Some Scars Remain" also brings to the fore the issue of confidentiality and its interpretation in the rural milieu. This issue is still preoccupying rural social workers. While the protection of the client is of the utmost concern, is it not true that in our attempt to maintain a securely confidential relationship we often isolate the natural networks of the community? Proximity and neighborliness are still being evaluated by rural workers in relation to confidentiality. The issues raised by Miss Bailey have not yet been resolved.

The merit of the article obviously transcends the use of words such as Missus and terms such as men's business that might offend the contemporary reader. But for the reader who might still be bothered by Springer's lines, even after tuning in to the language differences of the 1930s and 1940s, let me quote from Chambers's commentaries on Gertrude Springer and the Miss Bailey series:

> Mrs. Springer sought to give the kind of down to earth practical advice that untrained social workers in the depression so desperately needed: how to handle a drunk or abusive client, how to gather essential family data without offending its members, what to do in the face of emotional outbursts, how to keep the office running smoothly when welfare recipients pickets patrolled the corridors. The columns, which appeared (with but a few breaks) every month from March 1933 until the end of the decade, bubbled with wit. Designed to reach newcomers in relief work and to advise them on human relationships in their day to day rounds, the pieces featured one recurring theme above all others—that social workers must hold to their own humanity and must respect absolutely the right of their clients to direct their own lives. Thus social workers were

admonished never to use granting or withholding of relief
as an incentive to impose their own middle class standards
on others. The family's lifestyle was its own business
and its moral standards and values were to be accepted
and respected. [1]

Gertrude Springer's Miss Bailey series was an exponent of the best
of commonsensical and socially minded journalism, which never
sounded unprofessional in its simplicity or unintelligible in its professionalism.

The second excerpt in this part is an article that appeared in
the Survey Midmonthly in February 1941. Written by Louis Towley,
this article discusses the qualifications of a rural worker, a subject
that remained in vogue well into the 1940s but slowly disappeared
from the literature in the 1950s as professional social workers became more concerned with urban than with rural practice. Towley's
statements are still true in many areas of the country. His views
that rural social work is mostly public work (and by that he meant
public welfare work) were echoed by Ginsberg in 1976.

The existence of public programs and the absence of private programs carry several implications for rural social
workers. . . . The public, basic services must often expand their activities to include functions that they might
not carry in cities. For example, a public welfare office
might be charged with much more responsibility for family
counseling, community development, and social welfare
planning simply because it exists, is staffed with knowledge-
able people, and needs to help meet problems that occur. [2]

Today's concern with community level intervention in the rural
field is still one that prevails among rural practitioners. Towley's
commonsensical description that rural social work might, after all,
be a call of sorts is not out of place in the 1980s, when our concern
with scientific truths and methods has made the profession forget that
social work has always been, in the words of Porter Lee, a "cause
and a function," and that social work's uniqueness lies as much on the
first as on the second.

Finally, the third piece, a response to Towley's article from
the perspective of the 1980s, was written especially for this volume
by Naomi Griffith, a public welfare supervisor in Morgan County,
Alabama. Perhaps some explanations about the public welfare system
in that state will help the reader understand Griffith's perspectives.

At the county level in the State of Alabama, the Department of Pensions and Security is divided along the lines

of Public Assistance Eligibility and Social Services. The Eligibility Unit determines the client's eligibility for Aid to Dependent Children or Supplemental Assistance for the Elderly. It also administers Food Stamps and Child Support Recoupment as well as informing clients of the availability of Title XX Services. This unit does not make home visits, but rather sees the client in the office for the initial interview and for review of redeterminations of eligibility. The eligibility unit refers to the Service Units when it is felt that a client is in need of services in addition to public assistance.

Service Units are divided into Family and Children's Service and Adult Service. These units deliver Title XX services along with Child Welfare Services such as adoptions. In these units child abuse and neglect are investigated as well as adult abuse and/or exploitation. These social workers go "to the field" to see clients regularly. If a client is referred to DPS, the social worker seeks him out and assesses his need for services. The social worker explains services which are available through this public agency and might refer clients to other agencies. These service workers are the outreach arm of the agency. They respond to the request of a person for help, and they visit with persons whom others feel are in need.[3]

NOTES

1. Clarke A. Chambers, Paul V. Kellogg and the Survey: Voices for Social Welfare and Social Justice (Minneapolis: University of Minnesota Press, 1971), p. 144.

2. Leon H. Ginsberg, ed., Social Work in Rural Communities: A Book of Readings (New York: CSWE, 1976), p. 7.

3. Letter from Naomi Griffith to the author.

SOME SCARS REMAIN

Gertrude Springer

Miss Bailey knew as well as anyone that in going out like this she was breaking all precepts about client privacy. In fact, she knew it somewhat better than the young worker whom she was accompanying. He wasn't bothered too much by precepts and he had welcomed company for the long drive into the country to visit what the county welfare director had described as "that boxcar family."

On either side of the road stretched vast reaches of treeless country undulating to the horizon. There were few reminders in the tawny grass-grown pasture lands or the occasional stubble fields, that only a few years ago this had been dust-bowl country, victim of a scourge which only nature at its cruelest could inflict. To Miss Bailey the wounds of those devastating years seemed pretty well healed, but young Mr. Harmon knew better.

"Don't fool yourself, the scars are here. The emptiness of the country is one of them. See that little school house? It used to have nineteen pupils; now it has six. Those rises of ground over there used to have good stands of buildings, and the farms were well stocked and well cultivated. Now they're abandoned."

"What became of the buildings?" asked Miss Bailey, whose ideas of abandoned farms came from New England.

"Rustled," replied Mr. Harmon laconically. Then, in answer to Miss Bailey's questioning look: "Abandoned buildings don't last very long here. Lumber is too scarce. Piece by piece they just disappear. People don't figure it as stealing; it's just that they need the

---

Gertrude Springer was a native midwesterner who, after graduation from Kansas State University, pursued a career in journalism until World War I. The American Red Cross afforded her the opportunity of working in Italy and advocating for the little people and the man in the front lines. She joined Survey Midmonthly in 1930 and kept social journalism flourishing for the 12 years she stayed with Survey. She was a friend of most of the well-known social workers of the time, from Grace Abbott to Harry Hopkins. Her Miss Bailey column gave her fame among the thousands of less-known practitioners who staffed the front lines of public relief. In 1952 she received the Terry Award from the Annual Conference of the American Public Welfare Association for her creation of the "delightul and readable" Miss Bailey. Gertrude Springer died on July 17, 1953. "Some Scars Remain" originally appeared in Survey 78 (January 1942): 13-14.

stuff the other fellow has practically thrown away. It's an old custom of the country."

"What about the people? What's become of them?"

Mr. Harmon made a wide gesture in a general westerly direction. "Gone. Not all the Okies were from Oklahoma, you know. We contributed our quota. And a good many are still in our own towns, thanks to WPA."

Before Miss Bailey could put the obvious question, Mr. Harmon went on, "See those grain elevators over there? That's where we're going. That's where the boxcar family lives."

You couldn't miss the elevators. They stood up in the landscape like the Empire State Building on the New York skyline. Around them was a grayish patch which was undoubtedly the town, though in the great sweep of country it looked like a lone teacup on a banquet table.

The boxcar family, explained Mr. Harmon, was several kinds of headache, all tangled up with unpredictable human emotions.

"Such as?" asked Miss Bailey.

"We'el," replied Mr. Harmon, a little pink around his young ears, "I suppose you could call it love."

"Oh," said Miss Bailey.

Mrs. Boxcar, it seemed, had been the wife of a farmer who managed somehow, with relief and one thing and another, to get through the worst of the bad years. Then he died, thereby qualifying his four babies, all under five, for aid to dependent children. The farm already was practically lost and wasn't much good anyway even if the widow had wanted to stay on it, which she didn't. So with an ADC grant of $39 a month she moved, bag and baggage, into two decent rooms in town.

At first all that cash money seemed like munificence to her—"Her husband was one of those who never let his wife see a nickel even when he had it"—but pretty soon she found that it wasn't so much. And the children were more of a handful in two rooms than they had been running loose on the farm. "But I guess the real trouble," said Mr. Harmon thoughtfully, "was that she was lonesome for a man around. She was only twenty-five."

The man who came around was Mr. Boxcar, a bachelor neighbor in the country until he was "blown out," and went to town to go on WPA. Just about when his eighteen-months' layoff was coming up, he got a job at $70 a month taking out coal in the nearby strip-mines. With such an income the lonely bachelor could afford a wife and home. What could be more natural than that he should turn to the lonely widow?

The welfare department, said Mr. Harmon, had reservations about the match, though marriage of widows is usually counted as a satisfactory way to reduce the ADC case load. "But we knew that the strip-mines were due to shut down and that cuts in our WPA quota left him no chance there. So we advised her to wait and to hang on to her ADC status a little longer. But I guess they really were—well—'that way' about each other. You know how people are."

Yes, Miss Bailey knew.

"Anyway," went on Mr. Harmon, "the next thing we heard they were married and that saved us $39 a month. For awhile everything went fine. They moved into a little house, the kids had new hair ribbons and the Missus a permanent wave. Then the strip-mine shut down. The man had been working such a short time that his unemployment compensation didn't mean anything, and WPA is still laying 'em off, not taking 'em on. They had to move out of their house into whatever they could get. It turned out to be a boxcar."

It was indeed a boxcar, stripped of its running gear and set down endwise on the dusty road which presently would be Main Street. A rough door and window had been cut on the street end, but all the rest of it was just old red freight car.

The door was opened by a black-haired giant of a man, all bone and muscle. Crowding around his legs, their blue eyes bright with curiosity, were four stairsteps of towheaded children. Back in the dimness was a woman so young and pretty that Miss Bailey promptly forgave all. To be sure the children were far from immaculate, the splintery floor was unswept, dirty dishes competed with a stuttering radio for space on the table, but, since Miss Bailey's domestic experience did not run to keeping house in a boxcar, she was not inclined to be critical.

Miss Bailey need not have worried about intruding on the privacy of the interview. She heard none of it. This was men's business and the two men attended to it in the dark furthermost reaches of the boxcar. She was left to talk with Mrs. Boxcar. Just as the weather and the prevalence of colds were pretty well exhausted as topics of conversation, the men emerged from the gloom.

Mrs. Boxcar dropped the weather like a hot potato. "Well, what about it?" she asked sharply. Her husband shrugged his shoulders. "Says he can't do a thing. Says I'd better light out for some of these places where there's defense work, and send you back some money."

Mrs. Boxcar ruffled up like a little hen. "And leave your family and maybe get sick and nobody to take care of you? No, siree! Kids or no kids, if you go I go."

Mr. Boxcar smiled and patter her shoulder. "Honey, that's just what I've been tellin' him."

Neither Miss Bailey nor Mr. Harmon had much to say as they drove through Main Street and on into the open country. Finally she asked, "Is it true that you can't do anything?"

"I'm afraid it is. You see he's employable, and such little general relief as we have is strictly limited to unemployables. There's no way that I can think of now for him to get even food stamps. With harvest over there's no work for him here until the strip-mines open, months from now. Tough, isn't it, a big husky like that."

"Wouldn't he be better on the land? Can't the Farm Security people do anything?"

"Nope. I've tried 'em. They're very choosy, take only men who have been operating farmers, and Boxcar was never that; he really was just a farmhand. Of course he'd be better on the land. So would hundreds of farm people who were drawn into these little towns by WPA and now are stranded, rotting their lives out. WPA unsettled 'em in droves and now FSA piously resettles 'em one by one. What kind of a policy do you call that? And meantime the land that they left has been gathered in, usually for delinquent taxes, by a new kind of speculator who works it at the absolute minimum to get the maximum benefits under the Agricultural Adjustment Administration. Those guys don't give a whoop about producing. They're farming to get the most they can out of the government. And where does that leave Boxcar?"

Miss Bailey didn't know. Agricultural economics were not up her street. So she asked another question.

"How are the Boxcars, and the four babies, going to eat this winter, and keep warm?"

"Well, he still has a few dollars that he earned during harvest, and five or six bushels of potatoes that he dug on shares. He gets a quart of milk a day for milking three cows, and he knows where he can get some winter squash. For fuel he digs in the tipple and sifts coal out of the dust. He's worried, but he doesn't want her to know it. Honestly, he'd be an all-right guy if he just had work."

"What about the people who stuck to the land? Are they any better off?"

"They couldn't be worse than Boxcar, and some of them are better. Why, we have a woman, an ADC case—say, let's go see her. It isn't much out of the way."

As the car jounced over the rough dirt road Mr. Harmon told about Mrs. Birnoff. Her husband had been a fairly prosperous farmer until he fell sick. It was cancer and before he finally died debts had accumulated and much of the livestock had been sold. The day after the funeral the house burned.

"We first heard of her," Mr. Harmon went on, "when a neighbor told us that she was living on the prairie and that something ought to be done about the children. So we traveled out there and sure enough there was the furniture set out on the prairie with tarpaulins spread over it and the mother and her four little girls crawling in under at night. Nothing would induce her to leave the place, first because she knew that if she did the barn and sheds, ramshackle as they were,

would be rustled; and second because she was sure that if she could
get the few hundred dollars insurance on the house she could work
the place herself and make a go of it. She knew how to farm, but she
didn't know how to live in town and she didn't propose to lose all that
she and her husband had worked to accumulate. She's from the old
Russo-German stock that first settled this country and those people
sure aren't afraid to work.

"Well, we offered to do what we could and she took us up. We
made her an ADC grant of $39 a month and our attorney helped her
with her insurance claim and with adjustments so that in the end she
had a good quarter section free and clear, the most necessary farm
machinery, a couple of cows, a horse, and some chickens. Also four
little girls, the oldest only eleven.

"The matter of a house was a sticker. We suggested trying to
make the barn habitable, but she needed that for the stock and anyway
she had a better idea. Built out from the side of a hill was a big half-
dugout chicken house, and did she do a job on it! She cleaned and
scrubbed it, patched the roof, traded days' work for windows that she
put in herself, laid a floor of pounded clay mixed with straw, and
finally had a perfectly decent, snug, one-room house, a lot better,
she says, than her grandmother ever had. I hope she's home. She's
a great character."

But Mrs. Birnoff wasn't home, and the visitors could only wan-
der around, climbing down into the root-cellar stocked with heaps of
potatoes and winter vegetables, and peering through white curtains
into the half dugout with its neatly made beds and oil-cloth covered
table. As they were about to give up, Mr. Harmon's sharp eyes
caught a glint of light way off on the prairie. "Here come the kids
from school. See the sun on their dinner pail?"

"Ma," said the oldest girl was "getting in the millet." She'd go
get her. And go she did, bounding away like an antelope.

Mother and daughter rode the load of millet in together. Mrs.
Birnoff wore a man's overalls, a man's wide straw hat, a man's
heavy work shoes. Her skin was like coffee, her hands like oak, her
smile like sunshine. She was getting along fine, she said. Another
day and the millet would all be in. Had we seen the new root-cellar?
The roof of the house had a leak where the stovepipe came through,
but she knew where to borrow a soldering iron to fix it. One cow was
beginning to dry up but the other would soon be fresh. "Four kids
need a lot of milk." No, there was nothing she needed, she was getting along fine.

"But Mrs. Birnoff," said Miss Bailey, "don't you get lonesome?
You're so far from town or from neighbors."

Mrs. Birnoff laughed out loud. "Me, lonesome? When would I
have time to be lonesome? I've got four kids to bring up and that oldest
—already I see she's smart. She's got to have real schooling. No, I'm
not lonesome."

ALL THIS AND HEAVEN HELP US, TOO

Louis Towley

What a state agency wants in the way of a rural social worker is
not to be found in any objective statement of standards and qualifications. It is not so simple as that. Social workers as a whole are not
prefabricated. A rural social worker, particularly, is not easily
measurable by a yardstick. It is the difference between hiring a cook
and choosing a wife—although one school of thought holds that it's so
much the better if a wife can cook.

Personnel standards are not enough in the rural field even though
the local community bears with them. The worker must have the en-
dowment impossible to define in formally stated qualifications, that
will make paper criteria come alive. He, or more usually she, must
personify the technical terms by which personnel is judged and must
make them understood and accepted by the community. Without local
acceptance, no amount of merit plan, no personnel standards are
worth a whistle in a rain barrel.

This does not mean that an agency should sit back and wait for
the mountain. It means, rather, a constant process of education and
persuasion, a progressive stiffening of requirements, beginning with
standards that meet the realistic situation, but with alternatives that
point to the desirable goal. By constant education and effort, backed
up with staff performance, the community and its welfare board or
committee will be convinced that the best people are not too good for
this job. It is a slow process, but it is the only sound one.

The rural worker is the core of this education process, the
proof of the pudding. In the country rather more than in the cities,
the claims of personnel standards depend on the worker's performance.
The rural worker carries the brunt of the newest pioneering in public

---

Louis Towley (1904-59) was born in Minnesota and educated as
a student of literature. He spent his early years as a journalist,
working on a family newspaper. During the depression Towley found
his way into social work through the public agencies of Minnesota and
served as director of public assistance of his native state for many
years. He was a faculty member at the George Washington School of
Social Work of Washington University in St. Louis, Missouri, beginning in 1944. He was a much admired speaker and consultant for social work organizations. His style was pungent, whimsical, and always interesting. This article originally appeared in Survey Midmonthly 77 (January 1941): 49-51.

welfare and its helper, social work. She is the Fuller brush man without the free sample. In this almost virgin field the choice and decision
in personnel matters rests with men and women to whom social work
is a relatively mysterious profession, all the more mysterious because it has such a hard time explaining itself. The community knows
something of the money grant programs; to a degree they interpret
themselves—money talks. But the larger aspect of the work—service,
prevention, rehabilitation, treatment—is another language. Only one
person can translate this and make the soul of the work understood.
And that is the rural worker.

This talk of soul makes the job sound like a mission, but I really
don't think a "call" is necessary. A call is a nice thing to have, but
may be awkward to live with. Rather, I suggest that one must like
people more than they deserve and be able occasionally to restrain
the impulses that proceed from this liking. What is needed is sympathy and intelligence, and a rational control that will direct potential
energy and insight. One without the other two is ineffectual. Without
sympathy, one has little drive; without intelligence, one sits passive,
uttering restrained cooing sounds; without rational control, one will
fall on his face—bright, eager, young as that face may be.

All of this applies equally well to all social workers; there's
nothing rural about it. The qualities of urban and rural social workers
do not differ very much except in degree, in responsibilities, and, I
dare to suggest, in temperament. The basic desiderata are very much
the same.

As to academic equipment, a desirable present norm is a college
degree with one year's graduate training in social work, plus as wide
a background as possible. Given the realities of the times many agencies allow experience, even in related fields, to be substituted for
some of the academic points. This elasticity is necessary as a means
of bringing the local community along.

Integrity is perhaps the first quality of a social worker. It cannot be overemphasized, but of course if you have it no emphasis is
needed; and if you haven't, emphasis doesn't help very much. And
tolerance—plenty of that, but not too much of the speaking sort. Like
old-fashioned children, tolerance should be seen and not heard. It
should be lived, not talked about.

Intellectual honesty is the first requirement for anything beyond
temporary success. This means that you must find and face the facts
and not pass the buck.

Someone has said, and rightly, that a social worker must have
a passion for fairness and that this fairness should be employed in the
face of prejudice and pressure.

Patience you will need more than bread and wine. I suggest that
this patience owe nothing to Job and less to Griselda. It must instead

be that temporary armistice with disappointment that is not resigned to permanent failure—like a young man refused his first kiss.

These are a few of the basic qualities that all social workers must have. A more difficult question, because more intangible, is how to describe the traits and abilities needed in extra measure by the rural worker.

It must be remembered that rural social work is almost wholly public work. The distinction is simple and fundamental in its implications. It means that in all you do, you represent government—and if you think this is something to puff you up you will shortly be deflated. The representative of government finds that the cloak of authority is not a cloak at all, but a multiplicity of petticoats—and petty is the word. The worker that is wanted is one who rarely if ever will use authority as such.

The state agency and the county administrators want a worker who will like a rural environment and find it friendly and helpful. This is vital because the community is a major factor in rural social work. It is the far-from-silent partner in the whole enterprise. The worker deals not only with individuals and agencies, but often with the whole community. There are strata, to be sure, but there is not much segregation. The difference is significant. Economic inequalities may be great, but there is partially compensating social integration. The banker may hire his garbage hauled, but he stops to pass the time of day with the scavenger, may even ride downtown on the truck. Mrs. Banker inquires about the little scavengers and asks for their mother's recipe for corn muffins.

A successful rural worker must be able to represent the state agency to the community and the community to the state agency; in other words, to support each against the other—a task requiring not only whalebone and steel but a two-way stretch. This kind of support may be what the state agency means when it talks about flexibility. Undoubtedly the state agency is a trial to the county workers, the cross that they must bear. The state agency realizes its dour role and in its best moments tries to mitigate the results. Because it usually fails, it wants workers of a forebearing nature who can understand its position and survive its vagaries.

The agency wants workers who can see administration as the application of general requirements to specific needs. This view of administration, insufficiently recognized in a period that must stress mechanics, requires good sound sense, the ability to discipline oneself without being subservient, and the constant use of the complementary senses of humor and proportion. Can you, for example, keep as straight a face as your district supervisor when he presents the state's latest superhuman demand in the way of reports, checks, audits, procedures? There is more than a little of a certain Japanese politeness

underlying the conventions between state and county agencies. Until
you understand this and automatically can make the due allowance for
it, you will be vastly puzzled and more than a little disillusioned.
Once you grasp the point and can laugh about it, you will see these
are like most conventions: they lubricate contacts that otherwise·
might become heated.

It is a truism that administrators want workers who can follow
instructions. But they also want workers who can go beyond instructions and use their own ingenuity and originality. The reason for this
paradox lies in the fact that during the past eight years some ten to a
dozen major money-grant programs have been put in operation. A
money-grant program, particularly when it involves more than one
level of government, requires extensive policies, procedures, checks,
and audits that in turn require emphasis on routine and mechanics.
As a result of this constant and repeated emphasis, the staff of most
agencies has been conditioned by the very excellence of its routines:
it has come to see the end and being of its work in terms of routine.
These routines are necessary, but workers must rise above mechanics
to give that additional service that is the cohesive of a public welfare
program, the plus that adds depth to the work and stature to the worker.

A good state agency wants workers who can see beyond explicit
instructions into the implications and the purpose that underlie them.
This calls for an original habit of mind and more than a little nervous
energy, hard to find in these burdened days. Yet workers say that in
action independently planned, with its accent on service, they find release and refreshment. To be sure, workers who seek that release
may have to suffer for what T. E. Lawrence called sins of too great
individuality and common sense. But administrators like the kind of
worker who can retain perspective while going through the alarming
experience of paying dearly for a virtue.

This matter of individuality in workers is basic to a major question now arising in administrative practice: Within a prescribed minimum uniformity, how much latitude can the state agency give to the
worker's judgment and discretion? The answer to that question is the
next development in administration. The proper answer, I believe,
will put the accent on service, will recognize the family as a unit, and
will counteract, at least in part, the curse of the categories.

The temperament of the rural worker is important for a special
reason: few of them are fortunate enough to have a skilled supervisor
on whom worries can be sloughed, with whom troubles can be shared.
Each worker must restore his own balance. An even temperament is
advantageous, although the performers are valuable because many of
them, along with firecrackers in their makeup, have stable personali-
ties. A stable personality is to be preferred to an even temperament,
provided you can't have both. It gives the worker that quality of con-

stancy that wins and holds the respect, perhaps even the liking, of people in the community. Remember that contact with the county board is frequent and sustained. It involves a great deal of give and take, with the social worker usually on the taking end.

The even temperament or the stable personality or both, are important for another reason: in the country you don't leave your work and your community contacts behind when you leave the office. You carry them with you to your home and into your social relaxation. It is the rare worker who does not of necessity remain the "welfare" everywhere and always. Administrators do not want people who have to be on their guard all the time. They want people who can do their work and win their place naturally, without pose or tenseness.

All of this adds up to something very obvious. The worker must fit into the community, be an inconspicuous yet forceful part of it. She must be able to modulate from key to key, staying in tune whether the voice be that of harmony or counterpoint. She must have poise, adaptability, and enough force of character to be a person as well as a representative of the welfare office. She must stand for certain things without being what in gentler days was called a prig. Tact, of course, will be her shield and buckler. There may be a time, for example, when she must persuade the pastors and the priests of the community that the slot machines or the beer taverns are raising particular havoc with certain young people, not only from families across the tracks but from some of the pillar families of the community. It is best if that persuasion can be done without alienating the heavy taxpayers who own the joints. Don't be shocked at that compromise: it is only sound public-servant sense. Obviously this means an ability to organize people to do something about the problems you dig up. The community itself has to be caseworked. But as heaven is your help, never use that phrase.

Force of character and tact are needed in many circumstances. You attend a church supper and your neighbors on either side toss back and forth in front of you their distorted version of the latest unmarried pregnancy the records of which, as everyone knows, are confidential. Can you quietly set these good women straight with a minimum of facts and then later stand up under the accusation that you talked about the case? That sort of thing sometimes has to be done. It takes quick judgment, considerable quiet force, and the best sort of bourgeois tact.

The rural worker operates in a field requiring wide knowledge. Can you talk mortgagors, deeds, joint tenancy, harrowing, silage, overrun, hames, single-tree, Torrens title? This is not quite the language of psychiatric case work, but it is the language of your everyday work in a rural community, in whatever terms you may think. You need to know taxes, property valuations. You must be able to dig out the facts of local indebtedness. You need to have a working knowledge of sociology and economics, with special stress on the rural phase of Carlyle's dismal sciences.

All of this is random comment on some of the more important complementary intangible qualities the state agency and the county administrator want in a rural social worker. Does it sound like all this and heaven help us, too? After all, the qualities are not necessarily peculiar to any social worker. The ability to work with people, a controlled sympathy for them, understanding and originality in putting skills to work—these are basic. Flexibility in meeting different situations is a valuable ally. I do not mean that oozing type of flexibility that absorbs and envelopes and takes on protective coloration; rather I mean the flexibility that comes from tempering, a giving-way and a springing back, a shift in approach, without being shifty.

You must not gather from this that all a social worker needs is common sense. That is fundamental, as it is to any well-rounded person, but training helps make the fundamental equipment usable. Training is disciplined common sense.

Come to think of it, perhaps some kind of "call" is necessary; a sort of private dedication that you will sometimes laugh at until you come to see that a great work is only the sum total of many, very many, humble dedications—coupled with temper of mind and strength of character built upon the homely virtues of honesty, integrity, and industry.

PUBLIC WORK IN THE 1980s: MORGAN COUNTY, ALABAMA

Naomi Haines Griffith

To the average American social work practitioner, Morgan County, Alabama, would conjure up pastoral images of farms, bad roads, cotton, clapboard, and red clay poverty. This locale would appear to represent the epitome of rural social work where people are isolated and aloof but in desperate need. The county area is classified "rural" for although Decatur, its only real center of population, had around 46,000 people in the last census, the rest of the area is indeed "rural," even judging it by the current arbitrary population standards. According to national criteria, the social worker in Morgan County is a rural practitioner.

Generalizations, however, can be very misleading; therefore, to understand the role of the Decatur, Alabama, rural social worker, a look at this particular geographic area of practice is absolutely necessary. The term rural, applied solely on the basis of population, is at best nebulous and vague and in Morgan County it would be no exception.

Morgan County, Alabama, is a strange mixture of lonely, sparsely populated areas and industrial complexes that puff smoke along the banks of the beautiful Tennessee River. Diversified industry dealing in automobile parks, polyester fiber, chemicals, and paper line the river that was tamed in the 1930s by the Tennessee Valley Authority. The dams and accompanying power plants that provided cheap power in an area with a ready labor supply contributed heavily to the development of the Tennessee Valley into an industrial area, a peculiarity in most of the deep South.

Therefore, in this technically rural southern county, the social work practitioner can drive from the mammoth General Motors plant to the most stereotypical rural setting in less than 15 minutes. From the smokestack to the haystack is only a step comparable to the city resident's trip to the supermarket. The successful social worker in Morgan County, Alabama, is a flexible, adaptable, and resilient professional who is much like the social worker of the New Deal era. The

---

Naomi Haines Griffith is Child Welfare Supervisor II at the Department of Pensions and Security of the state of Alabama. Griffith received an M.A. from George Peabody College (1965) and an M.S.W. from the University of Alabama (1978). Prior to her present position in Alabama, she was with the Cumberland County Department of Public Welfare in North Carolina.

practitioner in this contrasting area must deal with the problem of the farm and factory family all rolled into one.

In Towley's 1941 article "All This and Heaven Help Us, Too," the author stands but one step into the New Deal and merely on the brink of the unbelievable growth that the next 40 years would bring in federally funded, bureaucratically administered social work. The dilemma of Towley's 1941 rural social worker, getting services to far-flung families, is still an accurate description of the current problem facing the public welfare social worker in this Alabama county. Towley uses rural social worker and public worker interchangeably, and this is probably the key to understanding the role of the rural Alabama social worker today.

While all social workers of the 1940s tenaciously carried the first blooms of federal New Deal programs to the families of their area, the 1980 social worker who assumes this role is the public welfare social worker, for the rural social worker today, in Alabama at least, is the outreach worker or field worker. When Towley used the term public, he was indeed futuristic, for Towley's worker has become the public welfare worker of today. Although the public welfare social workers in some areas of the United States have dropped "in home" work, Alabama's public welfare outreach effort is vital and basic. It is this practitioner who regularly seeks out and delivers services, whether county, state, or federal, to families in their own homes. The list of services has grown considerably since Towley's era. The public welfare social worker is still the liaison between the individual and the vast array of agencies that offer specific services in this area.

The role of Towley's rural social worker falls to the public welfare social worker in Morgan County, Alabama, and probably in most other areas of this country.* This is the practitioner who leaves a warm office, travels to the family at the end of the rutted, washed-out road, and explains the alternatives, services, and possible consequences that are present in the lives of the client. The public welfare social worker is the one who reaches out and makes the connection that completes the circuit of service.

---

*For example, neighboring Georgia is organized at the county level much like Alabama with the service unit social workers functioning as field workers. The local department is called Department of Family and Children's Services (DFACS) and is the only agency that functions in each of Georgia's counties as a home-visiting, outreach agency. Although a grant agency may appear in an area for a certain period of time, DFACS is the agency in each county that is available with continuity and ongoing bases.

This rural social worker in Alabama is an activist, an aggressive force who seeks out and intervenes. While numerous other agencies hang out their signs, define their roles very sharply, and wait for a client to approach them for service, the "public worker" (Towley's term) regularly catches families who fall between the gaps and circles of the myriad of social agencies that are the full-blown New Deal, New Frontier, and new Title XX. The public worker explains, interprets, and sells the services of all the other agencies.

These last 40 years have brought changes in the framework in which the Alabama public welfare social worker delivers services. In the 1930s she worked for the Alabama Child Welfare Bureau, protecting the welfare of children and families. Like Towley's description, the child welfare worker fought prejudice, suspicion, and misunderstanding and became the link between families and increasing services. She represented all of government, the object of distrust and disdain. Today the attitude of Morgan County people is much the same: general resentment of governmental intervention. However, creeping into this bastion of conservatism and self-reliance is a desire for a little taste of the readily available governmental fruits. Food stamps, subsidized housing, and other services are no longer objects of derision and disgust. Rather, for many of the staunchest individuals, these opportunities are seen as objects they "bought and paid for" and deserved.

It is this diverse, changing client population and the innumerable services available that are the greatest challenges to the public or rural social worker in Morgan County. This social worker must know and develop rapport with city dwellers, farm families, and hybrids of the two. Added to this is the task of "representing" (Towley's term) county, state, and federal services of many specialties. She does not represent them officially, of course, but she must be aware of all programs and services for, more than likely, she is the only person who reaches out and enumerates the possibilities. Federal services such as the Women, Infants and Children Program (WIC), rent subsidy, and CETA, added to a variety of state programs, including Crippled Children's Services, Vocational Rehabilitation, Work Incentive, and Child Support, to name only a few, are but the top two layers to county and private resources that the public or rural social worker must represent to the client. In this respect the rural social worker is the purest of all case managers, aware of the alternatives and willing to bring these to the attention of the client. She takes the same important step that Towley's rural social worker took: outreach.

As American society has seen the passing of the family doctor who makes house calls, social work has quietly witnessed the demise of the outreach, home-intervening social worker. As a medical specialist sits in an office awaiting a referral, so does the social work practitioner in most agencies today.

It is quite possible that the rural social worker has little, if anything, to do with rural in the traditional sense. Rural social work is possibly an approach to service delivery that was spawned out of necessity when client cars and phones were scarce and programs were new, but has now evolved into a philosophy of social work practice that involves a more aggressive, active, outreach approach to service delivery. Many social workers, with all their particular specialties and closely defined practice settings, choose to work with the highly motivated client who seeks out the social work practitioner, rather than taking the position of Towley's social worker that the people who needed services the most were unaware of their existence or unwilling to ask.

I have no doubt that rural social work is being practiced in Decatur, Alabama, as well as in outlying regions of Morgan County, if rural workers are indeed the social workers who function in all settings, know something about everything, seldom say "We can't help you," are usually available (without appointment), and make house calls. Rural social workers continue to fight the bureaucratic gnome on their days in the office and are often all things to all people on their days in the field.

2/ Rural Social Research and the Conditions of Rural Life

INTRODUCTION

One of the most striking historical facts facing students of social welfare research is the central role that the survey, as a tool of social science investigations, played in the development of the profession. From the early stages of social research, investigators painstakingly documented a variety of social conditions that plagued city and country alike. Although in the rural areas the very first exponent of organized social fact-finding had been the commission inquiry method (for example, the Country Life Commission), the survey soon overshadowed all other methods of appraisals of social conditions.

The beginning of the twentieth century witnessed an emphasis on scientific investigations and an invigorated faith in the value of fact-finding research for the resolution of the problems of poverty and social malaise. Facts were seen as the primary requirement for connected action. This dual commitment to research and remediation was characteristic of all the early social scientists, rural sociologists, social workers, clergymen, and social journalists, although through the years it has remained a feature only of those who, like clergymen and social workers, continue to espouse a "cause" in their professional commitments.

In September 1907 Paul Kellogg, "aged twenty-eight but already seasoned by ten years of writing and editing,"[1] moved to Pittsburgh following the invitation of Alice B. Montgomery of the Allegheny Juvenile Court.[2] Here he began the work that would eventually result in the most comprehensive survey of social conditions and exposé of socioeconomic problems of the city of Pittsburgh. The Pittsburgh survey proved to be "creative research and journalism at its best."[3] Chambers has suggested that "not until the Pittsburgh Survey was completed, and then, not again for many years, was there such a compendium of facts, the facts of human existence in modern industrial communities."[4] In 1909 Charities and the Commons changed its name to Survey, thus highlighting for nearly 50 years the central importance of the Pittsburgh findings and of social surveys as instruments of progress and reform.

In the rural field, the twentieth century had seen the introduction of rural social surveys by a number of religious organizations staffed by persons whose names are now associated with the early days of rural sociology.

Under the leadership of the clergyman and educator Warren
H. Wilson, the Board of Home Missions of the Presbyterian Church in the United States of America conducted
church and community surveys in counties in Pennsylvania (1910), Indiana and Tennessee (1911), Missouri
and Maryland (1912), Arkansas (1914), California (1915),
and Oregon (1916). . . . In Ohio, Paul L. Vogt undertook
a series of rural life surveys that were sponsored jointly
by the Ohio Rural Life Association and the Church and
County Life Department of the Federal Council of Churches.[5]

In later years the scientific method was behind the many survey activities of the Interchurch World Movement (1919) and the Country
Life Association (also 1919), and finally, the "breakthrough for the
support of social research at the experiment stations and with the passage of the Purnell Act in 1925."[6] Surveys of the rural village, farm
populations, rural-urban migration patterns, and so on flourished
through the years, reaching new pinnacles in the research units of the
FERA, the CCC, and, in later years, the WPA. The FERA-WPA
published over 20 monographs between the years 1935 and 1940 that
reported assessments of various social conditions prior to and following the intervention of those agencies.

It must be noted, however, that the passing of time brought forth
modifications in the nature and scope of the surveys performed. Kellogg's 1909 Pittsburgh survey had covered a variety of problems,
from conditions of labor and the study of the economic cost of typhoid
to living conditions and household budgets. The 1920s and 1930s saw
a general refinement and narrowing down of the scope of the areas to
be assessed, as most surveys concentrated on a particular topic or
field. Two new elements introduced in the prewar years were assessments of needs and resources and an eagerness to measure, even if
in rudimentary fashion, the impact of interventive social legislation.

But the importance of this new variety of survey as the major
source of data for rural research continued to diminish after World
War II. Although the basic fact-finding tool is still used at present,
its centrality has been lost to more sophisticated devices. Presently,
surveys—defined more narrowly than ever before—are used in conjunction with other research methods since, as shall be seen from the
examination of the Vinson and Jesberg's piece, they can still provide
valuable information to action-oriented social workers who must be
able to grasp the broad view of many social problems.

The three examples selected for this part of the Appendix constitute but an arbitrary selection of the many pieces that could have
been included. They do, however, illustrate the development of the
survey as a tool of rural social research through the seven decades

that concern this volume. The first article, "Rural Social Research —Methods and Results," is an abbreviated version of a paper presented to the National Conference on Social Work in 1927. George H. Von Tungeln, then a professor of sociology at Iowa State College in Ames, tried not only to convince his social work audience of the merits of social research, particularly of the survey method, but also attempted to point out to a group heavily imbued in the casework tradition that "the city . . . needs its social case experts as the country needs its community experts." This message endured many decades and is still applicable in the rural field. Writing about the merits of Von Tungeln's Iowa studies, Lowry Nelson suggested:

> Von Tungeln's studies were pioneering efforts and thus subject to the weaknesses and advantages of the survey method. The survey attempts to cover all aspects of social and economic life and as a consequence tends to be superficial. On the other hand, it provides the residents of a local community with a broad picture of their condition and an accumulation of data that can be used as a basis for planning. [7]

The second article, A. R. Mangus's "Spotlight on Rural Needs," is an illustration of the type of survey that became popular during the war and postwar years. Mangus's surveys were narrower in scope and dealt with only one topical area, in this case rural mental health, or in the terminology of those days, rural mental hygiene. An interesting feature of the work of the early rural sociologists is that their findings were not limited to describing the conditions of a given environment, but extended beyond description to provide guidelines for amelioration. "The facts speak loudly enough for themselves," says Mangus in his presentation. "They show that mental ill health and social maladjustment are no less a rural than an urban problem. They show that services are needed in Miami County to cope with these problems, no less than in her sister cities." Of course, it was the ameliorative emphasis that made these surveys useful and popular among rural social workers. As prescriptive statements began to be erased from the reports of rural sociologists because of the more scientific orientation of that discipline in later years, rural social workers became disinterested in what rural sociology could still offer to social welfare. The dialogue between the two fields is still less than affable. New statements of common purposes have not yet been pronounced.

The final contribution, Elizabeth A. Vinson and Kate M. Jesberg's "The Rural Stake in Public Assistance: Summary of Findings and Recommendations," is the most contemporary exponent of rural data collection. While the researchers had at their command a variety of means to gather their information, survey data were utilized as one tool in the construction of the rural poverty profile they offer the reader. What makes Vinson and Jesberg's work particularly useful to social workers is their action or ameliorative orientation. The authors suggest that their findings illustrate "specific characteristics of the rural poor that are pertinent to public policy decisions." While a myriad of characteristics could have been used to describe the rural poor, these researchers chose to present those characteristics that would affect or illuminate policy decisions, thus making their data all the more significant for professionals in the rural field. Vinson and Jesberg's "Summary" has been slightly shortened for presentation in this volume. Final comments by the principal author (Vinson) were prepared specially for this volume and have been included under the heading of "Follow-Up of the Project."

NOTES

1. Clarke A. Chambers, Paul V. Kellogg and the Survey (Minneapolis: University of Minnesota Press, 1971), p. 35.
2. Ibid., p. 33.
3. Ibid., p. 37.
4. Ibid.
5. Lowry Nelson, Rural Sociology: Its Origin and Growth in the United States (Minneapolis: University of Minnesota Press, 1969), p. 46.
6. Ibid., p. 86.
7. Ibid., p. 72.

RURAL SOCIAL RESEARCH—METHODS AND RESULTS

George H. Von Tungeln

Man is the label of heredity and environment. He is, in part, also the manufacturer of both his heredity and his environment. Scientific research and experimentation are the modern means for the accurate analysis and synthesization of heredity and environment as these forces of nature and nurture relate to the improvement of man, and as man relates himself to them and to their improvement both in his attitudes and his actions. This paper will deal primarily with research, the first of these two instruments of social progress. Furthermore, it will be restricted largely to rural social research.

The Purpose of or Objectives in Rural Social Work

Rural social research plays an important role in the answer to that perpetual dual question that socially conscious individuals and communities are always asking about their communities, namely, what can be done to improve local conditions and how can it be done? To answer this dual question specifically for any community, there is needed a type of research that discovers, analyzes, and correlates the inside, or taproot, forces that give rise to a community's social relationships, as well as the surface factors that serve as connecting links in those relationships. Such a type of research rests on the basic principle that social conditions are as open to correction as they are to creation. This involves social diagnosis, social prescription, social persuasion, and social production.

*George H. Von Tungeln (1883-1944) was born on a farm in Galconda, Illinois. He graduated from Central Wesleyan College in Warrenton, Missouri, received a master's degree from Northwestern University, and a doctor's degree from Harvard in 1913. Rural sociology was but a budding discipline during Von Tungeln's days. At the close of World War I, he undertook a number of social surveys of rural townships in Iowa under the auspices of the agricultural experiment station. In 1913 he offered the first courses in applied and rural sociology at Iowa State College in Ames. Von Tungeln remained a professor at that college for most of his life. This article originally appeared in Proceedings, National Conference on Social Work, 54th Annual Session (Des Moines, Iowa, 1927), pp. 331-40. This summarized version appears courtesy of the National Conference on Social Welfare.

But even more specifically rural social research may take as its purpose or objective one of the three following goals, or a combination of these: first, to give the students firsthand experience in social fact-finding; second, to ascertain facts on rural social conditions as such for the purpose of increasing the volume of rural social scientific knowledge; and third, to ascertain scientific facts regarding specific communities for the purpose of projecting and executing practical programs of local improvement and social progress. Any one of these objectives, within proper limits and safeguards, constitutes a very worthwhile goal in both social research and social progress. However, two or even all three of these goals may often be achieved in the same process, if careful planning and tactful leadership is exercised in connection with the work. If the three purposes can be served in the one process, the largest amount of social good will have been achieved, with probably the minimum expenditure of individual and social effort. This suggests that careful planning, a tactful setting up of the project, and skillful and thorough procedure are essential in scientific rural social research. This in turn brings us to a consideration of instruments and methods of rural social discovery, diagnosis, and treatment.

Instruments of Rural Social Research

In many fields of investigation experimentation is extensively used as an instrument of research. But experimentation has very rigid limitations in its direct application by the sociologist to at least the main part of his subject matter: man. Experimentation has a somewhat wider application to the activities of men and to social institutions and organization. But even in this phase of the field of social progress, experimentation of the purely hit or miss or trial and retention or rejection type is likely to be both extremely slow and very costly. The trial and retention or rejection type of experimentation has little to recommend it for the sociologist unless it is based upon a thorough preceding study of local conditions.

During the pioneer stages of rural social research, and even yet when very large areas are involved, it has been common to resort to the commission inquiry and report method of research. The Roosevelt Country Life Commission inquiry and report is a good example of this type of procedure in rural social discovery and social diagnosis. This commission went from place to place over the country connecting up with leading local individuals and institutions and thus sought to gain from them reliable information concerning local conditions. The information so gained was in a large measure somewhat better than average estimates. The scientific reliability or accuracy of information so gathered may, of course, well be questioned, but in the case of the Country Life Commission Report, and as is the case with most of such inquiries and reports, the report served a good purpose as a preliminary survey and contained enough of concise and suggestive information to center constructive thought upon this hitherto neglected field, with the result that it blazed the trail for the early organization of more serious and thorough research in this field. Commission inquiries and reports may, therefore, still be regarded as a constructive instrument of rural social research, particularly as a means of making preliminary or superficial surveys of large areas. Information secured through its use is more suggestive than scientific, and so suggests leads to be followed up rather than provides bases of complete discovery and thorough diagnosis.

The social survey is now undoubtedly the most commonly used instrument of rural social research. For that reason it will be considered in more detail than any of the other methods of social research. A rural social survey is a scientific inventory, analysis, and portrayal of the forces and factors that exist and are at work, both favorably and unfavorably, in a rural community. Social surveying is a type of photography. Social photography or social surveying differs, however, from ordinary photography. In ordinary photography the photographer usually does a lot of retouching on the negative so as to remove all the defects that the camera found in the subject, while in social photography, or social surveying, the photographer gives to the community the unretouched though clearly marked picture of itself and leaves the retouching for the community to do. The social survey is both a scientific and a practical tool of social construction.

The Rural Social Survey Setup

There are a number of important factors in the setting up and the execution of a successful rural social survey. First there is an important difference between the ways social construction work is carried on in the country and in the city. Most of you know how extensively the casework method is relied upon and practiced in our cities as a tool of social construction. Casework is a triangular system. At one corner of the triangle is the philanthropist, whether a private individual or the public, who furnishes the means for carrying on the work; at another corner of the triangle is the expert social worker who is employed by the philanthropist; and at the third corner of the triangle is the case that is to be assisted or reconstructed by the expert social worker. The philanthropist is not a social case, at least he does not regard himself as such. He is employing the social expert or caseworker to work with or upon someone else whom he regards as a social case. The philanthropist pays for the expert and the case gets her services. Of course, the philanthropist also gets the services of the expert, but it comes to him and the community indirectly through the direct expert service that the philanthropist provides for those individuals the employed expert assists.

In the country it is different. The country has not yet reached the case method stage in any large way. In the country the County Agricultural Agent and the Home Demonstration Agent are not paid by the one group of individuals primarily, so that they may directly serve or assist some other group. The very term agent in the title of these experts is significant. They are thought of as the direct agents or paid experts of those who employ them quite as much as that they shall serve as experts to others, as is the case of the social caseworker. The triangular system of the city, when applied to the country, is not a triangle but a straight line system. That is, at one end of the line are those who pay for the expert. At the other end of the line is the paid expert and he or she is to serve up and down that line and not off at a third corner of a triangle. These experts serve their employers directly and primarily in the capacity of agents and counselors.

These experts are not regarded as caseworkers but as expert advisers and agents. Farmers who employ them and expect to receive their services do not regard themselves as social cases any more than the city philanthropist regards himself as a case. The farmer, therefore, thinks in terms of community organization, community work, or cooperative work rather than casework. If once this can be genuinely understood, the running quarrel between the community organizationists and the social caseworkers as to which should be devoured or vanquished by the other will cease to be a quarrel, or even a serious argument. Casework is quite the proper thing in the city, with its heterogeneity of people and occupations, while community work is probably quite as proper in the country, where there is a homogeneity of occupation and also of people to a large extent, except in the South where there are two races on the farm. When your neighbor in town gets sick you probably cannot take care of or look after his work, for while he is perhaps a grocer, you are perhaps a doctor, a lawyer, or a druggist. In the country when a neighbor gets sick, his neighbors can look after his work for theirs is just like it. In the country there is but one occupation; in the city there are all the other occupations and professions except the one that is in the country. The city, therefore, needs its social case experts as the country needs its community experts. At least that is the way the farmer still sees it. So when you want to examine his children, he wants his neighbor's children examined also, and perhaps will suggest that you examine the school children. He calls it community work or community organization work because it is a community enterprise. If you want to call it casework only remember to include every farmer in the community, then it becomes a social or community survey or project.

Enough has now been said to explain why, as the writer sees it, the case method has not yet been widely introduced as a tool of rural social research, at least not under that name. This tool or method of social research will, therefore, be passed over by adding that perhaps this method of research hasn't yet got itself established in the rural districts because it is not so readily adapted to rural conditions.

Returning now to the social survey as a tool of rural social research, it is important that we note a few other facts that pertain to the survey setup and execution. One of the most effective, if not the most effective and important, uses to which the social survey can be put is to provide a scientific basis of local social progress. If it is to be so used, particularly in rural communities, it must have the active and sympathetic cooperation of the local people, both in the collecting of the survey data and in the use of the survey findings in a program of local social improvement. In order to secure such an active and sympathetic cooperation, both the object and the method of the survey must be sold and kept sold to the local people. They must see it and accept it as their survey, their project, their program of progress. Proper local preliminary preparation and education, the appointment of a local survey committee to serve as a buffer between the surveyer and the surveyed, or as a counselor to the former and a persuader of the latter, are very essential to the successful execution of a rural social survey. Without such local cooperation the survey is most likely to fall down in the first essential, namely, the securing of complete and reliable data. Unless such cooperation can be secured and maintained, the findings of the survey will also not be put to the most and best local use.

Before a group of this sort one needs only to say, in regard to the survey schedule, that it should meet the following essentials: first, be so carefully planned and phrased that the questions asked of the surveyed by the surveyer will be as uniformly interpreted by all the surveyed as possible, so that the data and information secured shall be both reliable and comparable; second, keep up interest and confidence in the survey on the part of the surveyed so that he may and will give the surveyer the truth, the whole truth, and nothing but the truth; third, secure complete and accurate subjective and objective information on that part of the community—individuals, organizations, and institutions—that the survey purports to cover.

Rural Social Survey Results

The phrase, results of rural social surveys, has come to have a double meaning. One meaning refers to rural social survey findings and the other to the effects produced by the survey, or what follows from the survey.

The two lines of emphasis that have been developed in rural social surveying, as outlined above, suggest a very wide range of survey findings. The very wide range of rural social conditions that prevail in the different parts of the United States suggests even as great a variety of findings within the scope of surveys of the same type that were made in different areas. Lack of modern conveniences in the farm home, illiteracy, unsanitary conditions, lack of a good water supply, overcrowded farm houses, lack of medical care, child labor, and rural poverty as shown by survey findings of many of the children's bureau's rural surveys stand out in contrast to findings of some of the midwest social surveys, which show that in some areas over 50 percent of the farm homes are modern, illiteracy not over 1 or 2 percent, many high school and a goodly sprinkling of college graduates on the farm, a doctor within 30 minutes or an hour of every farm family, and where an average farm family spends for family living expenses $1,680 per year, as shown by an Iowa Farm Cost of Living Survey.

But it must not be assumed that the midwest rural social survey does not reveal a variety of rural social conditions. Midwest rural social surveyers have reported in their published survey bulletins a wide range of conditions. For along with such findings as communities in which more than 50 percent of the tenants are sons or sons-in-law of their landlords and so will inherit part or all of the farms they now operate as tenants, where tenants who represent a younger generation of farmers are better educated than owners, where farmers' wives are better educated than farmers (a thing that means so much in the field of child care and child welfare), where radios are found in one-third of the farm homes, where there are well-booked home libraries, where over 40 percent of the children who graduate from the eighth grade school enter high school, there will also be found the fact that farm accidents run high, that hired-men families, although much younger than owner families, have nevertheless already had more deaths in the family than have farm owner families, that frequent movings of farm families fall most heavily on farm tenant school children, and even an occasional farm-owning family is found in which a child can live for six months without being given a name, and without his parents being able to state definitely the day of his birth or even be absolutely sure whether he was the eleventh or twelfth child that had been born to them.

As to what follows from rural social surveys as effect from cause is hard to say, for no one knows what would have occurred in

the same communities had they not been surveyed. It is reasonable
to believe, however, that a community that voluntarily submits itself
to be surveyed and genuinely cooperates in the making of such a survey, or even takes the initiative in having a survey made, will also
not utterly fail to use the findings of such a survey for its own improvement. Changes that have taken place in Iowa communities, as
shown by surveys, suggest that such is a reasonable assumption.
But at least one thing is certain: the survey gives the community a
good up-to-date inventory of itself that can serve as a scientific yardstick for gauging its own progress or regression from time to time.
To provide communities with such a scientific measuring rod may
well be one of the chief aims of rural social research.

SPOTLIGHT ON RURAL NEEDS

Arthur Raymond Mangus

Miami County, Ohio, is a typically prosperous Midwest rural county, similar in many respects to scores of counties in the great corn belt. The Miami River runs through it on its way to the Ohio, and most of its 50-odd thousand people live on farms and in small towns. Troy and Piqua are the two largest cities—9,697 and 16,049 each. The stresses and strains of modern urban life, about which nowadays we read so much, seem remote from its green hills and fertile fields.

Yet a study begun in April 1946 and now concluded shows that:

Approximately 10 percent of Miami County's men of military age were disqualified for military service during the war because of personality disorders and character defects.

One man in 100 was rejected because of mental and educational difficulties, and one man in 200 because of epilepsy.

During a six-year period, 1,168 children were referred to the juvenile court. In the peak year—1943—nearly 4 percent of all children of juvenile court age were so referred.

During the same period, 207 persons were committed to state institutions because of insanity, mental deficiency, or epilepsy. At current rates, it is estimated that one in 25 persons in the population at some time in his life will be committed to a state hospital for the mentally ill.

One in five children in the third and sixth grades of all public schools is judged poorly adjusted on the basis of personality tests and ratings.

Fifteen hundred divorce suits were filed in the years 1940-45, and nearly 1,000 marriages actually dissolved.

The picture of the spread and intensity of mental disturbance and social unadjustment in such a typically rural area comes from a

Arthur Raymond Mangus (b. 1900) is a native of Virginia and graduated from Illinois Wesleyan, the University of Chicago (1929), and the University of Wisconsin (1934). He was a senior research supervisor for the FERA-WPA and the author of a number of research monographs, Changing Aspects of Rural Relief (WPA Monograph no. 14, 1938) and Farmers on Relief and Rehabilitation (WPA Monograph no. 8, 1937). Mangus pioneered a number of studies on rural mental health. He taught rural sociology at North Dakota (1929-34), and at Ohio State University from 1939 until his retirement in 1969. This article originally appeared in Survey, July 1947, pp. 203-4.

study made under the auspices of the State Department of Welfare, the Ohio Agricultural Experiment Station, and the State University Department of Rural Economics and Rural Sociology. The research staff was assisted by a professional advisory committee drawn from the fields of psychiatry, sociology, psychology, education, and social work. Local sponsorship was given by the Troy and Miami County Public Health Department and the County Mental Hygiene Association, while schools, the courts, churches, service clubs, fraternal organizations, and many other public and private agencies enthusiastically cooperated in the project.

The facts speak loudly enough for themselves. They show that mental ill health and social maladjustment are no less a rural than an urban problem. They show that services are needed in Miami County to cope with these problems, no less than in her sister cities. Social planning and community organization to meet these problems are just as badly needed.

School-Age Focus

One phase of the study throws revealing light on the point where planning can be focused most constructively. Children in their grade school years show tendencies toward retardation, antisocial behavior, frustrations, and conflicts that lead back to deeper causes of trouble in their family life and social environment. When these tendencies manifest themselves, appropriate service could do much to avoid more serious difficulties later on.

For example, a special study of the children in the third and sixth grades of all city, village, and county schools showed that 12 percent—about one in eight—were age misfits in their respective classes. That is, they were one or more years older than the average child in their classes. These were children who had repeated one or more grades in school and as a result were generally cast in the role of failure by family, school authorities, and classmates. Boys were worse off than girls in this respect—one in six of the former was an age misfit, only one in 13 of the latter.

Personality tests showed that these retarded children generally were emotionally disturbed and socially maladjusted. As a whole they were notably lacking in self-confidence, self-esteem, and a sense of personal worth. Teachers rated the majority of them in the lowest 20 percent of their classes as far as personality adjustment was concerned, and a composite index rated 51 percent as below average in this respect. Not a single one showed superior personality adjustment.

Only 3 or 4 percent of this over-age group, however, could be classified as true mental defectives. Many were dull and borderline children, while 42 percent were definitely of normal intelligence with IQs of 90 and above. Facts such as these suggest that inability on the part of children to learn at the normal rate may itself be a cause of mental disturbance and unsocial behavior.

But they also emphasize the great opportunity that the schools afford in recognizing and identifying mental hygiene and behavior problems in their incipiency. This backlog of slow-learning children furnishes a fertile source of delinquency and other troubles that later become the concern of law enforcement authorities, our institutions, and the divorce courts. These disturbances often originate in unsatisfactory home conditions, and the schools frequently intensify the problems by failure to understand or meet the special needs of these handicapped children.

Evidence from the juvenile court further confirms this point. Juvenile offenders were generally from this same group that had not gotten along well in school. Indeed, of those who came before the court in 1944, only 63 percent were in school at all. The other 37 percent had left school on working certificates or for other reasons. Many of those still in school were outstandingly retarded and were finding little or no real satisfaction in their school work. Only one had finished high school. Although the median age was 16, the seventh grade was the median for educational accomplishment. Also, these juvenile offenders, retarded in school, were particularly prone to sex offenses, truancy, running away, and to charges of being ungovernable.

Coordination Needed

Offenses against the law, retardation in school, mental disturbances, and divorce frequently are but symptoms of frustrated needs for security and self-confidence. Punishment or giving "another chance" may be equally ineffective treatment for either child or adult. The child is apt to need expert help in working out his conflicts and meeting the threat to his security or self-esteem.

Thus the police officers of the county, like their urban counterparts, need help in securing information on which to make a sound decision regarding a juvenile offender. Without it, they can only guess whether to dismiss him with a warning, report him to the school authorities, refer him to a social agency, or send him to the juvenile court.

The county juvenile court soundly believes that the welfare of the community is best served by studying each child and treating him according to his personal and social needs. But the court needs to enrich its own services by cooperating with other agencies providing psychiatric, psychological, casework, or recreation services. At the same time, the court and other law enforcement agencies can assist social agencies in overall treatment plans by the constructive use of their authority.

In other words, this study in a typical rural county showed the same need for planning and coordination that similar studies have shown in urban areas.

Its social service resources were somewhat differently organized, and geographically the county is much larger than any ordinary city, but the fundamental problem is the same. The schools, social agencies, law enforcement agencies, churches, and other groups need to plan together for a unified and consistent approach to the prevention and treatment of mental and social ill health.

Under the guidance of the Miami County Mental Hygiene Association, a program of public education and social action to meet mental hygiene needs is being launched. It is hoped that this program will point up ways by which a rural and semirural area can mobilize services for the treatment and prevention of mental illnesses and for the promotion of mental health.

THE RURAL STAKE IN PUBLIC ASSISTANCE:
SUMMARY OF FINDINGS AND RECOMMENDATIONS

Elizabeth A. Vinson and Kate M. Jesberg

In recent years, most debate about public assistance has focused on urban conditions and concerns, despite the fact that 41 percent of the nation's poor live in rural America. Given the general absence of attention to rural poverty and the lack of advocacy for changes in public assistance programs from rural people and their representatives, one might have assumed that income support programs serve the needs of rural people better than the needs of urban residents.

The major finding of this study is contrary to that assumption. Regardless of how one may view the quality and quantity of public assistance programs in urban areas, the inadequacies, inequities, and gaps in coverage in public assistance programs in rural areas and rural states generally are greater and more widespread than in urban areas and states. The unmistakable conclusion is that public assistance policy ought to be as much a rural as an urban issue. In short, rural people have a major stake in improving public assistance programs.

This paper summarizes the National Rural Center's statistical research project on the rural poor and public assistance programs, and recommends some changes in policy. The highlights of the findings illustrate specific characteristics of the rural poor that are pertinent to public policy decisions; they demonstrate the inequities and

Elizabeth A. Vinson joined the National Rural Center when it was organized in 1976. She came to the NRC from the national office of the League of Women Voters, where she had worked in the legislative action branch, and from a career of political and volunteer activities in the arts. She is presently involved in organizing a project on the arts in rural America.

Kate M. Jesberg, MSW, ACSW, received her social work degrees from the University of Illinois, Champaign-Urbana, in 1976 and 1977. She came to the National Rural Center having had experience at the National Association of Social Workers national office, a Twin Cities Special Project of the AFL-CIO, the Illinois Department of Public Health, and the Illinois Department of Children and Family Services. Jesberg is presently legislative assistant on welfare issues in the office of the assistant secretary for legislation of HEW.

This article is excerpted from The Rural Stake in Public Assistance (Washington, D.C.: National Rural Center, 1978). Reprinted by courtesy of the NRC. Nonmetropolitan and rural are used interchangeably throughout this article.

inadequacies of public assistance in rural America and why the rural poor have a stake in improving public assistance programs.

Findings about the Characteristics and Location of the Rural Poor

The demographic findings are a reminder that public assistance programs in rural areas are important to large numbers of people—a significant portion of the nation's poor—and that the particular characteristics of the rural poor are a useful guide to public policy. For example:

More than 10.5 million poor people live in rural America. That is about 41 percent of the nation's poor people.

About 15 percent of the rural population is poor, while only 10 percent of the urban population is poor. In the nation as a whole, the rate is 12 percent.

About 57 percent of the rural poor live in husband-wife households, compared with about 38 percent of the urban poor. Most of the rural poor are members of the work force, yet the incidence of poverty remains higher in rural than in urban areas.

The rural poor are older, more disabled, and less educated than their urban counterparts, and yet only one-fifth of the rural poor receive all or some portion of their income from means-tested cash income support programs. This compares with one-third in urban areas, according to the project's findings.

Findings on Work Patterns and Education

Despite the fact that they are poorer, older, more disabled, and less educated, poor heads of households in nonmetropolitan areas have a higher attachment to the labor force than do their counterparts in metropolitan areas or in the nation as a whole. For example, one survey showed that 67.3 percent of rural poor households had at least one member who worked: more than 8 percent had three or more workers; more than 20 percent had two workers; and more than 38 percent had one worker.

In addition, rural poor heads of households had the highest participation in the labor force—57.5 percent. The comparable urban rate was 45.3 percent, and the national rate was 50.3 percent. Of those rural poor heads of households who worked part time, the main reason given for reduced work involvement was an inability to find work.

Most (87.3 percent) rural poor family heads are older than 25 years, yet almost 75 percent have not completed high school. Comparable urban figures are about 60 percent and the national average is about 66 percent. More than a third (36.2 percent) of all poor nonmetropolitan family heads over 25 years have not completed elementary school.

Findings on Poverty, General Characteristics, and Residence

The statistical profile by the National Rural Center also found:

Most poor rural people are white, but blacks, in all categories, have a two-to-four times greater likelihood of being poor.

Rural women who head families have a four times greater chance of being poor than rural men.

Eighty-three percent of the nation's nonmetropolitan poor live in 25 states—14 of which are southern, 8 midwestern, 2 western, and 1 in the northeastern section of the nation. Sixty-two percent of those nonmetropolitan poor people reside in 16 states—14 southern, 1 midwestern, and 1 western.

Most of those in rural poverty live in or near small towns and villages, not on farms. But the farm poor have the highest incidence of poverty of any residential category.

Findings about Benefits, Availability of Programs, and Participation

The overall question is whether public assistance programs serve the rural poor as well as they serve the urban poor. The pattern is not uniform nationwide. Some states in which a larger percent of the people live in nonmetropolitan areas have programs that compare favorably with those in states having a larger percent of urban residents. But—and it is a very important but—in all except five of the 25 states where more than 83 percent of the rural poor live, most public assistance programs serve the rural poor less adequately and less equitably than is true for their counterparts in urban states. In many states that are largely urban, the rural residents are less effectively served by public assistance programs than are their urban counterparts.

Aid to Families with Dependent Children (AFDC)

The AFDC program varies significantly in maximum payable amounts (MPAs) for a family of four in interstate comparisons and in average payments in intrastate comparisons. * Examples include the following:

Of the 19 states having 50 percent or more of their population in nonmetropolitan areas, only 5 have monthly payments above the national average.

Of the 12 states that rank among the top 25 as to percentage and number of nonmetropolitan residents, only 3 have annual MPAs above the median for all states.

Eighteen of the 25 states in which 83 percent of the nonmetropolitan poor live have MPAs that are below the median for all states. Fourteen of those states are in the South.

Participation in AFDC by poor female-headed families tends to be less in nonmetropolitan than in metropolitan states, and fewer AFDC participant families are lifted above the poverty threshold.

Among the 26 subregions in which rural and urban counties were examined, all but 3 showed lower AFDC benefits in the rural counties.

Aid to Families with Dependent Children
—Unemployed Fathers Component (AFDC-UF)

Twenty-seven states provide AFDC-UF. Most are northern and urbanized. For nonmetropolitan poor two-parent families, the situation is worse than it is for female-headed or single-parent families:

Although almost 60 percent of the rural poor are in husband-wife households, only 11 of the 25 states with the most rural poor provide benefits for two-parent families (AFDC-UF).

Twelve southern states have over half (54 percent) of all the rural poor in husband-wife households. Yet only one of those states (Kentucky) provides assistance through the AFDC-UF program.

---

*The AFDC program provides cash benefits to poor families with children—families in which one parent, usually the father, is absent from the home. In some states, families with an unemployed father present in the home may receive benefits.

Less than 5 percent of all the nonmetropolitan two-parent poor families in the 27 states examined in the intrastate rural and urban county comparisons are estimated to be receiving AFDC-UF benefits.

Supplemental Security Income (SSI)

The SSI program, established in 1972, brought important increases in benefits to the aged, blind, and disabled in all states through the federally financed floor, increased benefits, and indexing for inflation. Before SSI, states with larger nonmetropolitan populations paid lower benefits.

Because the SSI benefits for the aged, blind, and disabled is a federally set amount nationwide, the pattern of state supplements, rather than the benefit level, illustrates the contrast between metropolitan and nonmetropolitan areas.

Twenty-six states provide supplements to the basic federal SSI benefit for aged individuals living independently. Although almost half (12) of all states providing supplements have significant rural populations, they are not states where a significant proportion of the aged poor are located. (Supplementation by states is optional.)

Eleven states that rank in the top 25 of all states as to percent of nonmetropolitan population provide state SSI supplements to elderly individuals living independently (that is, not in institutions). *

In contrast, 11 states (largely southern) have almost 40 percent of the nation's aged poor, yet only 1 of those states (Oklahoma) provides supplements.

Food Stamps (FS)

The Food Stamp program, the only federal program that provides assistance based on need (income and assets), not categorically defined groups, offers important aid to rural poor people.

FS bonuses are about the only benefits available for the working poor in many nonmetropolitan states where AFDC-UF is not in effect or where it reaches very few people, and also for individuals and

---

*States may provide larger supplements to SSI recipients who are in nursing home centers or other domiciliary care institutions. Many more states provide that supplementation, even when they exclude the noninstitutionalized aged from supplementary benefits.

families in the nonmetropolitan states where there is little or no General Assistance (GA).

In ten states (mostly southern) it is the FS bonus that brings combined annual public assistance benefits for four-member, female-headed families above very low cash AFDC benefits ($720 to $2,376). Even so, the combined MPAs for AFDC and FS for four-member, female-headed families are below the median for all states in 18 of the 25 states where 83 percent of the nonmetropolitan poor live.

Despite the obvious merits of the program, fewer AFDC families participate in the FS program in nonmetropolitan areas than in metropolitan areas; bonuses in nonmetropolitan areas are generally lower; and in three-quarters of the 52 counties surveyed, nonmetropolitan poor people participated in the program at a lower rate relative to the incidence of poverty than was true in the metropolitan counties.

General Assistance

States that do not offer a General Assistance program are predominantly nonmetropolitan, and some states offer coverage only in parts of the state. In the latter cases, it appears that many more metropolitan than nonmetropolitan poor residents are served.

Of the 19 states in which 50 percent or more of the residents live in nonmetropolitan areas, only 8 provide GA statewide, 4 provide it in part of the state, and 7 provide no GA.

Of the 31 states having 50 percent or more of their population in metropolitan areas, 22 provide GA statewide, 4 provide it in part of the state, and only 5 have no GA program. Most of the states having no GA or partial state coverage are in the South and the Midwest.

In the 52 rural and urban counties, states providing GA pay less in benefits to nonmetropolitan than to metropolitan recipients.

Synthesis of the Findings on Public Assistance

These findings about specific programs illustrate why the non-metropolitan poor have an important stake in reform of the public assistance system. It is they who not only have the greatest degree of poverty but are also more inadequately served by public assistance programs. An examination of the 25 states in which 83 percent of the nation's nonmetropolitan poor live provides a brief but detailed synthesis of the assistance the majority of the rural poor may receive.

Sixty-two percent of all nonmetropolitan persons in poverty live in 16 states* that: pay less than the median MPA in combined AFDC (cash) and Food Stamp benefits for a family of four for all states ($5,220); and have a lower percentage of poor persons receiving AFDC and AFDC-UF or SSI than the national average percentage of poor persons receiving such benefits. Further, only two of those 16 states (Kentucky and West Virginia) offer the UF component of AFDC, and only one (Oklahoma) provides supplements to noninstitutionalized aged SSI recipients. Fourteen of those 16 states have more than 32 percent of their total population in nonmetropolitan areas. (Texas and Florida are the exceptions.)

Five of the remaining nine states of the 25 with the most nonmetropolitan poor (California, Pennsylvania, Michigan, Wisconsin, and Illinois) have MPAs above the median MPA for all states. In those same states, the percentage of poor persons receiving either AFDC, AFDC-UF, or SSI is above the national average. All five of those states supplement noninstitutionalized aged SSI recipients and provide the UF program. However, only one state (Wisconsin) has more than a third of its total population in nonmetropolitan areas.

Two states of the remaining nine (Ohio and Missouri) have a greater percentage than the national average of poor persons receiving either AFDC, AFDC-UF, or SSI, but have a lower MPA than the median. Neither of those states provides supplements to noninstitutionalized aged SSI recipients, but both provide the Unemployed Fathers program. Missouri has more than a third of its total population in nonmetropolitan areas, and Ohio has less than a third of its total population in nonmetropolitan areas.

The two remaining states (Minnesota and Iowa) in the grouping of nine states among the 25 with the most nonmetropolitan poor, have a higher-than-median MPA, but a lower percentage of poor persons receiving either AFDC, AFDC-UF, or SSI in comparison with the national average. Both states offer the Unemployed Fathers program, but only Minnesota provides supplements to aged noninstitutionalized SSI recipients. Both states have more than a third of their population in nonmetropolitan areas.

Thus, those states with the most progressive public assistance systems in terms of benefit amounts, participation, and coverage tend to be those with less than a third of their total population in nonmetropolitan areas. Although there are exceptions, those states with the

---

*Georgia, Alabama, Louisiana, Tennessee, Mississippi, Virginia, Indiana, Arkansas, Kentucky, Oklahoma, South Carolina, North Carolina, West Virginia, New Mexico, Texas, and Florida.

least adequate public assistance systems and the greatest poverty
have more than one-third of their population in nonmetropolitan areas.
Clearly the degree to which the state is rural cannot be cited as the
cause for inadequate welfare programs. Several highly nonmetropolitan states have relatively adequate public assistance systems. However, there is a strong correlation between states that have a significant proportion of nonmetropolitan population and those in which the
public assistance programs are characterized by low benefits, under-
participation, and limited coverage.

Recommendations

As was noted in the preface to this report, a principal concern
for the National Rural Center is equity for rural people, especially
the poor. The marked absence of equity in public assistance programs
in rural areas is undoubtedly the most significant finding of the report.
Significant, but not surprising.

Poverty is most frequently depicted as an urban phenomenon.
It is a fact that during the past several decades many of the rural
poor moved to the cities, only to become the urban poor. Despite the
flow of poor people to cities, however, many of the poorest, least
educated, and oldest rural people were left behind in rural areas.
That is still true, despite the pattern of reversed migration in the
1970s.

Poverty, then, is a national problem. And a national problem
should suggest an approach based on equal treatment. But is it treated
equitably? Indeed no. The rural poor are less equal and more easily
forgotten than their urban counterparts . . . or so the project's findings suggest.

Need, not category, should be the criterion for any equitable
and adequate reform of the public assistance system. The nationwide
standard for eligibility should be based on need (measurements of income and assets) rather than the categorical classifications now applied in AFDC, AFDC-UF, and SSI.

It seems so obvious and it has most certainly been said before,
but poverty is a matter of income and assets, not categories of personal or family status. The same criterion, if we are to treat one
another equitably, should apply to the working poor as well.

So obvious, so necessary, so fair. But, perhaps, so distant,
too. In the interim, four steps could help reduce the severity of rural
poverty. They are:

A minimum floor should be established for AFDC cash benefits.

The federal government should mandate AFDC-UF benefits for two-parent families, and eligibility requirements should be made more flexible and realistic.

The federal government should design a system of financial incentives that will stimulate expansion of General Assistance programs by state and local governments.

Food Stamp bonuses should be continued as a separate program to provide assistance to the poor who do not fit into certain categories —an essential aid to those poor people who live in states where AFDC-UF and General Assistance are not provided.

Again, these recommendations are the obvious ones—those that were brought to the fore by disparities in the public assistance programs surveyed by the project. The list is by no means inclusive, nor is it intended to be. Our task was to find, describe, and analyze the rural stake in public assistance . . . and finally to report it.

Follow-Up of the Project

Research into the practice of public assistance in the nonmetropolitan areas of the nation would have been completely justified for its contribution to understanding the public response to meeting the needs of very poor people living in nonmetropolitan states and areas. The project, however, had an additional and immediate purpose: to evaluate President Carter's "Better Jobs and Income" proposal submitted to Congress in 1977 and to develop information and data that would be useful in framing the legislation. Fortunately, the report, The Rural Stake in Public Assistance, was published in time to be useful in the congressional process. The Rural Center was able to provide information to national social welfare organizations about the importance of the president's proposals to poor families in the states where benefits are below national averages and where some programs are nonexistent. In that way, the Rural Center helped win support of several organizations that, in the past, had not been willing to settle for any but comprehensive welfare reform packages.

Two staff members at the Center worked with the offices at the Department of Health, Education and Welfare, having responsibilities for drafting legislative language and providing data to support the president's position. John M. Corman, the Center's president, testified before the House Ways and Means Subcommittee on Public Assistance, providing data and insights to show that, although a relatively modest set of reforms, the president's plan would go far to make the nation's public assistance system more equitable for people (urban and rural) in the largely nonmetropolitan states. We provided backup information and data for a lobbying effort by organizations in the national Rural Caucus. Many observers believe that the center's report and the efforts of its staff to provide data and information about poverty and existing programs in low-benefit, nonmetropolitan states, turned the tide in the House of Representatives. That is, the research and subsequent efforts stimulated the balance of support necessary to House passage of the important "Social Welfare Reform Amendments of 1979." That effort will be continued in the Senate in 1980.

3/ Social Work Education:
Rural Dilemmas of Past and Present

INTRODUCTION

One of the persistent predicaments of social work education has been the issue of levels of training (graduate versus undergraduate in years past; baccalaureate versus associate in present days). Social workers have been traditionally ambivalent about the advantages and disadvantages of professionalizing workers at lower levels of the educational continuum. On the one hand, the profession has had an expressed commitment to the incorporation of minority and less privileged groups into its ranks; public welfare work and undergraduate training have been the avenues of professional escalation for such groups. On the other hand, social work, like all professions, has wanted to retain whatever elitism it could to ensure its survival as an occupational group and has had to defend its status bitterly in the hierarchy of professions. For these latter purposes, increasing educational requirements and more selective entry into the professional ranks have always been prerequisites.

Some background comments might help highlight the nature of social work's ambivalence vis-à-vis levels of professional education other than the master's. In 1942 undergraduate social work education in the public universities was one of the major issues that led to the formation of the National Association of Schools of Social Administration (NASSA), apart from the American Association of Schools of Social Work (AASSW). Because of the bitter rivalry that ensued between the two organizations as accrediting bodies in social work education, it was not until the 1950s that the two merged into the Council on Social Work Education (CSWE), following painstaking compromise. It was not until the 1970s, nearly 20 years later, that the National Association of Social Workers (NASW) admitted to full professional membership those persons practicing in social welfare agencies who held baccalaureate degrees from accredited CSWE programs.

At present, although associate level social work training is mentioned in the Encyclopedia of Social Work as one of the four levels encompassed by social work education, associate level workers are generally referred to as technicians. They have not been recognized by the professional organization, NASW, as bona fide providers of professional social work services. [1]

The ambivalence of social work about its levels of education has always constituted a special rural practice dilemma. While in the early days of social work master's level workers were available in the cities, they were nonexistent in the hinterland where educational institutions offered only undergraduate courses, if any at all. This problem has not yet been resolved since many of our most rural states, for example, Wyoming, do not offer graduate social work education in their state universities. Furthermore, in a state such as Pennsylvania with large numbers of rural dwellers, the land-grant college does not offer graduate social work education either. The graduate schools in Pennsylvania are located primarily in the large private or state-related universities of the eastern part of the state.

The conflicts of accreditation in rural social work have been discussed in Chapter 2. The two excerpts in this part of the Appendix have been included to illustrate further the deep-seated roots and tenacity of many of rural social work's present educational points of contention. The first piece by Mattie Cal Maxted is entitled "The Need for Undergraduate Trained Social Workers in Arkansas." Maxted, with characteristic openness, discusses the pitiful conditions in which public agencies delivering services in rural states found themselves at the peak of New Deal welfare activity and in the early 1940s. Maxted was an ardent advocate of undergraduate education in the state universities. It was her firm conviction that undergraduate programs in the state schools served educational as well as public relation functions in rural and small communities. As a rural person and practitioner, she believed that social work had to take a realistic and unpretentious view of what were attainable educational levels for public practice in rural states. Because of her fervor, Maxted was actively involved in the NASSA and risked the criticism of many of her contemporary professional colleagues.

The second article by William E. Cole, "Training Social Workers for Rural Areas," represents another illustration of one of those persistent preoccupations of social work education in the rural field. The nature of the content required for successful rural practice has troubled social workers throughout the seven decades discussed in this volume. Although Cole's article reflects points of debate that were more on-target before national accreditation standards brought about the high level of uniformity that exists today in social work education, Cole touches upon many questions that are still asked today. Cole not only discusses content from related rural disciplines, but also goes on to list specific areas and courses he would like to see included in rural training. Although Cole's article was discussed at fair length in the text (see Chapter 3), it has been included in full because it provides the kind of definite suggestions and prescriptions that the more cautious contemporary rural educators are hesitant to give.

NOTE

1. See L. Diane Bernard, "Education for Social Work," in Encyclopedia of Social Work, vol. 2 (New York: National Association of Social Workers, 1977), pp. 290-300.

THE NEED FOR UNDERGRADUATE TRAINED SOCIAL WORKERS IN ARKANSAS

Mattie Cal Maxted

This paper is not a defense of less training for social workers but a plan for more training. To argue for undergraduate training for social workers when we have been thinking of training as graduate training sounds as though we were advocating less. The facts are that we may have thought of training for social workers as graduate training, but the greatest percentage of our social workers have had little or no training and for them any training, even though undergraduate, is an advance.

No profession begins by training a group of workers and then finding something for them to do. A need is present; someone fills the need as best he can; then it gradually becomes apparent that some particular kind of training is helpful to those who relieve that particular need, thus a profession gradually develops. So it was with social work. But social work as a profession probably had a more difficult and unique beginning than the other professions had, since we were just finding out something of how valuable a person a social worker could be, and something of the kind of training she needed, when along came the depression and almost overnight created the need for thousands of social workers when only a handful were available. Some parts of the country were affected more than others in that they had no social workers and had not the faintest idea of what the creature called a social worker was supposed to do. Therefore, some persons who were out of work and were so desperately in need of jobs that they would tackle anything were given the positions and were called social workers. The general public got the idea that any-

Mattie Cal Maxted (b. 1900) is a native of Ripley, Mississippi, but has spent most of her life in Oklahoma and Arkansas. Maxted holds a degree in social work from the University of Oklahoma and a law degree from Oklahoma City Law School (1929). She worked for the Provident Association in Oklahoma City, the FERA in Oklahoma, and Rural Rehabilitation in Arkansas. She was organizer and director of the undergraduate social work program at the University of Arkansas, Fayetteville, until her retirement in 1970. She was an early advocate of undergraduate education and an active member of the now defunct NASSA. Maxted is still active in personal and professional circles. She lives with her sister in Fayetteville. This article was presented at the Twenty-Sixth AASSW Annual Meeting, Chicago, January 1945. Reprinted by courtesy of the author.

one with a kind heart and common sense could do social work, and that even common sense was not too essential. Applicants for social work positions emphasized their need for work, not their qualifications for the job. We are reminded of a quotation from Mary Richmond written in 1897 in which she said, " 'You ask me,' wrote a clergyman, 'what qualification Miss Blank has for the position of Agent of the Charity Organization Society. She is a most estimable lady and the sole support of a widowed mother. It would be a real charity to give her a job.' " Another example is the person who was employed to distribute relief because he had failed in the grocery business.

The general public in a state must have a pretty clear idea of what social work is if it is ever to be able to secure and be willing to pay for a sufficient number of competent, well-trained social workers. It does not know this at the present time, partly because social work is new, and partly because there are few accepted patterns of achievement in social work. What did the social workers do for the Jones family? In Arkansas and most of our rural states the social worker was untrained, and often the sum total of what was accomplished was that the taxes were raised and the Jones family had three more babies for the public to support. Then they ask what can a trained social worker do for the Jones family? And every trained social worker knows that what a social worker can do for any family depends to a considerable extent on the resources available in the state and the community, and that those resources are not developed until there is a sufficient demand for them, and that there is not much demand until there are some trained social workers to use them, and so it goes on. Mr. Public is so confused that he decides that he can get on a while longer without those newfangled ideas.

Undergraduate teaching in the state colleges will help to remedy this situation. Over and over the students in the beginning classes in social work remark after a few weeks of study that they never knew there was so much to learn about social work. They say, "Why, the welfare director in our county is an old man who can scarcely read," or that it is an old lady who sits in the office and gives out a few grocery orders. During the summer terms of school when the classes are composed chiefly of teachers, frequently school superintendents and principals, they repeatedly say, "I never realized what a wide variety of activities social work embraced," or "I did not know that anyone could do anything about such conditions. I supposed they just existed. When I get back to my county I intend to see that we get a trained social worker." In my opinion, if undergraduate departments of social work never produced a single professional social worker, they would be worthwhile to the profession for many years to come since they make it possible to offer some instruction in social work to students who will be engaged in other activities, such as teachers, doctors, lawyers, ministers, housewives, and businessmen who will help interpret social work to the community. They will also be a source of recruitment for social workers since they will have contact with many young people whom professional social workers would never see.

Other results of the ignorance of the public concerning social work are the low salaries of the social workers and the low esteem in which they are held. Under the Arkansas Merit System, the salary of a typist ranges from $85 to $105 a month, and that of a telephone operator from $90 to $100; a senior stenographer begins at $110. The range of a visitor's salary is from $80 to $100 a month. But in spite of the clerical positions paying more, the educational qualifications for entrance are not as high as for that of visitor. The educational qualifications for typist, clerk, and stenographer are graduation from a standard four-year high school with the substitution of one year of successful full-time employment for one year of the required school education, with a maximum substitution of two years. The qualifications for a visitor are education equivalent to graduation from a standard high school plus two years of college, or a year of successful full-time employment substituted for one year of college work with a maximum substitution of two years.

Although the salaries in social work are low, many of the social workers are actually overpaid in view of their training and the quality of their work. At the present time one-third of the visitors in the State Department of Public Welfare in Arkansas have a high school education or less, only six of them are college graduates, and none of them has had any social work training. Few of the county directors have degrees.

The standard of performance must therefore be raised before the salaries will be increased. On the other hand, as salaries are increased, better qualified personnel can be brought into the field. To raise these standards one obviously must begin with the present workers and with such other suitable persons in the state as may be available. This is not an argument for a state residence requirement for social workers, but it must be recognized that the greater part of the social workers in any state will come from that state.

A large percentage of the workers in Arkansas feel that graduate training is so far above their present accomplishments that it is useless to try to attain it. Therefore, they make little effort to improve their work. Undergraduate training could be offered nearby in a familiar setting and would, as a consequence, not seem so unattainable. The present workers could be encouraged to begin their training. Many of them would then finish their degrees, and a few would want graduate training.

Another advantage of undergraduate training in social work is the possibilities for recruitment. It is during the undergraduate years that students decide on their careers. If no social work training is offered, many of the prospective workers are lost to other fields. Students are not much interested in a career unless they have some firsthand knowledge of it. If there are no teachers of social work in the school, how can they get their information? Teachers of the other social sciences have their own problems, and many of them know little about social work.

A third advantage of undergraduate training that can be offered within a state where one works is that such study offers an opportunity for the student to learn state conditions, problems, personnel, laws, and resources that one would not learn in a school in a distant state. Some of our administrators complain that workers who have attended a graduate school located in a large city, as most of them are, on returning to a position in a state where there are few resources are intolerant of the conditions they find and do not make much of an effort to use the resources that are available.

A fourth advantage of undergraduate training in a state is that the state has a stronger hold on its workers in that they often become aware of the possibilities for service and advancement in that state and wish to return after graduate training elsewhere. The home state does not then lose the cream of the crop to those states having graduate schools that, thereby, hold a favored position in choosing the best of the available supply. The director of the New York School of Social Work recently remarked that its students came from nearly every state in the union. It is not where the students come from but where they go that counts; at the present time they do not go to Arkansas. The Arkansas Department of Public Welfare has a scholarship scheme in which workers are given a year's leave of absence with part salary to attend a school of social work, on the condition that they work for the department for two years on their return. This privilege has been extended in particular to field supervisors. Last month Arkansas had three field supervisors out of a full staff of eight or ten. The workers completed their two years and left for better jobs. The state director of Social Service remarked that he would rather have a local graduate with undergraduate training in social work and two years of experience than a graduate of a graduate school of social work with no experience.

A rural state like Arkansas must also combat less desirable working conditions. Driving over rough county roads in an old jalopy in all kinds of weather, spending one's evenings in a dingy rooming house where one's every act is scrutinized by the landlady and all the neighbors does not compare well with city streets, plenty of amusement, and freedom to do as one pleases outside of working hours. The graduate trained social worker is, therefore, likely to try greener pastures since there are plenty available, and the postwar prospects are that there will be even more of them.

One of the most frequently heard objections to undergraduate training in social work is that students who get undergraduate training will consider themselves fully trained social workers and that the standard of training will thereby be lowered. The evidence appears to be quite the opposite, since undergraduate social work majors who plan to go into social work usually plan to continue their social work education. Of the eight graduates of the Department of Social Welfare at the University of Arkansas who have attended graduate schools of social work, seven probably would not have gone except for the interest that was created in the undergraduate department. The profession of social work has had difficulty not from those who have a little training, but from those who have no training and do not know that any is necessary.

If undergraduate training can contribute so much to a state, how can it best be utilized? It is rather generally agreed that the different positions in social work require different standards of skill. A visitor in a public assistance program, for example, could function with less training than a psychiatric social worker. Since there is not and will not be for some time enough graduate trained social workers for all the positions, the undergraduate departments could train visitors for most of the agencies and the graduate schools could train teachers of social work, supervisors, and specialized case workers.

It would appear that a plan could be worked out among the social agencies, the undergraduate departments, and the graduate schools whereby undergraduate training would be a recognized step on the road to professional social work education. In five or ten years most of the workers in a state could have at least a bachelor's degree with some training in social work. A plan of graduate training for everyone could then be undertaken.

To summarize, undergraduate training in social work would help enlighten the public concerning the nature and scope of social work. This lack of information contributes to low salaries for social workers, which makes inevitable poorly trained workers whose work is of an inferior quality. Undergraduate training would break this vicious circle by raising the standard of work. This would be accomplished by encouraging the present workers to begin their training, by serving as a recruiting station for new workers, by giving the workers a greater knowledge of conditions within the state in which they work, and by giving the rural states a greater hold on their workers. With a recognition of the different levels of social work and a coordinated program of training, much could be done to raise the present standard and to make social work a profession in fact as well as in theory.

TRAINING SOCIAL WORKERS FOR RURAL AREAS

William E. Cole

One need not repeat on this occasion that the field of rural welfare, generally, and the training of rural social workers, specifically,
have been pretty badly neglected. There are good reasons for this
neglect. In the first place, the case work services developed historically out of urban conditions and urban institutions, whereas the welfare needs of rural people, if met at all, were met through local or
state institutions, outdoor relief on a local basis, and through care
by relatives or other mutual aid arrangements that even today constitute an important part of the social organization and structure of
rural cultures. Also, there was always the stigma attached to receiving aid or welfare services that extend even into the present time.

Historically, the professional training of social workers developed in institutions with urban points of view and with programs designed to train workers for urban situations. This regime was, as a
practical necessity, forced upon the schools, because until the depression and the passage of the Social Security Act, and the attendant
state and local welfare organizations set up or approved to administer
categorical assistance, there was little firm demand for trained social workers in the rural field. By 1940, however, there were 70,000
social and welfare workers in urban areas and 12,000 in rural areas.
By this time rural social work had become an important segment of
the profession.

With the growth of social work activities in rural areas, and
with the growth of NASSA, increased attention has been given to the
wisdom of differentiated training for social workers. This differen-
tiation is based on two hypotheses: first, that the functions and activities of the rural social worker are different, and second, that the human resources and the physical facilities with which the social worker
works are different.

William Earle Cole (b. 1904) was born in Shady Valley, Tennessee. He received his B.S.A. at the University of Tennessee (1926)
and his A.M. and Ph.D. at Cornell University (1928 and 1930). He
taught education and sociology at Cornell and the University of Tennessee. He was social science analyst with the Tennessee Valley Authority and, more recently, a member of the Tennessee Commission on
Aging. This article was originally presented at the proceedings of
NASSA at the National Conference on Social Work, Cleveland, June
12-17, 1949. Reprinted by courtesy of the National Conference on
Social Welfare.

Training of rural social workers is only part of the problem—a major aspect being recruitment and selection for work in rural areas—and another is compensation, in view of travel and the fact that many states require the rural worker to maintain an automobile.

Every state department of welfare needs to have a recruiting program whereby their workers will be on the outlook for people who have potential for developing into effective rural social workers—people who are perhaps doing good work in some other field but who have the personality, desire, and background to profit from preprofessional or professional social work training. The schools likewise have a responsibility for screening their students for rural work on the basis of background, initiative, independence, and desire to be of service to rural people. These are important qualities in the rural worker. Only through recruitment, selection, training, placement, supervision, and in-service training may a generation of effective rural workers be trained.

On the basis of the jobs they have to do, I would like to indicate the following areas in which training is needed beyond the customary preprofessional and professional courses in psychology, sociology, the history of social work, social legislation, introduction to social work interviewing, case recording, research statistics, casework, procedure, law and social welfare, welfare administration, current problems in welfare administration, and so forth.

BASIC TRAINING IN STATE AND LOCAL GOVERNMENT

Even as yet, as Grace Browning indicated, "as the social worker takes the place in the official family of the rural county courthouse or town hall, she finds her service inevitably defined and bounded by the general framework of county or township government and by the more specific framework of her own administrative organization for welfare services."[1]

There are a substantial variety of welfare services either contributed to or performed by local units of government. In addition, local units contribute strongly to public assistance programs. This local participation in welfare programs and understanding of what the state and national government is trying to do and how this is reflected in the local area is something very important to welfare activity. It is an important aspect of the democratic process and must be cultivated if we are to avoid a centralized trend that can only result in what has come to be called "the welfare state," which is in reality not the welfare state but statism.

Rural welfare workers need to have some philosophy of the nature and significance of government. They need to know of the distribution of governmental powers and the welfare services available under each; of intergovernmental relations; of citizenship and its privileges, including civil rights. They also need some knowledge of parties and how the local political mind works; politics as a cause of rural conflict; government as a force in rural improvement; and ways and means of improving state and local government. Such knowledge should not only enable the rural worker to better develop her role in the local media, but should also serve her well as a political strategist in inspiring other people to political action. After all, as the Ogdens point out, "If the citizen of your community is alert to the need, if he conceives of his first job as political (in its broad sense) rather than economic, then your community is on its way to becoming a rural community."[2]

For persons who are in supervisory positions over rural social workers, I would recommend one other type of training in political science: work in agricultural politics and in the broad field of agricultural policy. Such training is necessary, I believe, for an adequate understanding of agricultural and rural life programs, but is most essential if there is to be coordination of the welfare services and the agricultural extension services. Such work is obviously of professional level caliber, whereas state and local government of the nature indicated may be offered at the preprofessional level.

BASIC TRAINING IN RURAL SOCIOLOGY

I cannot see how most social workers can work successfully in rural communities without some basic training in rural sociology. Furthermore, I do not see that being born and reared in a rural community is a substitute for such training, although it is of immense aid.

The social characteristics, cultural values, and group and institutional patterns of rural society are so vastly different from the urban that they warrant special treatment in an area best covered by rural sociology. Such work should cover what we know are the essential elements of the social psychology of rural peoples, cultural patterns, economic bases of rural life, the rural family, rural institutions and institutional trends, rural health, welfare, and recreation, the extension services, the country life movement, rural planning, and attempts at rural rehabilitation. In addition to aiding in the understanding of the human and institutional resources with which the rural social worker has to work, such training, as Lindstrom points out, should enable these young men and women "to become fully aware of the social problems which our increasingly complex civilization has imposed on rural life. These problems are just as important as are the sociological problems of our cities, and correct solutions to them are just as necessary. "[3]

COMMUNITY ORGANIZATION

The increasing importance of the small community in a democracy permeated by centralizing tendencies; the potential inherent within community organization for dealing with rural problems; and the community-centered aspects of social pathology emphasize as never before the importance of understanding the small community and of ways and means of organizing its resources in the interest of the welfare of its members. Added also is the fact that the rural social worker is frequently in a position to set in motion the mobilization of community resources in the interest of general community improvement or the mitigation of particular problems. As one regional child welfare consultant stated the situation to me:

> Rural social workers, as others, need to learn to share
> responsibility with the community, either that responsi-
> bility which the community is trying to carry or that which
> it does not yet recognize—share both the responsibility and
> the outcome and the further needs. This, of course, in-
> volves recognition of where the community is in its thinking
> and action (What does the community want to do? What has
> it tried? What has worked and what has failed?) and going
> on from there, not expecting the community to wholeheart-
> edly and unreservedly accept where the worker is as a
> place to start. The worker needs to know that he may have
> to create that interest and get that support as it may not be
> there just waiting for him to use it. To learn that before
> hand may save some disillusionment later. We may not be
> able to learn in its fullest implication, but we can get a
> warning that practically, theory and practice that fit the
> local situation are the determining factors in action. [4]

The purposes of community study and community organization are, as Hayes states, "to understand the nature of community life and the essential processes by which it may be developed in a balanced way. "[5] The aim, insofar as possible, is an

> adequate and balanced social structure and to aid in
> achieving this aim the rural social worker needs training
> in the structure and functions of rural communities and
> small towns and cities; in community leadership and in

ways and means of creating community consciousness and
intelligence. She or he needs to know ways and means of
implementing community programs and needs to have at
hand considerable knowledge of how specific communities
have attacked specific problems and in what ways. If at
all possible the worker needs to spend some time in small
communities observing the process of community leadership and community planning in action. Alongside the standard works in case work procedure on her library shelves
should be some of the standard works and reports of some
experiments in rural community organization. [6]

I rather feel that work in community organization should be given at
the professional level or during the time when the worker is on the
job as perhaps a phase of in-service training.

GROUP WORK

I believe there will be little debate that the most sadly neglected
aspect of rural social work is group work; even sad areas of neglect
are found in the youth-serving organizations in rural areas.

The field of group work is difficult to master, requiring a substantial program of study and, above all, field experience. I hold no
belief of trying to make group workers out of caseworkers, but I
would trust that they would have at least one course not so much in
preparation for group work activities they will direct, but in order
that they may develop some ideas of group work, will sense the possibilities of it, and will actively be in a position to share in the development of group activity programs in rural areas. Emphasis in such
training should be on the significance of the social processes in relation to group work, the understanding of groups, group work techniques, and the place of group work in the whole social work process.
These topics should be directed toward the group work needs of the
small community.

SOCIAL WORK REPORTING AND INTERPRETATION

Rural social work is in more need of reporting and interpretation than is urban social work. Furthermore, the rural social worker
may be the only avenue for motivating and planning such interpretation,
whereas urban communities are likely to have well-developed machinery for such interpretation.

Interpretation is needed not only for added support, but above
all for understanding of social work programs and activities in rural

communities. While the rural social worker should act as a channel for news materials and publicity materials originating in central offices of the state and national government, there is much on-the-spot interpretation, news gathering, and publicity that needs to be done. Much of this information is likewise of interest to state or regional headquarters of social work agencies. Frequently, cantankerous individuals and chronic opposers have to be dealt with; local legislative and administrative officials have to be dealt with. The modus operandi and the skills for dealing with such problems should be part of the standard equipment of the rural social worker. As one social worker phrased the responsibility of interpretation to me: "Challenging interpretation and performance on the job to the point that it is indispensable are strong influences in building support for the present and personnel for the future."

I would say that the locale—or training area—and the nature of field work experience for rural social workers are so important as to merit the setting up of some rural demonstration centers on an area, say a county, basis. After part of their classroom instruction, workers would be sent to these centers, where under excellent supervisors, to whom rural social work is important, they would go into the field not only to get firsthand experience with rural clients at an advanced level of training, but also to get firsthand experience in working with rural health, religious, economic, and welfare agencies in a total rural situation.

The lack of coordination in agricultural extension and welfare activities and among agricultural extension, social work, and other welfare activities in local units of government—especially counties and parishes—is a matter of grave concern. County agricultural and home demonstration agents frequently show little knowledge of social work or other welfare services, or demonstrate little interest in or knowledge of community organization or coordination of county programs. This is so acute it poses a problem of the type of training and in-service aid county agricultural and demonstration agents are now receiving in most states.

Perhaps, after all, we need a radical reorganization of these services. I would suggest that we need to have a rather broadly, but specifically, trained welfare worker at the head of these county services whose function it would be to see that the services of the county agent, 4-H club leaders, home demonstration agents, caseworkers, and group workers are coordinated into a unified program. Such people as I visualize it should have some training in rural sociology, community organization, agricultural policy, casework, and group work. Only through such radical reorganization and extension of the services affecting rural folk will it be possible to develop with them the full measure of services that they merit and need. Only through such coordination may the piping in of diverse, uncoordinated programs be prevented.

NOTES

1. Grace Browning, Rural Public Welfare: Selected Records (Chicago: University of Chicago Press, 1941), pp. 8-9.

2. Jean Ogden and Jess Ogden, Small Communities in Action (New York: Harper & Brothers, 1946), p. 233.

3. David Edgar Lindstrom, American Rural Life (New York: Ronald Press, 1948), p. xiii.

4. Letter to the author from Ann Sory, Child Welfare Consultant, Tennessee Welfare Department.

5. Wayland J. Hayes, The Small Community Looks Ahead (New York: Harcourt, Brace, 1947), p. vii.

6. Such as ibid.; Ogden and Ogden, Small Communities in Action; Joanna C. Colcord, Your Community (New York: Russell Sage Foundation, 1939); A. E. Morgan, The Small Community (New York: Harper & Brothers, 1942); A. B. Hollingshead, Elmtown's Youth (New York: Wiley, 1949); Clarice C. Platt and Arthur Dunham, Community Organization for Child Welfare in Carver County (New York: Association Press, 1949), and other Community Organization Monographs published by the same firm.

4/ Racial and Ethnic Minorities in Rural America

INTRODUCTION

Any attempt to document the lives and activities of racial, ethnic, or even religious minorities in the rural areas of the United States becomes a monumental task. The researcher soon discovers a myriad of complex problems that have determined and affected the role of blacks, Hispanics, Italians, Armenians, Jews, and a number of other minority groups throughout the country. Additionally, from a historical perspective, the task is further complicated by attempts to identify whether a given group constituted an ethnic, cultural, religious, or even psychological minority in a given place at a particular time. For the fact that a group might not be considered presently a minority population by the census does not preclude the possibility that the historical experiences of the particular group might have been minority experiences in the rural areas.

This possibility is well illustrated with a personal biographical sketch by Leon Ginsberg, who recounts:

> I come from a rather off-beat family. When most Jews came to the United States from Eastern Europe in the beginning of this century they came to places such as Boston and New York, primarily. Half of my family ended up in Weimar, Texas, and the other half in Kansas City. We had a small town tradition. [1]

Ginsberg's minority experiences must have certainly been quantitatively and qualitatively unique in small-town Texas.

Another good example of the problems of identifying minorities in the rural United States is provided by the story of hillbillies, well told by Kathy Kahn in Hillbilly Women. Hillbillies are inhabitants of the southern mountains who are of English, Scottish, and Scot-Irish ancestry. For all practical purposes, hillbillies are WASP and should have been part of the U.S. mainstream. Yet the experiences of isolation, scorn, and exploitation suffered at the hand of "speculators from the North"[2] were, and in some instances still are, quasi-colonial, minority experiences.

As Ginsberg has pointed out, the issue of rural ethnic minorities is far from simple. We tend to speak about fairly homogeneous rural communities; while this fact might be statistically correct, the experiences of the majority population, as well as that of the minority

groups, corroborate the fact that "rural America is almost as eth-
nically diverse as nonrural America."[3] Furthermore, certain occupational rural groups can be doubly counted as minorities. Migrant
workers as an occupational group, for example, constitute an experi-
ential minority (their lives being affected in similar discriminatory
ways), while at the same time encompassing a number of diverse ethnic groups such as whites, blacks, Mexican-Americans, Puerto Ricans, Native Americans, and others.

On the other hand, certain rural minorities constituted occupational majorities in specific trades and occupations in the history of
urban and small-town America. Carl Oblinger has pointed out this
fact in Interviewing the People of Pennsylvania: A Conceptual Guide
to Oral History, while at the same time suggesting that there is a
dire need for research on this phenomenon:

> Throughout Pennsylvania particular ethnic groups domi-
> nated certain industries and trades. In Philadelphia gar-
> ment centers, Jews and Italians predominated. In steel
> mills German and Irish workers held skilled positions
> and superintendent posts until the mid-twentieth century.
> Slaves carried out beachheads in certain semi-skilled
> jobs in the open hearth and mines. What other examples
> of ethnic occupational clusters existed? How was the
> monopoly of certain jobs maintained by certain ethnic
> groups? How long did it last? How was the monopoly
> dissolved?[4]

The fact that this volume concentrates upon the narrative of
events primarily related to social work activity in the hinterland
makes the selection of social and ethnic groups for analysis somewhat easier because of the unfortunate historical fact that social workers did not concentrate upon helping or embracing the cause of rural
minorities. Rather, at particular historical periods social workers
have shown solidarity with specific groups because the group developed
a strong enough political identity to demand the attention of social
workers. (An example would be the migrant workers in the Southwest
and California.)

The story of events associated with the move toward equality of
the 1940s, 1950s, and 1960s has been provided in Chapter 3. It will
be the object of the selections included in this part of the Appendix to
illustrate further the statements of the text, or to provide material
that will deepen the understanding of the role of social workers vis-
à-vis rural minorities. The selections included will focus upon blacks
and Mexican-Americans. While the author recognizes that many other
rural minority groups appear to have been left out of the narration, it

must be stated that material documenting social work interventions among such contemporary rural minority groups as the Puerto Rican mushroom pickers of the Northeast or the apple pickers of the Northwest is completely absent from the social work literature. Again, social workers are still demonstrating a considerable urban bias by ignoring these rural groups in their investigations and their writings, even if not necessarily in their service delivery. (For example, the author has had the opportunity of observing commendable work being done by grass-roots and governmental social service agencies on behalf of the Puerto Rican population of southern New Jersey and southeastern Pennsylvania. Yet, most of these efforts remain undocumented and cannot yet be retrieved for presentation in a volume such as this.)

The first piece included in this part of the Appendix has been amply cited in the text and illustrates the nature of social work efforts during the civil rights period in the rural South. The article, Lewis W. Jones's "Social Centers in the Rural South," illustrates not only that attitudes in relation to race relations in the southern states had begun to change by the 1950s but also that rural feelings and resistance about accepting change through formalized social service organizations had changed considerably by that time. It must be pointed out, lest the reader be misled into believing that the changes were radical, that the acceptance of outside services necessitated the legitimization of those services through the existing and well-established rural organizations. Even today, as incremental changes continue to penetrate the rural social scenario, contemporary practitioners will find that acceptance of services and outsiders is enhanced through the support of local organizations perceived by the people as legitimate rural entities, such as the rural churches.

The second article is by Peter H. Schuck, entitled "Black Land-Grant Colleges: Discrimination as Public Policy." This article further illustrates statements about the nature of movements toward equality that appear in Chapter 3. It was stated in Chapter 3 that a report of the Civil Rights Commission, "Equal Opportunity in Farm Progress" (1965), indicted the Department of Agriculture for consistently denying blacks access to many services. Schuck's material elaborates on that denial, tracing it back through its historical roots to the legislation that created the black land-grant college as a separate and unequal institution, and through the administrative decisions that maintained the established nonegalitarian system through discriminatory appropriations.

Schuck's article takes on additional meaning given the discussions in Chapters 2 and 3 regarding rural training and accreditation in social work education. Historical documents appear to point out that had social work been successful in making the connection with the agricultural and mechanical colleges that Smick[5] called for at the height of FERA activity in 1938, rural social work would have been assured a healthier livelihood through the years of rural decline that followed World War II. It was stated in Chapter 3 that "the failure to connect with the agricultural and mechanical colleges and their well-established rural connections, spelled, at worst, the demise, and at best, the retreat of rural training into a 30-year limbo." Schuck's article sheds new light onto the analysis of this phenomenon. Schuck documents the success of the colleges of 1890 in educating "a very significant share of students from low income families." Would the share of black social workers have been assured had the rural branch of the profession succeeded in working more closely with the land-grants?

On the other hand, Schuck also suggests that owing to the persistent segregationist practices that have characterized the land-grant system, and because of the funding patterns that have affected the relationships of the black land grants with USDA, "USDA has, in effect, barred the black land-grant colleges from exercising the vital function" of reaching and adequately serving the needier elements in the rural United States. With the wisdom of hindsight, one might wonder whether the failure of rural social work to connect successfully with the land-grant system did not save the social work field from similarly entrenched discriminatory practices. One can also speculate whether social work might not have aided Extension in concentrating on the less affluent segments of the agricultural economy had the profession become an active arm of the service. At any rate, Schuck's material deserves careful consideration given what is now known about rural social work education and about land-grant institutions.

Finally, the third piece included is one of the many testimonies submitted by citizens throughout the country to the Hearings before the Subcommittee on Migratory Labor of the Committee on Labor and Public Welfare of the United States Senate, Ninety-Second Congress, 1971/72. This particular statement by Jean Flores, community worker of Kings County, California, and the appendix to her statement, a letter from the Department of Public Welfare of Hanford, Kings County, California, have been included because they illustrate a small but positive role played by social workers in support of migratory workers when the Kings County Board of Supervisors rejected the Food Stamps Program in late 1971.

The Subcommittee on Migratory Labor conducted public hearings in Washington, D. C., San Francisco, and Fresno during the Ninety-Second Congress. The voluminous testimonies heard by the subcommittee that was presided over by Senator Adlai E. Stevenson III have been published in five parts by the U.S. government. In the introductory remarks at the beginning of the hearings, Stevenson stated that "the problems of the most severely disadvantaged people in rural America—migrant and seasonal farm workers—cannot be described, much less solved."[6] Stevenson recounted the efforts of the President's National Advisory Commission on Rural Poverty and concluded that "the melancholy facts about rural poverty" had changed little since 1967.[7] The subcommittee focused its attention on problems of rural minorities as they were reflected among migratory workers, small farmers, and small businessmen across rural and small-town America.

The expertise of many individuals and organizations was brought to bear on the compilation of data for the subcommittee, which now represents impressive documentation of the problems and aspirations of significant numbers of rural minorities. The Spanish Speaking Peoples Study Commission of the State of Illinois, for example, presented a description of the situation of Mexican Americans, Puerto Ricans, and Cubans in the rural areas of that state. Their welfare recommendations to the subcommittee were, in their own words, "modest indeed," and included the amending of Illinois Revised Statute 48 31.2—Child Labor—to provide coverage for persons under 12 engaged in agricultural pursuits (a matter that concerned social workers since 1911), and the amending of Illinois Revised Statute 23 110 to remove all residence requirements for public aid (a restriction now abolished by the federal courts).[8] Manual Leon, a vice-president of the Greater California Education project, founder of El Porvenir, a corporation for the betterment of all farm workers, and an active member of the campesino movement in the greater San Joaquin Valley, gave a stirring presentation in his native Spanish about the campesino as the backbone of agriculture and his desire to buy and cultivate his own soil,[9] a desire that is becoming increasingly unattainable in the reign of agribusiness.

In short, the subcommittee learned that the situation of migrant workers, all of them minorities, had not progressed much since The People Left Behind. Perhaps as an appropriate ending comment and preface to Flores's testimony, it befits to quote the introductory statements of Senator Stevenson, which are probably just as accurate today as they were in 1971.

> While the subcommittee's hearings are not directly related to specific legislative proposals, certainly the problems of rural America and farm workers cannot be considered without reference to the inadequacies, omissions, and deficiencies in our present laws.
>
> For all practical purposes, many farm workers are either specifically excluded from, or, at best, only minimally included under every major Federal or State social

or worker benefit program, such as collective bargaining, minimum wage, workmen's compensation, unemployment insurance, child labor laws, wage payment and collection laws, social security, welfare, and housing programs. Even when farm workers are covered, enforcement is often inadequate or nonexistent. Thus, the benefits which most U.S. workers take for granted have been systematically denied to farm workers.

Where legislation makes social and worker benefits available to farm workers, and this availability is known, farm workers are still effectively excluded by their inability to meet unfairly demanding conditions such as income standards and residence requirements. Even special programs that have been designed to benefit farm workers, like the Farm Labor Contractor Registration Act, the Migrant Health Act, food and nutrition programs, housing programs, manpower programs, certain programs under the Office of Economic Opportunity, and the Office of Education appear largely useless to farm workers because of inadequate enforcement, lack of awareness, apathy, discrimination, poor program design, and lack of funds.

Even when migrants are eligible for such assistance, they often cannot afford to spend the tremendous time and energy demanded by the redtape associated with aid programs. Many programs, by holding out false hopes and promises, actually add to the hopelessness of rural people.

Finally, legal obstacles, residence requirements, and high illiteracy rates all conspire to limit farm worker registration and voting participation in the political process.[10]

Only the future can tell whether these unfortunate circumstances will be erased in the next seven decades.

NOTES

1. Leon H. Ginsberg, "Social Work in Rural Areas," in Social Work in Rural Areas: Preparation and Practice, ed. Ronald K. Green and Stephen A. Webster (Knoxville: University of Tennessee, 1977), p. 4.

2. Kathy Kahn, Hillbilly Women (New York: Avon, 1972), p. xii.

3. Ginsberg, "Social Work," p. 7.

4. Carl Oblinger, Interviewing the People of Pennsylvania: A Conceptual Guide to Oral History (Harrisburg: Pennsylvania Historical and Museum Commission, 1978), p. 31.

5. A. A. Smick, "Training for Rural Social Work," Sociology and Social Research 22 (July 22, 1938): 540.

6. U.S., Congress, Senate, Committee on Labor and Public Welfare, Subcommittee on Migratory Labor, Farm Workers in Rural Poverty, 92d Cong., 1971-72, pt. 1, p. 3.

7. Ibid.

8. Ibid., pp. 86-87.

9. U.S., Congress, Senate, Committee on Labor and Public Welfare, Subcommittee on Migratory Labor, Land Ownership, Use and Distribution, 92d Cong., 1971-72, pt. 3B, pp. 1326-29.

10. Ibid., pt. 1, pp. 5-6.

SOCIAL CENTERS IN THE RURAL SOUTH

Lewis W. Jones

A new phenomenon in the South is the rural social center, largely a church-related activity, which has developed in response to the needs of rural people in a period of drastic social change. These centers could not have been developed in the places where they are before those places experienced the changes they have undergone in recent years. Existence of such centers through efforts of church organizations bespeaks a change in rural attitudes and outlook that foreshadows general acceptance of social work among rural people. Church denominations have built and financed them because, before other services, churches seem to know the unfilled needs of bewildered people. The rural South has changed in community organization and in the attitudes and thinking of people. The rural social center is a natural outgrowth of the increasing sense of public responsibility for community welfare.

These social centers are the vanguard of tax-supported social work for rural people. Until recently, organized social work has been regarded as an urban phenomenon.

> The modern concept of social problems is primarily a product of urban-industrial civilization, as in the modern approach to social welfare. Under the individualistic economy of an agricultural society, few social problems are recognized as such; they are considered individual or neighborhood problems rather than social problems in the broader sense. Why worry about contagious diseases when one lives miles from neighbors? Or poverty if it is isolated so that it does not inspire the pity of others? Or family conflict if it does not grate upon the nerves of irate neighbors

---

Lewis Wade Jones (1910-1979) was born in Cuero, Texas, and was a graduate of Fisk University, Columbia University, and the University of Chicago. Jones taught sociology at Fisk, Colorado College, and Tuskegee Institute, and was involved as director and researcher at the Rural Life Council of Tuskegee Institute. He was author of numerous publications of such varied subjects as cotton tenancy in the South, the country church, and education of the disadvantaged. This article, under the same title, originally appeared in Phylon 12 (Fall 1951): 279-84 and is used with permission.

who think the police should interfere? Or security if one
has land? Or child welfare as long as most children work
under their own father on the family farm? All the above
situations may, in an isolated farming economy, concern
relatives or neighbors, but not the state or society at
large.[1]

Landis, one of the few sociologists to consider the problems of social
welfare in the rural community, indicates the difference between rural
and urban areas. "In a strictly rural economy where primary groups
prevail, each kinship group or neighborhood carries the responsibility
for its own social inadequacies. . . . Social work is a technique for
seeking a solution to the individual's need in an anonymous world."[2]
Where primary group organization prevails, kin and neighbors feel
moral responsibility for the unfortunate or disadvantaged. Dependent
individuals have found security provided by members of groups to
which they belong. It was the rare instance in which the orphan child,
the aged, or the mental incompetent became a public charge.

Apart from the disadvantaged individual in a community, there
is the disadvantaged community. In such a community where all have
the same problems, there is no feeling of peculiar disadvantage since
isolation does not make possible ready contrast between the status and
condition of one rural community and another. This is different from
the city, where the juxtaposition of gold coast and slum permits ready
contrast, stimulating concern of the disadvantaged for their predicament.

Changes in rural communities are making the need felt for formal action in the interest of the disadvantaged individual and the disadvantaged locality group. Changes that disrupt established patterns
promote consciousness of their own inadequacies on the part of the
disadvantaged and develop an awareness of their needs by others. In
the first place, the ideas of self-containment and self-sufficiency are
being shaken as developments change the service-satisfaction pattern.
Service-satisfaction, in becoming town centered instead of community
centered, influences the relationships of rural people. Economic
changes about new productive patterns effect changes in communities
by changes in population that are due to changes in the labor requirements of agriculture. So schools, churches, lodges, and other community organizations find their groups being disorganized by migration of people who formerly constituted membership of these groups.

With the closing of the community store, the removal of the
local school through consolidation, and the dying of social organizations, something happened to the community spirit. Contact and association with neighbors is lessened and the bonds of identification
become loosened. The enlargement of the area of want-satisfaction

and the enlargement of experience through contacts with more people in casual contacts, the radio, and the movies permit comparisons with others and promote self-consciousness.

The need for social services appears in the new context where people find things happening to them other than their traditional experiences and problems that were accepted, resigned to, and for which there had been established ways of meeting and solving.

Problems of rural people in the South are perhaps more serious than they have been before. The rural center movement is in its beginning, called forth by the urgent needs of the times.

Various kinds of community centers have been developed in recent years to serve problem communities. These are almost entirely church related. Missionary organizations of several denominations have undertaken social welfare programs for rural people. The Methodist church's Bureau of Town and Country Work, the Congregational Christian church's American Missionary Association, the Catholic church, the Church of the Brethren, the Quakers, Town and Country Church of the Evangelical and Reformed church, the National Town-Country Church Institute of the Protestant Episcopal church— all have some work going in social welfare services for rural communities. Long before a hospitable opinion has been created in which public action may proceed to meet social problems, the church organizations have pioneered, often at the risk of unpopularity, to accumulate knowledge and know-how while serving.

Since the work is of quite recent origin, the activities of the community centers vary widely. Some closely resemble the settlement houses in city slums. Others adapt themselves to characteristic rural problems and conditions and have little resemblance to the urban settlement house.

The Rural Life Council of Tuskegee Institute, designed to serve the South, became aware of the need for such services as these centers rendered. In response to the expressed need, it called a conference at Tuskegee in 1949. Representatives of eight of the centers attended a two-day session where the work and problems of the centers were discussed. It was decided to establish a loosely organized body to be known as the Conference of Rural Community Centers. In 1950 the second meeting of the conference convened at Highlander Folk School at Monteagle, Tennessee. Ernest E. Neal, first executive secretary of the conference, stated that the purpose of the conference was to serve "as a clearing house to keep each project director informed of the activities of all the others and as an instrument for the sharing of resources and experiences."[3]

The Tuskegee Institute Rural Life Council, under the direction of Neal, recognized the usefulness of consultation on the activities and problems of the centers. Financing of the two conferences and circulation of a newsletter to the affiliated centers have been rewarded by increasing affiliation of centers whose representatives look with favor on the organization. At the 1950 conference, representatives of government agricultural agencies discussed the services available to farm people from their agencies. The centers were brought to realize the opportunity for them to provide coordination of the services of the agencies to the people they served.

Dorchester Community Center in Liberty County, Georgia, and Bricks Rural Life School in North Carolina have been developed by the American Missionary Association to serve Negroes. Dorchester Community Center has a modern building, in the open country, with facilities for club and recreational activities. Focus of attention at the center has been chiefly on the improvement of the economic condition of the people it serves. A program of improved agricultural practices has been promoted through a tractor cooperative and a credit union. An effective political organization is related to the center.

Bricks Rural Life School is a refreshing innovation in adult education that expresses the philosophy of Ruth A. Morton of the American Missionary Association, and the persistent work of its director, Neill McLean.[4] Bricks also has an economic-centered program. Basic is its credit union, which serves a serious financing need of small farmers. Its cooperative program includes one for livestock, soil improvement, wheat, molasses, and poultry. In addition to these cooperatives, it has a health program and a unique training program that advances farmers from sharecropping to ownership.

The Methodist Church, through its Bureau of Town and Country Work of the Woman's Division of Christian Service, has established 22 centers that are under the direction of Marjorie Minkler, executive secretary of the bureau. These centers serve white people, Negroes, and mixed groups of anomalous identification. Several of these centers are briefly described below.

The Mobile County Rural Center in Alabama serves a group of people of Indian-Negro-white mixture who have not been fitted into the South's two-race pattern. Denied admission to white schools and not deigning to attend Negro schools, this group of people went untutored until the Methodist Church supplied a school and teachers who were white but accepted the salaries of Negro teachers. A community program for the people followed establishment of the school.

Scott's Run Settlement House, near Morgantown, West Virginia, and Amherstdale Wesley House at Amherstdale, West Virginia, serve white people in rural industrial areas—coal-mining areas. Both of these centers have standard settlement house programs, but with peculiar adaptations to the needs of disadvantaged coal miners. A recreational program at Scott's Run serves not only the clients of the center but also meets the need for a gymnasium that the school authorities have not yet supplied from public funds. There are kindergartens where no tax-supported preschool provisions have been made. Club activities, a library, and other settlement house standard provisions are available for these coal-mining communities.

At Columbia, Mississippi, the Mississippi Rural Center is the near perfect projection of the Methodist Church philosophy for Negroes. It did not grow but was built. It is a complete social settlement. There is a health clinic with a full-time physician in charge. Recreation and hobby activities have been provided for all age groups. For farmers, on the economic side, there is a counseling service that makes referrals to agricultural agencies.

The Reverend Ora Huston of the Church of the Brethren has done more than many larger denominations have attempted. Where Mexican immigrants suffered in the midst of American apathy, a center was established. For this center buildings were constructed on a 200-acre farm. Now there is a manual arts shop for those who wish to develop manual skills. Club work common to social work is presented. Distinguishing this center is the English class to help children and adults secure the essential communication medium.

Social work activity that is not church related is to be observed in the programs of Highlander Folk School and the Rural Life Council of Tuskegee Institute. Both agencies have programs for rural community improvement that are not appreciably different from those of the church-related centers.

These centers could not have developed without indication of their need. Most of them are located in problem areas. In fact, they have been established to serve disadvantaged communities. This is something new in the rural South.

The newness of social centers may be associated with the recent awareness of rural locality groups that they are disadvantaged. Tuskegee's experiments in community rehabilitation have been undertaken in subsistence communities. These communities once were prosperous cotton areas. As fertility of the soil decreased, ownership of the land by Negroes increased. Now Negroes own infertile land and the institutions that normally belong to communities have disappeared.

Highlander Folk School is in an area that once was a productive coal-mining region. Mined out, this area has people living on a poor surface underneath which there once was wealth. Dorchester Community, with a high degree of ownership, is on land that grows food but has never provided an adequate cash income. The Mobile center is in an area that was productive of forests and was known as a logging area. Scott's Run and Amherstdale are mined out coal areas.

All of these areas belong in the category of diminished resources. Crops, trees, and minerals have been exploited, and in the wake of exploitation there are stranded people. These people live in rural slums. Their needs are those of the disadvantaged in America, urban or rural.

Other centers are found to be located in areas that are secure economically but that, due to changes in production, have undergone reduction in the number of people living in the areas. Such population decreases have seriously affected community institutions and community life. In one instance an abandoned church has been remodeled to serve as a community center. In another a school abandoned in the process of school consolidation has been converted into a community center.

Activities of the centers described show that they are attempting to fit the services rendered to the needs of the people. In some cases the chief focus of attention is on economic problems and in others on social needs. Most of them have a program for the promotion of associational activities where community life has become disorganized and lacking in satisfactions needed by people living together.

NOTES

1. Paul H. Landis, Rural Life in Process (New York: McGraw-Hill, 1948), p. 463.
2. Ibid., p. 464.
3. Proceedings, Conference of Rural Community Centers, Second Annual Meeting, p. 4.
4. A full description of the Brick School is presented in Extension Division Bulletin, New Dominion Series, no. 117, June 1950, Charlottesville, Virginia.

BLACK LAND-GRANT COLLEGES:
DISCRIMINATION AS PUBLIC POLICY

Peter H. Schuck

More than 50,000 black students (one out of every nine black collegians in the United States) attend a unique group of institutions of higher learning—the black land-grant colleges. They are unusual in terms of their historical roots, their student bodies, their educational mission and accomplishments, and their legal and political status. But what distinguishes them most dramatically from other public colleges is the shockingly discriminatory treatment they have long received at the hands of the states and of the federal government, particularly the U.S. Department of Agriculture (USDA), established by President Lincoln in 1862 as the "people's Department."

The 16 black land-grant colleges, all located in the southern and border states, are a diverse group. The largest, Southern University A&M College in Baton Rouge, Louisiana, has an enrollment of almost 10,000, but Delaware State College enrolls barely more than 1,000 students. Lincoln University in Missouri and Alcorn A&M in Mississippi are each more than a century old, while Fort Valley State College in Georgia and Prairie View A&M College in Texas were established in 1947. These black land-grant colleges also differ enormously from one another in terms of curriculum, intellectual attainment, and academic focus. But for all their differences, certain similarities are striking.

Each of the black land-grant colleges was founded as part of a system of legally sanctioned segregation. The Morrill Act of 1862, which sought to democratize American higher education by instructing "the industrial classes in the several pursuits and professions of life," provided little comfort for southern blacks since the colleges established with the funds in these states were white preserves, barred by custom (and later by law) from admitting them. In 1890 Congress enacted the Second Morrill Act, which increased federal assistance to the original institutions and also authorized the creation of black land-grant colleges. The act provided that where separate colleges for whites and blacks existed, Morrill funds were to be "equitably divided."

The southern and border states implemented the 1890 act by establishing separate land-grant colleges for blacks. These "Colleges

---

Peter H. Schuck is a lawyer and was consultant with the Center for the Study of Responsive Law. He is presently Associate Professor of Law at Yale University. This article originally appeared in Saturday Review, June 24, 1972, pp. 46-48. All rights reserved.

190

of 1890" have, along with the other black institutions, traditionally been, and still remain, the major route for ambitious blacks to an inexpensive college education and entry into the professions. Of the 470,000 blacks enrolled in colleges in 1970, 36 percent attended predominantly black institutions, over a third of these in the black land-grant institutions. In the South these proportions are far higher.

What is more important, the black land-grant institutions educate a very significant share of students from low-income families. According to the Carnegie Commission for Higher Education, the average family income of 37.6 percent of black students entering black colleges in 1968 was less than $4,000. Yet the black land-grant colleges, as well as the predominantly black colleges, generally have had, in the commission's words, "remarkable" success in training such "high risk" students.

Despite this long-standing record of success where other colleges have failed—perhaps because 93 percent of the budgets of the 1890 institutions are devoted to teaching—the continued viability of the 1890 colleges (and other black public colleges) is endangered by two major threats: formal integration and continued segregation. As John Egerton has documented in Black Public Colleges: Integration and Disintegration, integration of public higher education in the South has increasingly meant the destruction of black public institutions and, with them, of the only hope of tens of thousands of blacks for a college education. Several of the 1890 colleges, including West Virginia State and Lincoln University, now are predominantly white. In many other states, among which are Tennessee, Florida, and Virginia, another pattern is becoming all too clear. These states have moved either to upgrade neighboring white institutions or to establish new, competitive, predominantly white college facilities close to the black colleges. In either case the result is the same: the black colleges find it impossible to hold their white students and steadily more difficult to attract the most talented blacks. Lawsuits challenging the legality of these practices have been filed in several states.

As plaintiffs in these cases argue, this form of "integration" may well end with blacks paying a terrible price, not simply in terms of reduced black student and faculty enrollment but also in the destruction of extremely serviceable institutions uniquely capable of fulfilling the educational and social-mobility needs of black Americans.

Destruction through integration, however, is but one threat to the 1890 colleges. Destruction through segregation is another. To be sure, the land-grant colleges, like all public colleges, are nominally integrated, and the black colleges slightly more so than the white. According to the Department of Health, Education and Welfare's Office for Civil Rights, the white land-grant colleges in dual-system states are about 5 percent black, at the same time that the 1890 colleges are about 7 percent white.

Nevertheless, the funding patterns of the white and the black land-grant colleges confirm what the law denies: inequality and segregation are alive and well in the land-grant college system. An examination of these patterns reveals a number of suggestive facts.

First, the 1890 institutions receive very little revenue from private sources. The Ford Foundation's $100-million program of assistance to black higher education applies only to private colleges and will not affect these public institutions.

Second, state appropriations for the white and black land-grant colleges are unequal, and the disparity in these appropriations to the white and black land-grant colleges on a per capita basis during fiscal 1970 were $1,585 and $1,180, respectively. In fiscal 1971 the corresponding figures were $1,763 and $1,260, respectively. Thus, while per capita state appropriations increased for both groups, the share of such appropriations going to the 1890 black colleges declined from 74 percent to 71 percent. In individual states the situation is often much worse (and only occasionally better). In Texas, for example, the per capita share of the 1890 college (Prairie View) was only about 28 percent of that of the 1862 college (Texas A&M) in fiscal 1971.

Third, as unequal as the state aid to black and white land-grant colleges tends to be, federal grants-in-aid are far more unequal, and the gap continues to widen. Between fiscal 1968 and 1970 the per capita amount going to the 1890 colleges declined both absolutely (from $352 to $310) and proportionately (from about 50 percent to 44 percent).

The inequality of federal assistance is nowhere more egregious than with respect to funds disbursed through the USDA. Of the approximately $76.8 million in USDA funds allocated to land-grant schools in 1970, about 99.5 percent went to the 16 white land-grant colleges; the 1890 colleges received a grand total of $383,000 (or 0.5 percent).

The land-grant college system is built around three activities—resident instruction, agricultural extension, and agricultural research. Two of them—agricultural extension and agricultural research—are supported by the USDA and state matching funds. The third, resident instruction, is supported at the federal level mainly by HEW.

The Cooperative Extension Service of USDA, established by the Smith-Lever Act of 1914, provides federal funds for extension services at the land-grant colleges. The act stipulates that where a state has separate land-grant colleges the USDA appropriations for extension work shall be divided "as the [state] legislature . . . may direct." Senator Hoke Smith of Georgia, author of the act, made the purpose of this provision crystal clear: "We do not . . . want the fund if it goes to any but the white college." His purpose has been admirably served. In each state where white and black land-grant colleges exist, the state legislature has directed that all federal extension funds go to the 1862 college. USDA has complied.

Much the same situation exists for agricultural research. Under the Hatch Act of 1887, USDA appropriations for research in states with two land-grant colleges are divided "as the legislature of such State shall direct." In the case of forestry research, the McIntyre-Stennis Act of 1962 permits the governor of each state to designate the recipient of federal funds. Again the pattern of discrimination repeats itself. In fiscal 1971 all $28,883,229 appropriated by Congress for agricultural and forestry research went to 1862 colleges; 1890 colleges got nothing.

These functions—agricultural extension and agricultural research—are critical to the ability of a land-grant college to attract and retain talented faculties and students, to keep abreast of developments in modern agricultural technology and education, and to reach and serve adequately the needier elements in rural America. Extension, in particular, is the crucial link between the small farmer and USDA programs, such as credit and subsidies. Yet USDA has, in effect, barred the black land-grant colleges from exercising those vital functions.

USDA officials invariably justify their policy on two grounds. First, they contend that black land-grant colleges lack the research and extension capabilities of their white counterparts. While this is obviously (and circularly) true, USDA and others recognize that the black land-grant colleges possess certain formidable strengths, which for lack of funds have never been fully exploited. A joint committee study conducted by the USDA and the Association of State Universities and Land-Grant Colleges showed that 1890 colleges maintained programs involving nutrition, environmental quality, psychology, consumer education, rural development, community health, and outreach to the rural poor. The committee report conceded that the extention service had abandoned its original concern with the rural disadvantaged in favor of "an increased involvement with people in the middle- and upper-income levels." But the report omitted criticism of USDA policy toward the black schools, concluding simply that the 1890 colleges "have a contribution to make to the efforts of cooperative extension."

USDA's other justification for its nonsupport of black land-grant colleges is more difficult to refute but equally invalid. USDA contends that it is the states, and not USDA, that decide how USDA money will be spent. The issue, like most concerning the 1890 colleges, is part legal and part political. The various federal acts do permit each state to divide USDA funds between the white and the black land-grant colleges as the state legislature directs. At the same time they also include provisions requiring the withholding of all research or extension funds from a state if any of the designated appropriations are "misapplied." Other federal departments have, on a number of occasions, withheld money under these statutes. In some instances political manipulation of funds was the reason given, whereas in others the state seemed to be using federal money poorly. Yet USDA has never withheld funds because of a state's rural discrimination or its denial of equal protection of the laws.

The Civil Rights Act of 1964 sought to put the enormous potential of federal assistance programs at the service of racial justice. Title VI of that act provides that "no person . . . shall, on the grounds of race, color, or national origin, be excluded from participation in, be denied the benefits of, or be subjected to discrimination under any program or activity receiving federal financial assistance." In addition, the act requires that each federal agency promulgate regulations implementing Title VI and providing for the withholding of federal assistance in the event of the state's failure to comply.

USDA issued its Title VI regulations in 1964 and has consistently failed to enforce them ever since. In 1965 the extension services were still formally segregated and still unequal, with white agents based at white schools serving only white farmers and black agents based at black schools serving only black farmers. All top administrative posts were held by whites, blacks supervised only other blacks, and all other aspects of the services were rigidly segregated. After a series of very critical reports by the Civil Rights Commission and USDA's own Office of Inspector General (OIG), Agriculture Secretary Orville Freeman finally ordered the merger of the segregated extension services in each state. The result was that virtually all extension activities were thereafter based at the white campuses, many black extension personnel lost their jobs, and those who remained were almost always demoted in favor of their white counterparts. A new round of investigations by the OIG in 1969 and the Civil Rights Commission in 1970 and 1971 disclosed that little progress had been made.

In addition, private lawsuits have been brought against the Mississippi and Alabama extension services alleging flagrant violations of the civil rights laws. On September 1, 1971, U.S. District Judge Frank Johnson ruled in favor of the plaintiffs in the Alabama action, and in an exhaustive opinion he detailed the systematic racial discrimination still practiced by the extension service at Auburn University (the white land-grant college in Alabama):

> The racial discrimination in this case has so permeated
> the employment practices and services distribution of the
> [Alabama extension service] that this Court finds it neces-
> sary to enter a detailed and specific decree, which will not
> only prohibit discrimination but which will also prescribe
> procedures designed to prevent discrimination in the future
> and to correct the effects of past discrimination.

Yet despite the well-known illegal practices described by Judge Johnson, and despite the clear language of Title VI and of USDA's regulations, USDA has never made the slightest move to withhold any funds for these violations.

This is not to say that the Nixon administration has been wholly indifferent to the plight of the black land-grant colleges. Former Agriculture Secretary Clifford Hardin, evidencing greater courage than his Democratic predecessor, accepted, first, a proposed allocation of about $4 million for the 1890 colleges in the 1972 budget for extension and research and, then, an amendment by Democratic Representative Frank Evans of Colorado, increasing this allocation to $12.6 million ($4 million for extension, $8.6 million for research), mostly under a 1965 law permitting USDA to grant research funds directly to institutions.

Although this is certainly a welcome development, this new fund is small, relative to the need, and leaves completely unchanged the venerable system whereby basic programs of southern agricultural research and education remain firmly and exclusively in the hands of the white land-grant colleges, colleges that have concerned themselves largely with the promotion of agricultural technology and the interests of white, relatively prosperous farmers. Every indication suggests that the "people's Department" will continue its refusal to enforce the law against states discriminating in the allocation of USDA funds.

STATEMENT OF JEAN FLORES, COMMUNITY WORKER, KINGS COUNTY, CALIFORNIA

Miss Flores. The statement that I have to make is regarding Kings County. The area of Kings County is 1,395 square miles and has a population of 66,300 as per census of 1965. The area of the county is 892,000 acres, 95 percent of the land is privately owned with 506,528 acres in farms, and 342,041 acres in other lands.

The above indicators reveal that Kings County is a largely agricultural area. One of the biggest growers in the state controls Kings County. J. G. Boswell, who obtained $4.5 million in subsidies from the federal government, is the largest landowner in Kings County. Agricultural prosperity blossoms out for the grower-controlled county. For the farm workers in this area it means poverty. An example of this is that 60 percent of the residents of this county are on welfare. These residents are on welfare because there is no work available, which reflects the subsidies that growers receive.

California growers are enriched and empowered not only by subsidized irrigation water (the world's largest welfare program some have claimed) but also the biggest growers, J. G. Boswell and Sawyer, who control Kings County, strengthen the control of our lives through political manipulation, which brings them the tax franchise subsidies of soil conservation programs, marketing order, acreage allotment for crops, guaranteed prices, and so on, as has been stated over and over again today. These government programs are administered entirely by local committees of farmers, the big growers control the committees that parcel out subsidies.

The size of some of these subsidies strains the imagination. The following growers rake in subsidies, welfare in Kings County: J. G. Boswell, with $4.5 million; Sawyer, $1,015,860; South Lake Farms, $1,468,696; West Lake Farms, $622,569.

Senator Taft. Excuse me, could I ask the witness to identify these subsidies?

Would you identify the subsidies and where you obtained them? Are they under the control of the support program? Are these crop subsidies, cotton mostly?

This statement is taken from U.S., Congress, Senate, Committee on Labor and Public Welfare, Subcommittee on Migratory Labor, Land Ownership, Use and Distribution, 92d Cong., 1971-72, pt. 3B, pp. 1342-44.

Miss Flores. Yes, sir, which is largely cotton area in Kings County, one of the reasons that no work is available.

The above is a sample of California farmer welfare recipients. A total of 84 farming operations in California received direct price support payments of over 100,000 in 1966. This story has been repeated over and over. The government makes laws to limit subsidies and the grower finds ways to continue to collect subsidies. The process for them seems to be very simple.

Another example of the kind of power that is controlled by the big powers is the Williamson Act that has recently passed in the Kings County at the same time the food stamp program was turned down. The food stamp program in Kings County would have cost $80,000 to be exact. Cost of commodities versus food stamp program is the same. At the same time the grower-controlled board of supervisors passed the Williamson Act, which represented a $500,000 tax cut to the rich growers. Middle-income people become the victims of rising taxes and place the blame on welfare recipients as a scapegoat. No one realizes the huge tax gifts that continually go to growers. The grower-controlled board of supervisors continue to divert public attention away from their own action and make the food stamp program and welfare a scapegoat for rising taxes. The large growers continue to manipulate Kings County.

The pity of all of this is that it took 1,500 farm workers to camp in front of the courthouse for 21 days and nights just to force the board of supervisors to comply with the law. The board of supervisors were not in compliance with distributing commodities as per regulations. It took a court order and demonstration to bring the board into compliance.

The Social Workers Organization of the Welfare Department in Kings County supported the poor of that county. It takes no imagination to see the outcome of the poor in this county. Health problems in this county are beyond belief. The County General Hospital does not provide adequate services. There is one intern doctor available at all times for the county.

I have some news clippings that represent some of the statements that I have made.

Attachment to the Statement of Jean Flores

Department of Public Welfare
Hanford, CA

February 17, 1972

Mr. J. E. Yenger
Chairman, Kings County
  Board of Supervisors
Courthouse
Hanford, CA

    Dear Mr. Yenger: In recent weeks the level of hunger in America has received widespread attention. President Nixon has stated that it is his policy to eliminate famine in the midst of great wealth. It is the feeling of Kings County Social Workers Organization that implementation of the Food Stamp Program in Kings County would eliminate much of the problem.

    The one major problem to the adoption of the Food Stamp Program has been the increased cost to the county. It however must be understood that if the present Commodity Distribution Program is to be operated under the State Plan, the total costs of the Food Stamp Program (Bank Issuance) versus State Commodity Distribution Program would be nearly identical. In the case of the Food Stamp Program (County Issuance) versus the State Commodity Distribution Program, the costs would be considerably less. It therefore must be realized that operating the Commodity Program in accordance with the State Plan will be just as costly yet fail to inject the stamp program's economic benefits into the county.

    The Commodity Distribution Program deals essentially in surplus foods as a means of farm price support. The only benefit to the local economy is this indirect one. The Food Stamp Program increases the purchasing power of the household to the extent of the bonus value and the entire purchasing is handled at local retail outlets.

    The Commodity Distribution Program provides no choice of foods to the participating household, and the nutritional value and balance are secondary and are determined by the available commodities. Since commodities are distributed only semimonthly without regard to eating habits or available household storage facilities, they are subject to waste and spoilage.

    Low income families and public assistance recipients prefer food stamps because they may be used to purchase any domestic food through normal retail outlets, allowing for free choice without the stigma attached to welfare commodities. It is for these reasons that the Kings County Social Workers Organization supports the adoption of the Food Stamp Program.

5/ National Advocacy Efforts and Health Care

INTRODUCTION

The first two excerpts have been chosen to appear in this part of the Appendix for a number of reasons. First, they illustrate the previous statements that contemporary social work is characterized by the presence of a number of national advocacy bodies (see Chapter 4). Second, they highlight a corollary of that statement, that is, the fact that rural social work as it has developed through the past seven decades could not exist without the support of persons and organizations involved in rural advocacy. Third, the excerpts not only encourage social workers to become significantly involved in political issues affecting rural people but also stress that most welfare issues, from rural roads to rural health, are political in nature.

Finally, the first two excerpts in this part of the Appendix relate to a topic that has not been stressed in the text of this volume because it is, in and of itself, far too complex and awesome to be addressed in a broad stroke narrative. That topic is rural health in all its dimensions. While attention has been given in the text to the development of mental health services in rural areas after the passage of PL 88-164 in 1963 and to the role of social workers following the comprehensive act, a similar legislative gain is still missing in the broader health field. Perhaps the two excerpts contained in this Appendix will be, as David Raphael implies in his address, warning signs of things yet to come.

The first document, Lorin E. Kerr's "The Road We Have Come: Rural Health Needs and Nonresponse," reviews from a historical perspective the health needs that have affected rural people through contemporary times and the characteristic responses that have, according to the author, exacerbated rather than diminished those needs. Kerr's views are political. His perspective is clear; there is no doubt in his mind that the solution to many of the problems of rural health lies in the passage of comprehensive health service legislation supported through progressive taxation. His position is similar to that pioneered by Gifford Pinchot in relation to federal government intervention on relief prior to the enactment of the FERA in 1933. "Is this nation, as a nation, to reach out a hand to help those of its people who through no fault of their own are in desperation and distress?" asked Pinchot in 1933. Pinchot firmly believed, somewhat like Kerr, that "the force behind the stubborn opposition to federal relief was fear lest the taxation to provide that relief be levied on concentrated wealth—fear lest the policy of years, the policy of shielding the big fortunes at the expense of the little ones, should at long last be tossed into discard."[1] Whether Kerr's statement will prove to be prophetic of things to come only time will tell. Momentarily, let them be presented as illustrative of the position of a person and an organization concerned with remedying rural health problems.

The second document, David Raphael's address to the Rural America Conference on the Rural Northwest, clearly exemplifies the political dimensions of most of the issues that concern human service practitioners. There are no purely ameliorative issues in public welfare; for those who still doubt that every remedial measure is the result of a political process, let Raphael's statements present a summary and examples. Raphael stresses the fact that progress has been made, yet the road ahead in rural health issues is still, at the end of the 1978-79 congressional year, tortuous and prolonged. Jay Feldman, rural health expert of Rural America, summarized the accomplishments and disappointments of the Ninety-Fifth Congress's measures.

> The 95th Congress adjourned in a whirlwind October 15, 1978, and as the dust settles it appears that the health concerns of rural people were met with mixed success. Community health centers and migrant health services, technical assistance and research and demonstration projects have received legislative authority to try and meet the needs of rural people. However, hopes for the enactment of rural health planning amendments were killed when the House adjourned without taking action on the "Health Planning and Resources Development Amendments of 1978."[2]

The third and final piece represents a bridge between a focus on the provision of general medical services in rural areas and a focus on the provision of psychiatric services. "A Decade in Rural Psychiatry" is the personal account of a psychiatrist who chose to serve on the staff of a general hospital.

Harvey Gurian's views are personal and reflect ambivalence on a variety of points. First, the author expresses the kind of ambivalence about the community mental health system that has not been reflected in the text of this volume, an ambivalence derived not from conflict with community mental health principles but with its administrative mandates. While Gurian still feels the community mental health program is important, his decision was that "someone else had better do it." Gurian's decision was based on the political (rather than the therapeutic) nature of the task, an observation to which Raphael clearly alluded in his paper, and a point that should be kept clearly in mind by anyone undertaking a managerial position in rural health. Furthermore, Gurian expresses ambivalence about rural psychiatry itself, an ambivalence that leads him to state that "intimate contact with the community and a community oriented setting" might not be the best way to describe rural psychiatric practice in his part of the country. These statements are of concern to all interested in rural areas. While they reflect Gurian's position in 1971 when national attention had not yet been refocused on rural America, the question remains whether they are still valid at the end of the decade, when migration patterns have been reversed and rural areas have been experiencing a return to the mainstream of national life.

NOTES

1. Gifford Pinchot, "The Case for Federal Relief," Survey Graphic, vol. 67 (January 1, 1932); also in Emilia E. Martinez-Brawley's Pioneer Efforts in Rural Social Welfare: First-Hand Views since 1908 (Philadelphia: Penn State University Press, 1980), pp. 216-24.

2. Jay Feldman, "Legislative Report," Rural America, November 1978, p. 1 (mimeographed).

THE ROAD WE HAVE COME: RURAL HEALTH NEEDS AND NONRESPONSE

Lorin E. Kerr

In 1944 Fiorello H. La Guardia stated with his inimitable vigor that "when knowledge is not applied, it's wicked." In the same presentation at the Annual Meeting of the American Public Health Association (APHA) in New York, Mayor La Guardia went on to say that "people have a right to medical care."

During the same meeting there was discussion of the problem of medical service for migrant workers and the excellent way in which it had been handled by the Farm Security and War Food Administrations. The APHA also adopted as its official policy a landmark report on medical care in a national health program.

This action put APHA squarely on record in favor of a national program that would make available for all people of the United States complete and adequate medical care of all essential types. It made it clear that such an end can be attained only by a decentralized but federally aided program; that it must be supported by compulsory insurance plus taxation or by taxation alone; and that it should be ad-

Lorin E. Kerr was born in Toledo, Ohio, in 1909. He received his B.A. from the University of Toledo and his M.D. and MSPH from the University of Michigan, Ann Arbor. Kerr entered the field of public health in 1937, working for the city of Toledo. He was a county health officer in Michigan and in his native Ohio. In 1944 he began working for the U.S. Public Health Service in charge of the medical health program for migrant and imported workers in seven northwestern states. In 1947 he was assigned to Washington, D.C., with the Division of Industrial Hygiene of the U.S. Public Health Administration. In 1948 Kerr began working for the United Mine Workers of America (UMWA) as assistant to the executive medical officer of the welfare and retirement fund. In 1969 the UMWA established its own Department of Occupational Health, of which Kerr became director and in which he continues to be employed. Kerr is one of the few physicians employed full time by a labor union.

This is a slightly revised and shortened version of the statement presented at the National Rural Health Conference held in conjunction with the Third National Conference on Rural America, Shoreham-Americana Hotel, Washington, D.C., December 5, 1977. A similar position was presented by Kerr in his testimony before the Subcommittee on Health and Scientific Research, U.S. Senate, February 9, 1978.

ministered by a single public health agency at the federal, state, and local levels.

This action was built upon the long and often isolated struggles to solve the onerous problem of paying doctor and hospital bills. Many of these involved rural groups banned together in health cooperatives such as the one formed in Elk City, Oklahoma, in 1929. While health co-ops were given impetus by some urban workers, they became the mainstay of the Farm Security Administration (FSA) in working with low-income farm families throughout the nation. Eventually there was an amalgam of the FSA program with the federal effort to overcome the unhealthy plight of migratory farm workers, particularly during World War II.

What has happened in the ensuing years? We have studied, reported, recorded, and proved beyond a doubt—in fact, the documentation is truly mountainous—that very little has changed. The litany of death and disability is essentially the same. The health facilities are in short supply and the same is true of all types of health personnel. The costs are astronomical and there is no indication that they will lessen or level off at any point in the foreseeable future.

Two years ago at the First National Conference on Rural America, it was the considered opinion of the 1,500 attendees that "nowhere in the United States is the need for an improved health system more pressing and nowhere is it less adequate than in rural America." It was agreed that the situation is getting worse, not better, despite the cheerful reports of the American Medical Association and some government officials. In the last 30 years the net efforts of tardy and miserly government efforts have not improved conditions so much as they have just barely prevented them from becoming scandalous.

An impressive array of health experts at the 1975 conference delineated, one after another, the nation's rural health problems. Today conditions are still the same. For example, infant mortality rates in rural medically underserved areas are double and triple the national norm, ranging in some cases up to 35 and 40 deaths per thousand live births. Of all women of childbearing age, 20 percent are rural, but they account for 50 percent of all maternal deaths. The message of these figures on infant and maternal mortality is quite clear—rural America offers a more hazardous environment than urban America.

Rural residents have a higher incidence of chronic conditions including digestive, respiratory, and circulatory health problems. They have 22 percent more ulcers, 26 percent more cases of hypertension, and 29 percent more strokes than city residents.

Work-related death and disability in rural communities have long constituted a major health problem that has only recently begun to attract serious national attention. Statistics for several decades have shown that traditional rural occupations such as mining, lumbering, and agriculture are among the most dangerous to working people. This was found even though our system of collecting information concerning all work-related injuries is inadequate, particularly in relation to farm accidents and the effects of pesticides on humans. The mortality rate for rural workers is almost double that of their urban counterparts. Overall, our national record is extremely poor compared with other industrialized nations of the world.

In other areas of prevention, 30,000 communities lack a centralized sanitary water system, and this does not include isolated populations; sewer facilities are a serious problem for millions. In West Virginia 60 percent of all homes have dangerous sewer systems. Of rural children 60 percent or less are immunized against communicable diseases.

One of the most serious health problems confronting the rural poor is undernutrition and hunger. It is estimated that less than half of the 26 million Americans who cannot afford an adequate diet are receiving assistance through federal food programs. A majority of these Americans live in rural America.

Briefly, this is the status of health in rural America. In this century we have managed to reverse the traditional relationship between urban and rural areas as far as the public's health is concerned. Today, on the basis of most indicators, rural America is far less healthy than the dominant, more urbanized part of society.

Most of us know that the distribution of health resources and personnel in rural America is as bad, and in some cases worse, than the distribution of other vital resources. The quickest way to learn what is wrong with our health system in general is to observe its particular malfunction in rural areas. At the heart of the crisis lies the gross maldistribution of physicians and other health personnel. Overall the United States averages one doctor for every 665 persons. In urban communities the ratio is one doctor for every 500 persons; in rural America, for every 2,400 residents there is only one physician. Looked at another way, although roughly a third of our national population resides in rural areas, they are served by only 12 percent of the nation's doctors and 18 percent of the nurses. The shortage means hardships for doctors, as well as patients, for rural physicians must work longer hours and see more patients.

Experience indicates that decent medical care can be provided with one doctor per 1,000 people. There is obviously a shortage of doctors and other health personnel, and those we have are distributed without much regard to need. But this is not a new problem.

Fifty years ago C.-E. A. Winslow, a widely acknowledged health expert, noted that state after state was complaining "of a grave lack of medical services of any kind in rural districts." He also said that there was no attempt to meet this need with community grants to physicians who will consent to practice in such regions. Winslow was of the opinion that money alone was not the answer. The solution required good laboratory and hospital facilities and the ready availability of consultation with other well-trained physicians.

Nearly three generations later states are still complaining—but more loudly because the situation has worsened. Today it is estimated that to remedy the doctor deficit in rural areas would require over 100 percent of the U.S. and foreign medical school graduates for a full year—almost 20,000—not counting deaths and retirement.

But the real remedy involves much more than locating 20,000 physicians—even if it could be accomplished—in doctorless rural communities. The problems I have described are manifestations of sorely needed changes in our entire national delivery system that must be effected in the immediate future. More than 60 years ago Congress first held hearings on national health insurance. It was nearly 25 years before the next congressional hearings occurred. Since 1943 numerous proposals have been introduced, but none achieved passage until Medicare and Medicaid were enacted in 1966. Today there is a wide variety of measures again before Congress that bear the label of national health insurance. The major proposal supported by organized labor and many other groups is the Kennedy-Corman Health Security Bill. This bill has been improved by two sets of earlier hearings. While it will assure the payment of doctor and hospital bills it does not resolve the basic problems, which are still the prevention of disease, reorganization of delivery of services, and financing. The absence of adequate cost controls, such as continuance of the fee-for-service method of paying doctors, will undoubtedly permit the cost of medical care to rise from its current level of nearly 8 percent of the gross national product to somewhere around 12 to 15 percent in a very short time.

On October 18, 1976, in a historic statement, four former presidents of the American Public Health Association declared their conviction that only a national health service act rather than national health insurance could solve America's health problems. They stated:

> We are fearful that a national health insurance measure will be enacted into law that will repeat the serious mistakes of Medicare and Medicaid, and that will fail to address the really critical issues confronting this nation with respect to health care for the people. All of the many proposals introduced in Congress that are described as national health insurance bills are essentially financial mechanisms for providing guaranteed payments to the providers of health care services. They contain virtually no

provisions for the reform or alteration of the American health care system. It has become more and more apparent, not only to health professionals and scholars but to much of the general public, that there are fundamental flaws in our system of providing health services which must not be incorporated into a new health system.

The former presidents ended their statement as follows:

We therefore call upon Congress to enact legislation to create a national health service which would be financed through progressive taxation, provide comprehensive health care with an emphasis on prevention and positive health promotion to all persons in the United States without charge and without any form of discrimination, to be controlled by the public in local communities with safeguards over quality and efficiency of health services delivery and expense, and with remuneration of providers based not on fee-for-services but on adequate salaries, as in all other public services.

Two days later APHA, at its annual meeting, called for a community-based national health service program embodying the recommendations of the four former presidents.

Congressman Ronald V. Dellums on May 4, 1977, introduced the National Health Service Act H. R. 6894. The bill is now being revised and will be reintroduced when Congress reconvenes after the first of the year. The major provisions of the bill assure that all residents of the United States will be included without exception; all health services for prevention, diagnosis, treatment, and rehabilitation will be included and there will be no charges; and care will be provided primarily in publicly owned community health centers equipped with modern diagnostic and treatment facilities.

Special efforts will be made to close the gap between urban and rural areas by giving priority to the construction and staffing of health centers in the small towns serving rural communities. Improved transportation and communication facilities will be developed to make the services of these health centers easily accessible.

The Dellums Health Service Act states that all health personnel will be salaried. Fee-for-service practice will be eliminated in the national health service. For those doctors who wish to remain in private practice, there undoubtedly will be a small part of the population willing to pay their fees.

Training for the health professions will be tuition-free and graduates will serve for several years in underserved rural areas. Living allowances and free child care services, as needed, will remove major barriers to training. Admission policies for medical schools will favor not only those previously underrepresented—minorities, women, rural and working-class students—but will draw a considerable portion of the student body from health workers, such as nurses and technicians who already have demonstrated their commitment to improving the health of people.

The basic unit of the national health service will be the community served by a single health center, with a population varying considerably according to circumstances, but usually of 25,000 to 50,000.

The administration will be headed at each level—federal, state, and local—by a Department of Health. Each department will be responsible to a governing board, of which two-thirds of the membership will truly represent the people being served and one-third of the health workers providing the service. All health centers, hospitals, and other health facilities will likewise be governed by these citizen-dominated boards.

The keystone of the national health service will be the promotion of health and prevention of disease. At every level there will be strong divisions of disease prevention in the health departments that will take all available measures for the prevention and control of infectious, noninfectious, occupational, and environmental diseases. Priority in research will be given to prevention.

The national health service will be consumer oriented rather than provider oriented. Health workers will be expected to have the welfare of the people they serve as their primary aims. In fact, a portion of the health service bill will be devoted to the provisions necessary to ensure the observance of these health rights.

The nearly 9 percent of the gross national product (GNP) that we now spend for health services in the United States is too much for what we get. Much of it goes for unnecessary operations, unnecessarily high incomes of private practitioners, and unnecessary waste and duplication. For 8 percent of the GNP, which is the limit on expenditures set by the Dellums National Health Service Act, a national service will ensure the provision of a high quality of general services. In addition, it will also ensure the provision of all the services badly neglected at the present time, such as dental care, mental health, and services for the chronically ill and aged.

A half century ago Winslow proposed that essentially the same program we are discussing today would solve the health problems he was observing in 1926. He anticipated criticism of the projects for organizing the medical service he outlined. Some he felt would be sound and significant, others merely superficial and frivolous. He added that "the habit of condemning any attempt at intelligent community action by labelling it as 'socialist' and 'bureaucratic'" is un-worthy of serious-minded men: "Some things are better done by the individual, some better by the state; and catchwords will not help us to determine to which class a given activity belongs. "

While it is likely that the same criticisms will be leveled at the Dellums Bill, a national health service is the only logical and rational way to solve our country's health problems.

In conclusion, I want to return to prevention because it is the crux of the action needed to reorganize the nation's health care de-livery system. It has never come of age because medical care is usually limited to those services for which payment is made on the archaic fee-for-service basis. This method of paying doctor bills is well suited for episodic services, like the repair of a faulty television set. But only when this piecework system of paying doctor bills is changed can the full force of preventive medicine become effective. A new national health care system must emphasize priority for pre-ventive community health efforts. It would certainly pay off in the long run, both in terms of a healthier nation and reduced costs, since preventive services are far less expensive and more cost effective than sickness services.

We must implement the philosophy of prevention that is best expressed by Milton J. Rosenau, M.D., an acclaimed public health leader who said in 1913:

> Preventive medicine dreams of a time when there shall be enough for all, and every man shall bear his share of labor in accordance with his ability, and every man shall possess sufficient for the needs of his body and the demands of health. These things he shall have as a matter of justice and not of charity. Preventive medicine dreams of a time when there shall be no unnecessary suffering and no pre-mature deaths; when the welfare of the people shall be our highest concern; when humanity and mercy shall replace greed and selfishness; and it dreams that all these things will be accomplished through the wisdom of man. Preven-tive medicine dreams of these things, not with the hope that we, individually, may participate in them, but with the joy that we may aid in their coming to those who will live after us. When young men have vision the dreams of old men will come true.

LEGISLATIVE ISSUES AND RURAL HEALTH

David Raphael

I have been asked to share with you some of our thinking and recent experience on the rural health legislative front and the politics of rural health. As a nonprofit, tax-exempt organization, we are prohibited from becoming directly involved in the legislative process, but we are trying to take a very direct and active role in the politics of rural health.

RURAL HEALTH AS A POLITICAL PROBLEM

Rural health is a political problem. It seems to me that it is at least as important for us to approach rural health needs as a political issue as it is to wrestle with some of the technical problems associated with delivering health services.

A few examples may show what I mean. To help illustrate the point, let me borrow from some of our experience in the rural housing area, because I think it has direct relevance to rural health interests.

Several years ago a number of us working through the National Rural Housing Coalition tried to get a couple of rural members of Congress to introduce a major rural housing bill. The first part of the bill proposed a number of useful but limited amendments to the existing Farmers Home housing programs, while the second part called for a major assault on the housing problems of the rural poor by creating a new Emergency Rural Housing Administration. Our potential congressional sponsors looked at the bill and were aghast—not by the price tag or the scope of the major provisions—but because the very act of introducing a rural housing bill was without precedent.

"This is just not the way things are done here," we were told by the Congressman from Georgia, who was known as "Mr. Rural Housing" by his colleagues. He explained that as long as he could remember, housing legislation had always been drafted by HUD, then a few minor amendments for Farmers Home programs would be tacked on at the end. The only real point in those rural amendments was to

David Raphael is executive director of Rural America. This is a slightly shortened version of the statement presented at the General Health Session of the Rural America Conference on the Rural Northwest, Seattle, November 1978.

give progressive rural members of Congress some reason for supporting the clearly urban-oriented legislation. The urgency of small town and rural housing needs and the unique problems of delivering housing services in smaller rural communities were never seriously considered.

The idea of rural housing interests originating a piece of serious legislation was so revolutionary that it frightened our friend from Georgia. But he introduced the bill anyway, and it turned out he was able to muster enough support to get at least half (the more modest half) of it through.

In many ways, those of us working on rural health issues are even less advanced than the rural housing people were in 1974 with respect to dealing with this kind of political problem. At least in the housing area, federal policy recognizes the special needs of rural people and their communities and has established a separate agency, the Farmers Home Administration, to deal with them. We have no similar institution or structure to rally around in rural health—only a couple of rural and migrant health offices within HEW that are sometimes there and sometimes not, depending upon who is in charge.

Additionally, and of equal importance to the structural problems, is the organizational problem. Until very recently, there has been no effective rural voice or coalition at the national level that could help focus public attention on the full range of rural health issues. The individuals and organizations actively concerned with rural health have been extremely slow in developing effective coalitions and action programs in order to confront the underlying political issues. However, that movement has begun, and its effects should be increasingly felt in the future.

The most visible result of the political process that is under way was the passage last year of the Rural Health Clinics Act. That bill represented the first exclusively rural piece of health legislation introduced in the Congress since the New Deal. Although modest in scope, and simply trying to correct obvious inequities in existing Medicare and Medicaid legislation, the Rural Clinics Bill encountered a lot of stiff resistance. Again, much of it simply reflected the fact that this was just not the way health issues had been dealt with on the hill. Along the way, we heard a lot of screams about how the bill was discriminatory, that rural people would be getting benefits not available in urban areas, how the potential costs might bankrupt the republic, and the like. But in the end, the sponsors and friends of rural people prevailed, and this historic piece of legislation is in place and is hesitantly being implemented. In addition to its obvious benefits to the rural elderly and poor, the act represents an important precedent in the drive to improve rural people's access to improved health care.

This year a significant amount of health legislation was passed by the Congress, and a number of important rural health initiatives undertaken. Our resources have been limited and the troops even scarcer, but I believe that important progress was made in a number of areas, particularly by focusing attention on such issues as community and migrant health centers, health planning in rural areas, and public health services in rural America.

COMMUNITY HEALTH CENTERS

In preparing testimony before Senator Kennedy's Health Subcommittee, we uncovered and documented evidence that the community health center program, funded under Section 330 of the Public Health Service Act, was seriously biased against small town and rural people. While rural areas account for more than half of the medically underserved people in the nation, less than 25 percent of the Section 330 funds go to support rural health centers and clinics.

Although disturbing, the figures on how HEW allocated its health center funds were by no means surprising. It reflects the all too familiar pattern of general neglect and outright discrimination against rural people in the allocation of federal resources and benefits. What was surprising was the administration's official reaction when the facts were published. Congress seemed genuinely concerned over the obvious maldistribution, but it was HEW that went to considerable lengths to justify the present imbalance.

At first, the response was to point to all those Rural Health Initiatives (RHI) projects that had been funded in recent years in an attempt to show how much the rural program had expanded. It was even implied that since HEW funds nearly 500 rural health clinics in rural areas, compared with approximately 160 in urban areas, the rural poor were really very well off. (The facts are that federal funding for the 160 or so urban health centers more than triples the funding available to all 500 RHIs and other rural projects.)

Subsequently, HEW argued that if urban clinics were receiving three times as much money for each medically underserved person in their area as rural clinics, it simply reflected the greater costs in serving people in urban as opposed to rural places. After all, was it not natural that it would cost more to provide services in metropolitan communities? That is, of course, nonsense, since no attempt has ever been made to compare levels of service and relative cost between urban and rural health centers. The fact is that the neighborhood health center program, and the community health center program that followed, recognized the need for a comprehensive range of health services, and funded them, but largely in the cities.

In the end, the disproportionate cost argument was dropped in favor of one that pretty crudely told Congress that the only way to achieve equity in community health services would be to expand the level of funding sufficiently to offset the past discrimination. Since neither Congress nor the administration wanted to talk about money, the matter was left pretty much the way it stood—at least for now.

PUBLIC HEALTH SERVICES

Historically, federal support of public health service has been based on two factors—population and medical and financial need. This year the public health lobby put together a strong and needed effort to increase support for public health services. The only trouble was the proposed new funding formula completely abandoned need as a criterion for receiving public health funds, basing it almost entirely on population. The effect of the change would have been to perpetuate present inequities and enable the rich and populous states to get richer.

When we approached supporters of the measure (such as progressive, publicly oriented groups like the American Public Health Association [APHA] and the Association of State and Territorial Health Officials [ASTHO]) with our concern about the impact of the bill on poorer more rural states, the reaction was quite surprising and unanticipated. It went something like this: Well who are you and why should you be concerned? Since no rural group was present when this strategy was agreed upon two years ago, you've got no standing and no right to come in at this time. Don't raise questions about equity, poverty, or need because you will wreck the entire bill that we have been working on for so long.

Despite the reluctance of the very groups who should have supported changing the formula, a couple of courageous senators and congresspeople amended the bill without, I might add, jeopardizing the whole public health movement as some had feared and predicted. As it stands, the victory for poor and rural people may be more symbolic than real, but an important concept has been kept alive, and in the process a new dimension of the politics on rural health has been illuminated.

REVOLT IN NORTH DAKOTA

Finally, no discussion of the politics on health could be complete without dealing with the role of organized medicine. In North Dakota this year, a fairly simple health initiative was put before the voters of that state. In view of the failure of our national government to move on either containing skyrocketing medical costs or establishing a rational system for the delivery of health care services, over 16,000 people of North Dakota—nearly 10 percent of the state's voters—decided to go ahead on their own.

Their proposition was simple, straightforward, and quite modest. It authorized the state health commissioner to establish an effective statewide cost containment program, not just on hospital costs, but a full range of physician and laboratory charges. It also instructed the state government to investigate the most effective means of establishing a comprehensive health insurance program, and to report back to the voters after a year or two of study.

For those of you who follow such things, you probably know the North Dakota health initiative was effectively defeated last week. However, it cost its opponents a wad of money to beat it. From the beginning, the measure was attacked by the medical industry in the state. It is estimated that anywhere between $300,000 and $1 million was raised by the AMA and others to oppose it. The state's television audience was subjected to a fearful campaign, threatening all sorts of horrors from outright socialism to the wholesale abandonment of North Dakota communities by private physicians. To those in the rural parts of the state, it was an empty gesture since most physicians had pulled out years ago anyway. However, the assault was effective, particularly when you keep in mind that polls in early September (before the AMA campaign) showed the initiative leading by 2 to 1.

For many of us, the point is not that the initiative in North Dakota lost or that organized medicine again took an unconstructive position on a critical health issue. The point is that some people's voices are beginning to be heard, even if faintly at first. The point is that we now perceive a growing popular movement toward effectively dealing with the politics of health, and specifically the politics of rural health. There is a stirring among people in many parts of the country, reflected in such diverse actions as the recent health initiatives in North Dakota and Oregon, in the local self-help projects emerging in many rural communities, and in the formation of such regional and national health coalitions as Northwest Chicano Health, RANCHO, and our own Rural Health Council.

At this point, that movement has a lot of needs. It needs the resources necessary to offset the television blitz that can be expected on major health issues. (In North Dakota, there was practically none.) That movement also needs the resources, materials, and trained rural people to assist local communities to provide their own health services, and those coalitions working for policy changes need the support and strength of local organizations and individuals and some clear directions and action strategies.

In the case of the Rural Health Council of Rural America, we have begun to identify the basic policy issues. That initial attempt is contained in the Rural Health Platform that was developed by the participants at last December's national rural health conference and has been adopted by the Rural Health Council. It needs to be continually updated and refined. It also needs to stimulate discussion at the regional, state, and local levels about the unique health problems confronting rural and other disadvantaged people in those areas. I hope it will be possible for this conference to contribute to that process of organizing people around common concerns, strengthening existing coalitions that can help speak on behalf of the citizenry, and also to contribute to the further development of an effective action agenda on rural health that recognizes the political as well as the technical issues involved.

A DECADE IN RURAL PSYCHIATRY

Harvey Gurian

Can one organize and present, in a meaningful way, a decade
of experience in rural psychiatry? Because my experience encom-
passes the chaotic 1960s, it might be worthwhile to try to evaluate it
—not only in terms of day-to-day stresses, but also from a broader
viewpoint—to try to discover how the events of the 1960s have shaped
me, personally and professionally, as a psychiatrist operating in a
rural area. Has my professional course deviated from that of psychiatry as a whole? How much do national trends influence a psychiatrist who is isolated from his psychiatric colleagues? What changes
have occurred in me, and how much can I attribute those changes to
the rural setting in which I have been working?

In December 1959 I arrived, young and fresh, at the Mary Imogene Bassett Hospital in Cooperstown, which is located 200 miles
northeast of New York City in a relatively poor area of the state. For
eight years I would be the only psychiatrist for miles around. I had a
strong medical orientation. I was eager to become a white-coated
doctor in the mainstream of medicine, which was why I had come to
Bassett, a small but renowned teaching and research hospital affiliated
with Columbia University College of Physicians and Surgeons.

Bassett serves as a referral center for a wide area and treats
patients with a variety of complex medical problems. It also serves
as the primary medical facility in its immediate area. It is gener-
ously endowed with private funds and has a closed, full-time, salaried
staff. The hospital offers straight and rotating internships and resi-
dencies in all major specialties. Its laboratory and clinical research
involves the departments of internal medicine, surgery, radiology,
and pathology.

When I joined the staff, the hospital had 96 beds and psychiatric
patients were admitted to medical and surgical wards. A new facility
with 186 beds, including a 16-bed psychiatric unit, was opened in 1970.

Harvey Gurian graduated in medicine from the University of
Toronto in 1949 and was trained in psychiatry in the New York State
hospital system. Since 1959 he has been psychiatrist-in-chief at Mary
Imogene Bassett Hospital in Cooperstown, N.Y. Gurian is certified
in psychiatry and neurology and is also a Fellow of the Royal College
of Physicians and Surgeons of Canada. This article originally appeared in Hospital and Community Psychiatry 22 (February 2, 1971):
56-58.

The psychiatric staff now includes a resident and two rotating interns, another full-time psychiatrist who restricts his work to child psychiatry, and two clinical psychologists. The state hospital that serves the area is 80 miles away, and there are no other psychiatric resources in the county.

In 1959 I arrived eager to provide all kinds of services to everyone. I wanted to teach and to learn. I had had much clinical, evaluative, and management experience, but not as much psychotherapeutic and teaching experience as I would have liked. I was ambitious, idealistic, and naïve. It was naïveté rather than courage that caused me to venture here alone. I was interested in community mental health. In my previous position at Middletown (New York) State Hospital, I had worked closely with the courts and had run a community clinic. But I had not been without psychiatric resources, and I was not in a place where psychiatry was more or less new.

Now, a little more than ten years after my arrival at Bassett, I find myself transformed. Perhaps after surviving the 1960s we are all transformed. The world seems a thousand years older—and so do I. How have I changed? I am not as naïve as I used to be. Also I am not as idealistic. I am much more skeptical and I am too cynical, perhaps because I have had to cope with a good deal of professional loneliness. And I find, a little to my surprise, that my orientation is no longer strictly in the traditional medical model.

One paradox is that although I have been desperate for psychiatric colleagues for most of the decade, I have also seen myself developing professionally. (My cynical self suggests that the absence of colleagues may be what has allowed me to develop.) But it is true that with our model communications, cultural isolation can hardly exist and changes penetrate everywhere, as if by osmosis. As Marshall McLuhan says, we are all now in the same global village. But for more than eight years I was the only psychiatrist here, and one needs ego infusions to maintain one's identity.

With concepts as subjective as those of psychiatry, the lack of colleagues often affects the manner in which a decision is accepted. The consensus of several psychiatrists carries far more weight than the opinion of one. Working alone, therefore, is a severe ego threat. Even such a simple problem as setting limits for a patient can be difficult when the patient is able to mobilize support against the decision not only from his friends and relatives, but also from the psychiatrist's own medical colleagues. When the inherent difficulties of psychotherapy are thus compounded, it is difficult to keep one's cool. One either leaves, builds formidable narcissistic defenses, or learns to live with periodic turmoil.

The problem of professional loneliness is directly related to the staffing problem, which is at the root of many of the difficulties of rural psychiatry. Competent staff are, for the most part, hard to come by. Urban psychiatrists do not want to come to a rural area for a variety of valid reasons, many of which are reflected by the experiences I have mentioned. Sufficient staffing would go a long way toward relieving the problems, but I would be surprised if there were many rural areas with that kind of luck. The problem is circular: one has difficulty in getting staff, which leads to situational stresses, which leads to difficulty in getting staff.

There is another type of isolation—that of ideology. Rural areas more than urban areas are inclined to be politically conservative, so a certain type of cultural alienation goes along with the professional loneliness. As Rogow says, psychiatrists, more than other medical specialists, tend to be liberals. "Basically the liberal point of view is more deterministic and less directive than the conservative point of view," he writes. "Liberalism doesn't involve doing something to someone nearly so much as does conservatism, which tends to be more authoritative and directive, and psychiatrists are a low authority group. That is, we value independence, free choice, minimum coercion."[1]

The medical model is, almost by definition, inclined toward conservatism. The relationship involves the patient's being dependent on the physician for diagnosis, medicine, and counsel. Although I was eager to pursue the medical model when I arrived here ten years ago, I now find myself much further from it. I incline more toward an interpersonal, shared, I-thou model. I find it hard to see my patients as sick in the medical sense.

That is interesting, because before I came here I had spent almost ten years working in a state hospital and had become progressively more plagued by psychiatry's isolation from medicine. The main attraction Cooperstown had for me was the general-hospital setting. I felt a strong medical identification and felt that psychiatry was a branch of medicine in every sense of the word. I think my dissatisfaction with the state-hospital system was similar to the general professional dissatisfaction that ultimately led to the community mental health movement. We were becoming increasingly aware of the detrimental effect state hospitals had on patients and staff, and ideas about milieu and therapeutic communities were pervading psychiatric thought.

In response to those trends, I left the state hospital to become not only a rural psychiatrist but also a rural general-hospital psychiatrist, a situation that is even more unusual and, I believe, more difficult to sustain. It soon became clear that first I had to select the patients I would treat, which of course involved refusing to treat some; no other physician in the hospital refused to treat patients. Second, my relationships with patients were different from those of my colleagues in other specialties. The nonpsychiatric physician diagnoses, usually treats quite definite conditions, and makes all the medical decisions himself. It is quite clear where his responsibility begins and what the patient's reciprocal responsibility should be. That is not so in psychiatry. The boundaries of responsibility are more vague, and therapist and patient may well differ about the nature of the problems.

As I struggled with those difficulties, often under the quite disapproving eyes of my medical colleagues, I found that in many instances I had to abandon the medical model. I could not do so in all cases, of course, because sometimes that would have been most inappropriate and, indeed, damaging to the patient. But although I have abandoned the medical model to some extent, partly as the result of the stresses I have experienced here, I find I am heading in the same direction as many other psychiatrists all over the country—toward an interpersonal, open encounter with the patient.

One wonders at the influence the communications media have had on this change. They have caused us to become increasingly involved and concerned with others, and have also led to antiinstitutional attitudes and new respect for the individual and for interpersonal relationships. At the same time, we are moving toward massive systems of managing large numbers of people. It is to be hoped that the changes will balance one another out.

When I came here, I was interested in community mental health and hoped to help develop a program. I still feel that a community mental health program is important, but that someone else had better work in it. When the local community mental health board first organized a program in 1967, I became the director, serving without salary in order to get things going. I found, however, that I could not develop the community program and the hospital program at the same time, and resigned from the former after one year. So far, no successor has been found, but the board is actively seeking to hire a new director.

My own reasons for preferring to develop the hospital's psychiatric department rather than venture into community mental health probably have a good deal to do with my own personality and prejudices. I find myself uninspired by most of the programs that have developed in the name of community mental health. There is much talk today about public health models and caretaking systems, and for all practical reasons the responsibility for developing services is squarely on the psychiatrist. Two things trouble me about that approach: it assumes that the types of treatment we have to offer are more effective than they really are, and it fails to recognize that a massive caretaking system is basically incompatible with individual responsibility and personal growth for both patients and therapists. Thus, in the end, I think the approach is self-defeating.

Community mental health programs emphasize community control. Although one does not question that concept, there is a lack of consensus about what aspects of the program the community should control. If it turns out to mean that the community is to define the job of the psychiatrist, his goal may be a contented board rather than effective services. Like most rural communities, Cooperstown has been oversold on the public health model of psychiatry, and, perhaps justly, feels that a highly paid community psychiatrist should be expected to deliver the goods. In this essentially poor farming area, one is expected to be conservative, careful of funds. There is never quite enough money to meet all needs. Because the community psychiatrist will obviously have to deal with county officials, he will be more likely to need political than therapeutic qualities.

But dealing with the local community is only one part of the problem. State and federal governments are now trying to outdo one another in setting up various new controls to regulate the psychiatrist's approach. Thus the community psychiatrist will have to contend with three governing levels, local, state, and federal, each of which makes very specific demands on him. He can seldom satisfy both the public —the consumers—and the administrative suppliers—the governments.

In the fashion of the day, we find front-line general psychiatrists caught between the power of the people and the psychiatric establishment. I am sure I would not have stayed in this rural area for ten years had I been supported by community mental health funds rather than by the hospital.

There can, of course, be no quarrel with the basic idea of providing a spectrum of services as close to home and as economically as possible, and giving priority to those not well served by existing systems of mental health care. In a rural community, however, a lot of professional staff support is needed from top-level central administration in order to develop new programs. Clinicians, not administrators, should be the ones to help decide what types of treatment are to be developed. To protect the local mental health staff from well-intentioned but ill-thought-out pressures, funds should come directly from state and federal governments, not from the county alone.

There is one area in which psychiatry certainly has not done all it should, and I must take my share of responsibility. This is the area of community education about mental illness. I am continually amazed and dismayed at the naïveté with which people react to mental illness or psychiatric problems of any kind. The stigma that mental patients still bear today was demonstrated vividly by comments the patients in our new wing overheard while visitors were touring. The most commonly heard remark—incredible, surely, in this day and age —was, "Why, you can't tell them from ordinary people."

My question after ten years in this picturesque resort and farming village is, What is rural psychiatry? When I first was recruiting staff, I would tell prospective house officers that for a year they would be away from the ivory tower of the large metropolitan centers and in intimate contact with the community in a community-oriented setting. Alas, everything has gone topsy-turvy. I have the strange sensation that it is I who am living in an ivory tower looking wistfully over agricultural and wooded countryside to where the action really is—in the cities. Now instead of offering psychiatric residents community involvement, I offer them respite and a rest cure.

McLuhan has said, "There is no rural America; everyone is urban today." I cannot define rural psychiatry, but, like many others, I have experienced psychiatry in a rural setting. There are some advantages; I have discussed only the problems. But to end on a happier note, it is interesting that a rural psychiatrist can achieve and maintain professional growth today because of the advance in communications technology, and that he can do so in spite of the difficulties that result from professional loneliness.

NOTE

1. Arnold A. Rogow, The Psychiatrists (New York: Putnam, 1970).

6/ An Eye toward the Future

INTRODUCTION

This volume began by discussing the resurgence of social work in rural areas as a field or specialty that deserved the attention of practitioners and educators. The narrative of related occurrences throughout the seven decades indicated that there have been periods of intense activity in rural social work, followed by periods of withdrawal of the specialty into latency. The current of events throughout the years waxed and waned the attention of service providers and policy makers who focused alternatively on rural and urban America. It is only fitting that this volume should end with an eye toward the future. If at present rural social work activity is experiencing a rebirth, what will happen in years ahead? Will social work, in its fickle commitments, soon abandon the social welfare gains achieved by rural dwellers? Will the fashionable aspects of rurality that grew during the 1970s recede again in the decade of the 1980s?

Unfortunately, the predictive value of history has not ever been proved successful. To claim that history can chart the path of the future is to disregard, in ahistorical fashion, the lessons of the past. As any amateur will quickly point out to presumptuous historians, the lessons of history have never prevented the crueler but more real lessons of experience. At the end of a historical volume one must look elsewhere, to the futurists, perhaps, for help in making educated guesses of what is likely to come.

Researchers have pointed out that "the 1970s will undoubtedly be remembered as a decade of important social and economic changes that had profound effects on our country. Among these significant changes have been the decline in some central city and metropolitan populations and the revival of population growth in the more rural areas."[1] Among the factors cited for the renewed growth of rural areas are the residential preferences of Americans, which seem to be shifting from urban to rural. While the rural to urban migrations of the 1950s and 1960s were associated with the search for livelihood and economic mobility, the urban-to-rural migrations of the 1970s seem to be connected to more subjective factors. The contemporary urban-to-rural migrants seem to be searching for the improvement of the quality of their lives in nontangible ways. It looks as if Americans have redefined, in broader terms, the old creed of Jeffersonian agrarianism. This new form of agrarianism seems to suggest that rural life in all its forms (not just farming) is more independent, more natural, and more gratifying.

Social workers during the 1970s have observed that groups are returning to the rural United States. Those rural dwellers who fled to the cities in the 1940s are now retiring and coming back with more resources and increased benefits to their villages and hometowns. Retirement communities are dotting the countryside and providing new resources for adjacent rural towns. Young intellectuals and craftsmen are returning to the rural United States in search of greener pastures. As has been amply documented by social workers from the West, the quest of energy sources is bringing back, or sometimes shifting around, large numbers of people to rural regions rich in natural resources.[2] All these phenomena have had positive and negative consequences for rural social work. Since narration is the prerequisite of historical analysis, these phenomena must be recounted as an important part of the story to be told before anyone can proceed to analyze its positive and negative effects.

The final excerpt in this volume is a shortened version of an article that appeared in the Futurist in 1975. Written by Calvin L. Beale, "Renewed Growth in Rural Communities" describes in careful detail the reversed trend of U.S. migration. Beale's descriptions should be heeded by rural social workers, for in spite of the fact that the incoming rural populations are not likely to be the immediate clients of social work, their arrival in the hinterland will have profound consequences for those who are now receiving social services. The expanding rural tax base that the incoming populations are likely to provide will benefit the social service system. Furthermore, the shifts in population clusters will have profound political consequences for the rural areas. As another futurist has stated, "If the current U.S. migration to rural areas continues, government and business policies that assume an increasing concentration of the nation's population in urban areas may have to be changed or abandoned."[3]

As the seven decades of this story come to a close, new and crucial developments are occurring. Gasoline has become a problematic and expensive commodity. Foreign countries such as Brazil are developing gasohol from their agricultural products. Coal is regaining its royal status and transforming ghost towns and quaint rural villages into social service predicaments. It is obvious that one must be cautious in one's desire for prediction. Rural change is becoming far too rapid for any predictive statements. Any conclusions can be presented only as questions. Will the value of the futurist perspective provided by Beale in the final excerpt hold its merit through the next decade? Or the next seven?

NOTES

1. Gordon F. DeJong, "Urban Migrants to the Countryside," Pennsylvania State University College of Agriculture, Agricultural Experiment Station, Bulletin 825, June 1979, p. 1.

2. Judith A. Davenport and Joseph Davenport III, <u>Boom Towns and Human Services</u> (Laramie: University of Wyoming Public Service 43, 1979).

3. William N. Ellis, "The New Ruralism: The Post Industrial Age Is upon Us," <u>Futurist</u> 9 (August 1975): 202.

RENEWED GROWTH IN RURAL COMMUNITIES

Calvin L. Beale

The vast rural-to-urban migration that was the common pattern of U.S. population movement since World War II has halted and, on balance, even reversed. In the eyes of many Americans, the appeal of major urban areas has diminished in recent years and the attractiveness of rural and small-town communities has increased. The result is a new trend that is already having an impact and modifies much that we have taken for granted about population distribution.

Rapid rural out-movement has occurred since 1940 when the United States began rapidly increasing its defense effort. The country-to-city movement continued apace in the 1950s as farms consolidated and the worker-short cities welcomed rural manpower. From 1940 to 1960, a net average of more than 1 million people left the farms annually (although not all moved to metropolitan cities) and a majority of nonmetropolitan counties declined in population despite high birthrates. (In general, Standard Metropolitan Statistical Areas —here called metro areas—are designated by the government wherever there is an urban center of 50,000 or more people. Neighboring commuter counties of metro character are also included in these areas. All other counties are nonmetro.)

By the mid-1960s, this massive movement had drained off so much population previously dependent on agriculture and other extractive industries that the peak of potential migration was reached and passed. Yet the impact of the movement had not been well recognized by cities or reflected in public policy. By the time that alarm over rural-to-urban migration arose around 1965, the economy of the nonmetro areas, as well as the social outlook and affluence of metro residents, were already changing in ways that would lead to a halt in the net outflow. Since 1970 changes in rural and urban population flows have occurred so rapidly that nonmetro areas are not only retaining people but are also receiving an actual net immigration.

The Reversal

The remarkable recent reversal of long-term population trends is demonstrated by growth in nonmetro counties of 4.2 percent between

Calvin L. Beale is leader of the Population Studies Group, Economic Development Division, Economic Research Service, Department of Agriculture, Washington, D.C. This is a shortened version of an article that appeared in Futurist 9 (August 1975): 196-202.

April 1970 and July 1973, compared with 2.9 percent in metro counties. This is the first period in this century in which nonmetro areas have grown at a faster rate than metro areas. Even during the 1930s depression there was some net movement to the cities. As late as the 1960s, metro growth was double the rate in nonmetro areas.

During the 1960s nonmetro counties of today were averaging a 300,000 loss per year from out-migration. Thus far in this decade, they have averaged a 353,000 in-movement per year, while metro areas have dropped from 600,000 net immigrants annually to 150,000.

A common first reaction to these data and the basic change they indicate is to ask whether the higher nonmetro growth could be simply increased spillover from the metro areas into adjacent nonmetro counties. To examine this local question, nonmetro counties were classed by whether or not they are adjacent to a metro area. As might be expected, adjacent counties have had the higher population growth since 1970 (4.7 percent) and have acquired about five-eighths of the total net in-movement into all nonmetro counties. However, the more significant point is that nonadjacent counties have also increased more rapidly than metro counties (3.7 percent versus 2.9 percent). Thus the decentralization trend is not confined to metro sprawl; in fact, it especially affects nonmetro counties well removed from metro influence. Their net migration pattern has shifted more than that of the adjacent counties, going from a loss of 227,000 annually in the 1960s to an annual gain of 130,000, a shift in the annual average of 357,000 persons. On a slightly larger base, adjacent counties have shifted from an average annual loss of 72,000 persons in the 1960s to an average gain of 222,000 from 1970-73, an annual shift of 294,000 persons.

Increased retention of population in nonmetro areas is characteristic of almost every part of the United States. As measured by migration trends, all states but three (Alaska, Connecticut, and New Jersey) show it, and two of the three exceptions are the result of military base cutbacks. Nonadjacent counties have had some net in-migration in every major geographic division.

There were still nearly 600 nonmetro counties declining in population from 1970 to 1973, but this was less than half as many as the nearly 1,300 declining in the 1960s. The largest remaining block of such counties is in the Great Plains, both north and south. Former large groups of declining counties in the Old South and the Southern Appalachian coal fields have been broken up except in the Mississippi Delta.

Factors Affecting Growth

Major centers of nonmetro population are found in counties with cities of 25,000-49,999 people. These counties contain a little more than a sixth of the total nonmetro population. Their growth rate for 1970-73 was 4.2 percent, identical with that in all other nonmetro counties. Thus recent nonmetro population growth has not gone disproportionately into counties with the largest nonmetro employment centers. Since these counties have a favorable age structure for childbearing, their rate of natural increase was higher than that of the rest of nonmetro counties, but the rate of immigration was lower.

At the other residential extreme are the completely rural nonmetro counties, which are not adjacent to a metro area and have no town of even 2,500 inhabitants. In the 1960s they had considerable out-migration and declined by 4.5 percent. However, from 1970 to 1973 their population grew by 3.0 percent. This is below the nonmetro average but a definite reversal of the previous trend. Natural increase of population in the completely rural counties has been very low since 1970 because of the comparative shortage of adults of childbearing age (resulting from past out-migration), and the growth of older populations of higher mortality as retirement settlements spread. The growth in these counties has come principally from in-migration, with a rate nearly double that of counties with cities of 25,000 or more people.

The decentralization trend in U.S. manufacturing has been a major factor in transforming the rural and small-town economy, especially in the upland parts of the South. From 1962 to 1969, half of all U.S. nonmetro job growth was in manufacturing. However, population growth has not been high since 1970 in areas with heavy concentration of manufacturing activity. Counties with 40 percent or more of their 1970 employment in this sector contained about 16 percent of the total nonmetro population and grew by 3.3 percent from 1970 to 1973. This increase required some net in-migration and was slightly above the total U.S. growth rate, but was well below the increase of 4.2 percent of all nonmetro counties. Thus, although growth of manufacturing has been a centerpiece of the revival of nonmetro population retention, the recent reversal of population trends has not been focused in areas already heavily dependent on manufacturing. Growth of jobs in trade and other non-goods-producing sectors has now come to the fore. From 1969 to 1973, manufacturing jobs comprised just 18 percent of all nonmetro job growth, compared with 50 percent from 1962 to 1969.

Retirees Moving to Rural Areas

A second and increasingly important factor in nonmetro development has been the growth of recreation and retirement activities, often occurring together in the same localities. Recreational employment is not easily assessed, but by menas of net migration estimates by age, it is possible to identify counties receiving significant numbers of retired people. Using unpublished estimates prepared by Gladys Bowles of the Economic Research Service in joint work with Everett Lee at the University of Georgia, counties were identified that had a net in-migration from 1960 to 1970 of 15 percent or more among white residents who were age 60 and over in 1970. Migration patterns at other ages were disregarded and may have been either positive or negative. These counties, which had already become a source of non-metro population growth in the 1970s, are by far the most rapidly growing class of nonmetro counties in the 1970s that I can identify.

Although a number of the retirement counties are in the traditional Florida and southwestern belts, it is the spread of retirement settlements to other regions that is a key characteristic of recent years. Clusters of nonmetro retirement counties are found in the old cutover region of the Upper Great Lakes (especially in Michigan), the Ozarks, the hill country of central Texas, the Sierra Nevada foothills in California, and the east Texas coastal plain. In general, coasts, lakes, reservoirs, and hills are favorable locations.

Although I have used the term retirement counties, this is too narrow a label for a number of the counties described. In about five-eighths of the cases, in-migration rates were highest at retirement age and lower (or at times negative) at younger ages. But in the other three-eighths of the retirement counties, in-migration was higher at some ages under age 60 than it was above that point. These areas often attract younger families because of climate or amenities, or because manufacturing or other employment may have begun to flourish as well. Indeed, the very influx of people into attractive areas for noneconomic reasons can stimulate follow-up types of job development—a case of supply creating demand. Further, it should be noted that for many people today, retirement may at first mean simply an optional departure from a career job and pension system at a comparatively unadvanced age; for example, most federal government workers can retire at age 55. Increasingly large numbers of such people then move to a different place where they may or may not re-enter the labor force.

The nonmetro counties with net in-migration of 15 percent or more of whites at age 60 and over grew by an average of one-fourth in total population in the 1970s. The pace of their growth has risen further, with a 12.3 percent population increase from 1970 to 1973.

The very rapid growth of these counties suggested a look at counties with a more modest level of in-movement of older people. Counties of 10 to 14.9 percent retirement-age migration rates in the 1960s were examined and proved to have grown in population by 6.4 percent from 1970 to 1973. This is a little more than half the total growth rate for counties with higher retirement rates in the 1960s.

However, the counties with modest retirement rates in the 1960s have had a relatively more rapid buildup in their total growth trend since 1970. During the 1960s, their overall growth of 9.3 percent was well below the national average, but their growth since 1970 is well above the national average. The two classes of retirement counties have between them 8.7 million people in 377 counties, and make up an increasingly significant part of the total nonmetro population.

State Colleges Stimulate Growth

An equal number of nonmetro people live in counties having senior state colleges and universities. The expansion of these schools has been substantial since the end of World War II, with many evolving from teachers colleges into major institutions. Some observers tend to denigrate the importance of nonmetro population growth stemming from college growth, as if it were somehow less real or permanent in its consequences than other growth. But the rise of nonmetro state schools has greatly increased availability and quality of higher education in nonmetro areas and has also made the affected towns more attractive for other development. In fact, many new metro areas over the last two decades have come from the ranks of college towns. From 1970 to 1973, nonmetro counties containing senior state colleges and universities grew in population by 5.8 percent, well above the nonmetro average, despite the slight national downturn in college enrollment rates that began at this time.

Eventually these counties should experience a drop in students as the decline in the birthrate since 1960 affects enrollment. But towns and counties containing state colleges are unlikely to return to their earlier size or status. Perhaps equally important to nonmetro areas has been the founding of numerous community junior colleges and technical schools typically do not have residential facilities and thus do not swell the local population with students, but they have made it much more feasible for nonmetro residents to obtain post-high-school education. They are often able to cooperate with business firms in providing specific skills needed for new or expanded plants. More than 150 nonmetro counties acquired public community colleges or college-accredited technical education centers during the 1960s.

Residential Preferences

A change in attitudes may be of equal importance to economic factors in producing the recent reversal in migration. In the middle 1960s Americans became aware of the great disparity between the

actual distribution of the U.S. population by size of place and the expressed preferences of people. Millions of people presumed heretofore to be happily content in their big city and suburban homes said,
in response to opinion polls, that they would prefer to live in a rural
area or small town.

When researchers James J. Zuiches and Glenn V. Fuguitt subsequently reported from a Wisconsin survey that a majority of such
dissidents in that state preferred their ideal rural or small-town
residence to be within 30 miles of a city of at least 50,000 people,
there was a noticeable discounting by urban-oriented interests of the
message of previous polls. It appeared that basic trends were not
being altered. Rather, only additional sprawl within the metro areas
was implied. However, a second finding in a later national survey by
the same researchers greatly modified the significance of the prefer-
ance for a close-in rural or small-town location, although it received
little notice. By a very wide margin (65 percent to 35 percent), the
big city people who preferred a nearby rural or small-town residence
ranked a more remote rural or small-town place as their second
choice, and thus as preferable to the big city. Therefore most of this
group were positively oriented toward nonmetro locations compared
with their current metro urban residence, regardless of whether an
opportunity arose to relocate within 30 miles of the city.

A second statistic foreshadowing the 1970-73 trends reported
here appeared in another national survey done for the Commission
on Population Growth and the American Future. The survey found
that three-eighths of the people expressing a desire to shift to a different type of residence declared they were "very likely" to make
such a move within the "next few years." An additional fourth thought
they would eventually make such a move at a later time. The very
likely group would have translated into a potential of about 14 million
people of all ages moving from metro cities and suburbs to smaller
places and rural areas. The expectation of making a move was highest among comparatively young and well-educated persons (where migration rates in general are highest), and thus was not primarily a
nostalgic hope of older people of rural origin.

I suggest the pattern of population movement since 1970 reflects
to a considerable extent many people implementing a preference for a
rural or small-town residence over that of the metro city, quite apart
from the fact that improved economic conditions in nonmetro areas
make such moves feasible. The environmental-ecological movement,
the youth revolution with its somewhat antimaterialistic and antisub-
urban component, and the narrowing of traditional urban-rural gaps
in conditions of life all seem to have contributed to the movement to
nonmetro areas.

Future Impact

How long will the 1970-73 trend persist and what is its larger meaning? It is doubtful that the United States is dismantling its cities. However, except for Boston, all of the largest U.S. metro areas have had major slowdowns in growth. The largest eight areas—which contain a fourth of the total U.S. population—grew by less than one-third the national growth rate from 1970 to 1973, whereas they were exceeding the national growth in the 1960s. Small and medium sized metro areas have had increased growth and net in-movement of people since 1970, and thus are behaving demographically more like the nonmetro areas than like the larger metro places. The trend that produced the turnaround in nonmetro population is primarily a sharply diminished attraction to the more massive metro areas, and a shift down the scale of settlement—both to smaller metro areas and small towns and rural areas.

Much is said in the literature of demography about the modern demographic transition, and the process by which nations go from high fertility and high mortality through a period of rapid total growth as mortality drops, to a subsequent condition of low growth as fertility also falls, with the whole process accompanied by rapid urbanization. But in a nation where this process is essentially completed, another aspect of demographic transition may emerge in which the distribution of population is no longer controlled by an unbridled impetus to urbanization. Under conditions of general affluence, low total population growth, easy transportation and communication, modernization of rural life, and urban population massings so large that the advantages of urban life are diminished, a downward shift to smaller communities may seem both feasible and desirable.

The trend in the United States since 1970 was not foreseen in the literature of scientific and public discussion of even three or four years ago. Its rapid emergence is basically the result of innumerable private decisions—both personal and commercial—which collectively and subtly have created a pattern of population movement significantly different from what went before. Long held social truths—such as the view that the basic movement of population is out of nonmetro areas and into metro areas—are not easily cast off. But this one seems to have reached the end of its unchallenged validity. Much new thought is needed on the probable course of future population distribution in the United States, uncolored by either value-laden residential fundamentalism or by outmoded analytical premises.

BIBLIOGRAPHY

Abbott, Edith. Social Welfare and Professional Education. Chicago: University of Chicago Press, 1942.

_____. "Twenty One Years of University Education for the Social Services, 1920-1941." Social Service Review 15 (December 1941): 670-705.

Abbott, Grace. "Developing Standards of Rural Child Welfare." Proceedings, National Conference on Social Work, 54th Annual Session. Des Moines, Iowa, 1927, pp. 26-37.

_____. "Improvement in Rural Public Relief: The Lesson of the Coal-Mining Community." Social Service Review 6 (June 1932): 183-222.

Abrams, Harvey A. "The Role of Social Work in Relocation for Employment." Social Casework 49 (October 1968): 475-80.

Adams, Frank, and Myles Horton. Unearthing Seeds of Fire: The Idea of Highlander. Winston-Salem, N.C.: John F. Blair, 1975.

"Advisory Commission Criticizes Aid Programs for Rural Poor." Congress and the Nation, 1965-1968, vol. 2. Washington, D.C.: Congressional Quarterly Service, 1968, p. 578.

"Agriculture." Congress and the Nation, 1965-1968, vol. 2. Washington, D.C.: Congressional Quarterly Service, 1968, pp. 555-58.

Aleshire, Ruth Cory. "Problems of Adoption in Rural Areas." Proceedings, National Conference on Social Work, War Regional Conference, 70th Annual Session. New York, St. Louis, Cleveland, 1943, pp. 417-25.

Allen, Frederick Lewis. Since Yesterday. New York: Harper & Row, 1968.

Alling, Elizabeth T. "Rural Social Work." Survey 46 (June 25, 1921): 438-39.

Alper, Minnie. "Supervision in a Rural Setting." Proceedings, National Conference on Social Work, 66th Annual Session. Buffalo, N.Y., 1939, pp. 295-303.

American Association of Schools of Social Work. Education for the Public Social Services: A Report of the Study Committee. Chapel Hill: University of North Carolina Press, 1942.

_____. Professional Education: Five Papers Delivered at the 26th Annual Meeting. New York: AASSW, 1948.

Amerman, Howard A. "State War Fund Experiences in Rural Areas." Proceedings, National Conference on Social Work, 71st Annual Session. Cleveland, 1944, pp. 415-21.

"Antipoverty Program." Congress and the Nation, 1965-1968, vol. 2. Washington, D.C.: Congressional Quarterly Service, 1968, pp. 748-50.

"Appalachian Development Bill Fails in 1964." Congress and the Nation, 1945-1964, vol. 1. Washington, D.C.: Congressional Quarterly Service, 1964, p. 1331.

"Appalachian Regional Commission." Congress and the Nation, 1965-1968, vol. 2. Washington, D.C.: Congressional Quarterly Service, 1968, pp. 3120-85.

Arendt, Hannah. Between Past and Future. New York: Viking Press, 1961.

Armstrong, Robert G. "Wanted—A Technique for the Rural County." Survey 59 (December 1927): 382-83.

Atkinson, Mary Irene. "The Rural Community Program of Relief." Proceedings, National Conference on Social Work, 61st Annual Session. Kansas City, 1934, pp. 166-77.

Auerbach, Arnold J. "Some Observations on the Black Aged in the Rural Midwest." Journal of Social Welfare 2 (Winter 1975): 53-61.

Ausubel, Herman. Historians and Their Craft: A Study of the Presidential Addresses of the American Historical Association, 1884-1945. New York: Russell and Russell, 1965.

Axinn, June, and Herman Levin. Social Welfare: A History of the American Response to Need. New York: Harper & Row, 1975.

Baer, Betty L., and Ronald Federico. "Educating the Baccalaureate Social Worker." Report of the Undergraduate Social Work Curriculum Development Project, Cambridge, Mass., 1978.

Bailey, L. H. "Rural Development in Relation to Social Welfare." Proceedings, National Conference on Charities and Corrections, 35th Annual Session. Richmond, Va., 1908, pp. 83-91.

Barzun, Jacques, and Henry F. Graff. The Modern Researcher. Rev. ed. New York: Harcourt, Brace and World, 1970.

Baskett, Janet Davidson. "Undifferentiated Case Work: The Surest Approach to Rural Social Work. Its Challenge and Its Opportunity (from the School)." Proceedings, National Conference on Social Welfare, 54th Annual Session. Chicago, 1927, pp. 109-14.

Bast, David. Human Services in the Rural Environment Reader. Madison: University of Wisconsin, Extension Center for Social Service, 1977.

Bast, David, and Julie Schmidt. Second Annual Northern Wisconsin Symposium on Human Services in the Rural Environment Reader. Madison: University of Wisconsin, Extension Center for Social Service, 1977.

Bellack, Arno E. "History of Curriculum Thought and Practice." Review of Educational Research 39 (1969): 283-92.

Benjamin, Paul L. "Illegitimacy in a Rural Community." Survey 46 (June 4, 1921): 305-6.

Bentz, W. Kenneth, J. Wilbert Edgerton, and William G. Hollister. "Rural Leaders' Perceptions of Mental Illness." Hospitals and Community Psychiatry 26 (December 1975): 143-45.

Bernstein, Irving. The Lean Years: A History of the American Worker, 1920-1933. Cambridge, Mass.: Riverside Press, 1960.

Berry, Wendell. The Unsettling of America: Culture and Agriculture. San Francisco: Sierra Club, 1977.

"Bigger Slice Goes to Poorer Areas." Business Week, November 27, 1965, pp. 54–55.

Bisno, Herbert. The Place of the Undergraduate Curriculum in Social Work Education. New York: Council on Social Work Education, 1959.

Bizzell, W. B. "Rural Housing and the Tenant Farmer." Survey 54 (April 3, 1920): 26–28.

Blackburn, John O. "The War in Viet Nam and the War on Poverty." Law and Contemporary Problems 31 (Winter 1966): 39–44.

Blackey, Eileen. "Social Work at the Grass Roots." Survey 71 (September 1935): 264–66.

Blickstein, Steve. "Appalachia: The Road Back." Sales Management 95 (August 20, 1965): 23–25.

Boehm, Werner W. Objectives of the Social Work Curriculum of the Future: The Comprehensive Report of the Curriculum Study, vol. 1. New York: Council on Social Work Education, 1959.

Bogue, Mary F., and Magdalen Peters. "Two Experiments in Training for Supervisory Personnel in N. J." The Family 16 (February 1936): 295–301.

Bookman, C. M. "F. E. R. A. Yesterday—Today—Tomorrow." Survey 70 (June 1934): 194–98.

Boone, Richard W., and Norman Kurland. "A Look at Rural Poverty." New Generation, Summer 1968, p. 3.

Bottorff, Katherine Piatt. "Tragedies of Village Slums." Survey 28 (September 21, 1912): 767–69.

Branson, E. C. "The North Carolina Scheme of Rural Development." Proceedings, National Conference on Social Work, 46th Annual Session. Atlantic City, N. J., 1919, pp. 546–49.

Brawley, Edward Allan, and Ruben Schindler. Community and Social Service Education in the Community College: Issues and Characteristics. New York: Council on Social Work Education, 1972.

Breckinridge, Sophonisba P. "What We Have Learned about Emergency Training for Public Relief Administration." Proceedings,
National Conference on Social Work, 62nd Annual Session, 1935.

Brooks, Margaret M. "Rural Worker's Diary." Survey 79 (May
1943): 143-45.

Broudy, Harry. "Can Research Escape the Dogma of Believable Objectives?" School Review 79 1 (November 1970): 43-56.

Brown, Bertram S. "Community Mental Health Centers in Rural
America." In The Mental Health of Rural America: The Rural
Programs of the National Institute of Mental Health, edited by
Julius Segal, DHEW publication no. ADM76-349. Washington,
D.C.: U.S. Department of Health, Education and Welfare,
1973, pp. 50-51.

Brown, Josephine C. "A City Case Worker for the Country." The
Family 3 (December 1922): 187-93.

_____. "In Service Training for Public Welfare, the Hows." Survey
75 (November 1938): 347-48.

_____. "In Service Training for Public Welfare, the Whys and Whats."
Survey 74 (October 1938): 210.

_____. Research in Rural Social Work—Scope and Method. Social
Science Research Council Bulletin no. 5 (1932).

_____. The Rural Community and Social Casework. New York:
Family Welfare Association of America, 1933.

_____. "Rural Social Work." Social Work Yearbook 1935. New York:
Russell Sage Foundation, 1935.

_____. "The Use of Volunteers in Rural Social Work." Proceedings,
National Conference on Social Work, 49th Annual Session.
Providence, R.I., 1922, pp. 267-70.

_____. "What We Have Learned about Emergency Training for Public
Relief Administration." Proceedings, National Conference on
Social Work, 62nd Annual Session. Montreal, 1935, pp. 237-45.

Brown, Sara A. "How Shall Country Youth Be Served?" The Family 7
(December 1926): 259-60.

Browning, Grace A. "The Application of Basic Concepts of Case Work to Rural Social Work." The Family 19 (March 1938): 8-14.

_____. Rural Public Welfare: Selected Records. Chicago: University of Chicago Press, 1941.

Brungardt, Theresa S. "Fun for the Older Person in the Country." Proceedings, National Conference on Social Work, 73rd Annual Session. Buffalo, N.Y., 1946, pp. 221-27.

Brunner, Edmund de S. "Some Critical Situations." Rural America 8 (June 1930): 3-4.

_____. "The Teaching of Rural Sociology and Rural Economics and the Conduct of Rural Social Research in Teachers' Colleges, Schools of Religion and Non-State Colleges." Social Forces 9 (October 1930): 54-57.

Brunner, Edmund de S., and J. H. Kolb. Rural Social Trends. New York: McGraw-Hill, 1933.

Bruno, Frank J. Trends in Social Work, 1874-1956. New York: Columbia University Press, 1957.

Buck, Roy C. "An Interpretation of Rural Values." A Place to Live: The Yearbook of Agriculture, 1963. Washington, D.C.: U.S. Department of Agriculture, 1963, pp. 1-12.

Burr, Walter. "The Philosophy of Community Organization: The Rural Community Ideal." Proceedings, National Conference on Social Work, 52nd Annual Session. Denver, 1925, pp. 396-99.

Butterfield, Kenyon L. "The American Country Life Movement." Rural America 6 (November 1928): 3-5.

_____. "Rural Advance." Survey 31 (December 27, 1913): 352-53.

Cairns, Lucille. "An Experiment in Training for Rural Social Work." The Family 16 (June 1935): 114-17.

Campbell, John C. "Social Betterment in the Southern Mountains." Proceedings, National Conference on Charities and Corrections, 36th Annual Session. Buffalo, N.Y., 1909, pp. 130-37.

Campbell, Paul. "Implementing Rural Social Work Content: Need Is Not Enough." Roundtable paper, Council on Social Work Education Annual Program Meeting, New Orleans, February 1978, pp. 1-11. Mimeographed.

Campbell, William Giles, and Stephen Vaughan Ballou. Form and Style: Theses, Reports, Term Papers. 5th ed. Boston: Houghton Mifflin, 1978.

Cannon, M. Antoinette. "An Experiment in Providing Instruction for Relief Workers." Bulletin of the New York School of Social Workers, October 1935.

Caudill, Harry M. Night Comes to the Cumberlands. Boston: Little, Brown, 1962.

Chambers, Clarke A. California Farm Organizations. Berkeley: University of California Press, 1952.

_____. "The Discipline of History in a Social Welfare Curriculum." Paper prepared for the Minnesota Resource Center for Social Work Education, 1971. Mimeographed.

_____. "FDR, Pragmatist-Idealist." Pacific Northwest Quarterly 52 (April 1961): 50-55.

_____. The New Deal at Home and Abroad, 1929-1945. New York: Free Press, 1965.

_____. Paul V. Kellogg and the Survey: Voices for Social Welfare and Social Justice. Minneapolis: University of Minnesota Press, 1971.

_____. Seedtime of Reform: American Social Service and Social Action, 1918-1933. Minneapolis: University of Minnesota Press, 1963.

_____. "Social Service and Social Reform: A Historical Essay." Social Service Review 37 (March 1963): 76-90.

Chicago School of Civics and Philanthropy. "The New Profession and Preparation for It." Chicago School of Civics and Philanthropy Bulletin 1 (1910): 173.

"Child Welfare Studied in Oklahoma." Survey 39 (March 30, 1918): 713-14.

"Chronology of Legislation on Civil Rights." Congress and the Nation, 1945-1964, vol. 1. Washington, D. C.: Congressional Quarterly Service, 1964, pp. 1615-40.

"Chronology of Legislation on Welfare." Congress and the Nation, 1965-1968, vol. 2. Washington, D. C.: Congressional Quarterly Service, 1968, p. 751.

Chute, Charles L. "The Cost of the Cranberry Sauce." Survey 27 (December 2, 1911): 1281-84.

"Civic Improvement." Survey 24 (September 17, 1910): 867.

"Civics and Country Life." Survey 24 (September 17, 1910): 867.

"Civil Rights Commission Reports, 1959 to 1965." Congress and the Nation, 1945-1964, vol. 1. Washington, D. C.: Congressional Quarterly Service, 1965, pp. 1609-14.

"Civil Rights in Social Work." Social Work Journal, vol. 29 (October 1948). Special issue.

Clarke, Helen I. "General Welfare and Social Security Legislation." Sociology and Social Research 29 (January-February 1945): 165-79.

_____. "Social Work Education in Wisconsin." Mimeographed. New York: Council on Social Work Education Archives, American Association of Schools of Social Work Curriculum Files, January 11, 1945.

Clopper, Edward N. "Rural Child Delinquency." Survey 46 (August 10, 1921): 607-8.

Close, Kathryn. "Social Workers along Three Fronts." Survey 78 (June 1942): 164-83.

Cochrane, Hortense S. Rural New York: The Plight of Rural Women in Upstate New York. Conference Proceedings. Syracuse, N. Y.: Syracuse University Printing Services, 1977.

_____. "Social and Economic Factors Influencing Human Services in Rural Areas." Address to the Planning for Rural Health Care Conference, Upstate Medical Center, Syracuse, N. Y., September, 1977.

Cohen, Jerome. "Selected Constraints in the Relationship between Social Work Education and Practice." Journal of Education for Social Work 13 (Winter 1977): 3-7.

Cohen, Wilbur J. "A Salute to Twenty-Five Years of Social Security." Public Welfare 18 (January 1960): 17-39.

Colby, Ira, and Gary Smith, eds. Social Work in Rural Virginia Institute Reader. Richmond: Virginia State Chapter of the National Association of Social Workers, 1978.

Colby, Mary Ruth. The County as an Administrative Unit for Social Workers. U.S. Children's Bureau Publication no. 224, 1933.

Colcord, Joanna C., and Russell H. Kurtz. "Dislocated Farm Folk." Survey 71 (August 1935): 246-47.

_____. "Rural Rehabilitation." Survey 70 (October 1934): 327-28.

Cole, William E. "Training of Social Workers for Rural Areas." Paper presented at the National Association of Schools of Social Administration meeting of the National Conference on Social Work, Cleveland, 1949.

"Commission on Country Life, a Report." Rural America 7 (January 1929): 5-8.

"The Common Welfare." Survey 26 (August 18, 1911): 747-49.

"Congressional Rural Caucus." Rural America 1 (March 1976): 1.

Copp, James, ed. Our Changing Rural Society. Ames: Iowa State University Press, 1964.

Cottrell, Louise. "Organization Needed to Support and Free the Local Worker for Undifferentiated Case Work." Proceedings, National Conference on Social Work, 54th Annual Session. Des Moines, Iowa, 1927, pp. 118-22.

Council on Social Work Education. Black Perspectives on Social Work Education: Issues Related to Curriculum, Faculty, and Students. New York: Council on Social Work Education, 1974.

_____. Memo no. 74-310-17 on Seminar on Social Work in the Rural and Small Community. Council on Social Work Education, December 16, 1974, New York.

_____. Training Social Welfare Manpower: The Essential Task. New York: Council on Social Work Education, 1969.

Cross, William T. "Rural Social Work." Proceedings, National Conference on Social Work, 44th Annual Session. Chicago, 1917, pp. 639-45.

Curti, Merle. "American Philanthropy and the National Character." American Quarterly 10 (Winter 1958): 420-37.

Daniels, Jonathan. "National Defense and the Health and Welfare Services in the United States, I: From the Viewpoint of the Local Community." Proceedings, National Conference on Social Work, 68th Annual Session. Atlantic City, N.J., 1941, pp. 88-98.

Davenport, Judith A., and Joseph Davenport III. Boom Towns and Human Services. Laramie: University of Wyoming Public Service, 1979.

Davies, Joann. "The Country Mouse Comes into Her Own." Child Welfare 53 (October 1974): 509-13.

Davies, Richard O. "The Politics of Desperation: William A. Hirth and the Presidential Election of 1932." Agricultural History 38 (October 1964): 226-34.

Davis, Michael. "A National Health Program." Proceedings, National Conference on Social Work, 71st Annual Session. Cleveland, 1944, pp. 382-91.

Dawkins, O. C. "Kentucky Outgrows Segregation." Survey 86 (July 1950): 358-59.

Deardorff, Neva R. "The Place of a Professional School in Training for Social Work." American Academy of Politics and Social Science Annals 121 (1925): 172-75.

_____. "Red Cross Home Service: 1919." Survey 44 (January 24, 1920): 470.

Deaton, Robert. "Social Work Continuing Education for Rural Areas: Beginning Where Generalist Preparation Ends." Roundtable Discussion Paper, Annual Program Meeting, Council on Social Work Education, February 1978, pp. 1-4. Mimeographed.

Deiman, Harry. "The Institutional Church for the Rural Community."
    Survey 30 (May 24, 1913): 280-82.

DeJong, Gordon F. "Urban Migrants to the Countryside." Pennsyl-
    vania State University, College of Agriculture, Agricultural
    Experiment Station, Bulletin 825, June 1979, p. 1.

Devine, Edward T. "Social Reconstruction." Survey 42 (June 7,
    1919): 402-5.

Donovan, Timothy Paul. Historical Thought in American Postwar
    Patterns. Norman: University of Oklahoma Press, 1973.

Douglas, H. Paul. How Shall Country Youth Be Served? A Study of
    the "Rural" Work of Certain National Character-Building Agen-
    cies. New York: George H. Doran, 1926.

Douty, Esther Morris. "FERA and the Rural Negro." Survey 70
    (July 1934): 215.

Drew, D. C. "The Rural Work of the Young Men's Christian Associa-
    tion." Proceedings, National Conference on Social Work, 49th
    Annual Session. Providence, R.I. , 1922, pp. 327-31.

Dumpson, James R. "Our Welfare System—Radical Surgery Needed."
    Public Welfare 23 (October 1965): 226-34.

Dunn, Lovla. "Public Welfare in 1945." Public Welfare 3 (January
    1945): 1.

Dusseldorp, Wilma Van. "The Development of Social Agencies in
    Rural Communities." The Family 14 (March 1933): 20-24.

Eastman, Fred. "Farmer Smith and the Country Church." Survey
    30 (May 17, 1913): 243-44.

_____. "Recreation and the Country Church." Survey 31 (October 18,
    1913): 76.

Eicher, Lydia S. "Undifferentiated Case Work: The Surest Approach
    to Rural Work: Its Challenge and Its Opportunity (from the Pub-
    lic Department of Welfare)." Proceedings, National Conference
    on Social Welfare, 54th Annual Session. Des Moines, Iowa,
    1927, pp. 115-17.

Eisner, Elliott. "The Curriculum Field Today: Where We Are, Where We Were, and Where We Are Going." Paper presented to the Society for Professors of Curriculum, 1976. Mimeographed.

_____. "Educational Objectives: Help or Hindrance?" School Review 75 (Autumn 1967): 250-81.

_____. "Instructional and Expressive Objectives: Their Formulation and Use in Curriculum." AERA Monograph Series. Chicago: Rand McNally, 1969, pp. 1-19.

Ellis, William N. "The New Ruralism: The Post Industrial Age Is upon Us." Futurist 9 (August 1975): 202-8.

Ellsworth, Clayton S. "Theodore Roosevelt's Country Life Commission." Agricultural History 34 (1960): 155-72.

Encyclopedia of Social Work. Vols. 1 and 2. New York: National Association of Social Workers, 1977, 1979.

Ezekiel, Mordecai. "Experimental Social Science." Rural America 13 (May 1935): 3-4.

Farley, Jennie. "Chenango Development Project—People-Mobile Project Evaluation." U.S. Educational Resources Information Center, ERIC Document ED 096 093, October 24, 1971.

Farm People and Old-Age Survivors, and Disability Insurance in the United States. OSAI-868-0-674463. Washington, D.C.: U.S. Government Printing Office, 1963.

"The Federal Role in Civil Rights." Congress and the Nation, 1945-1964, vol. 1. Washington, D.C.: Congressional Quarterly Service, 1965, pp. 1596-99.

Felix, R. H. "State Participation in the National Mental Health Program." Proceedings, National Conference on Social Work, 74th Annual Session. San Francisco, 1947, pp. 461-68.

Fetterman, John. Stinking Creek. New York: Dutton, 1967.

Fink, Richard L. "The Role of Mental Health Programs in Rural Areas." In Social Work in Rural Areas: Preparation and Practice, edited by Ronald K. Green and Stephen A. Webster. Knoxville: University of Tennessee School of Social Work, 1977, p. 328.

Fisher, Helen Dwight. "The Boy, the War and the Harrow." Survey 39 (March 30, 1918): 704-6.

Ford, Arthur M. Political Economics of Rural Poverty in the South. Cambridge, Mass.: Ballinger, 1973.

Frazier, E. Franklin. "Family Life of the Negro in the Small Town." Proceedings, National Conference on Social Work, 53rd Annual Session. Cleveland, 1926, pp. 384-89.

Fremon, Suzanne, and Morrow Wilson. Rural America. New York: H. W. Wilson, 1976.

Fuller, Wayne Edison. RFD, the Changing Face of Rural America. Bloomington: Indiana University Press, 1964.

"Further Comments on Undergraduate Training." The Family 24 (June 1943): 153-56.

Galarza, Ernesto, Herman Gallegos, and Julian Samora. Mexican-Americans in the Southwest. Southwest Council of La Raza, 1969.

Gardiner, Elizabeth. "A Maternity and Infancy Program for Rural and Semi-Rural Communities." Proceedings, National Conference on Social Work, 53rd Annual Session. Cleveland, 1926, pp. 396-99.

Gartner, Alan. The Preparation of Human Service Professionals. New York: Behavioral Publications, 1976.

Gerson, Samuel, and Jeanette Gerson. "The Social Worker in the Rural Community." The Family 16 (January 1936): 263-67.

Gertz, Boris, Jill Meider, and Margaret L. Pluckman. "A Survey of Rural Community Mental Health Needs and Resources." Hospitals and Community Psychiatry 26 (December 1975): 816-19.

Gilbert, Louise. "Foster Care in Rural Areas." The Family 28 (February 1947): 67-72.

Giles, H. H., S. P. McCutchen, and A. N. Zechiel. Exploring the Curriculum. New York: Harper & Row, 1942.

Ginsberg, Leon H. Conversation between Leon Ginsberg, Commissioner of Welfare of the state of West Virginia, and the writer. Morgantown, W. Va., August 9, 1978.

_____. "Education for Social Work in Rural Settings." Social Work Education Reporter 17 (September 1969): 28-32, 60-61.

_____. "Social Problems in Rural America." Social Welfare Practice 1969, Selected Papers, National Conference on Social Welfare, 76th Annual Session. New York, May 1969, pp. 176-86.

Ginsberg, Leon H., ed. Social Work in Rural Communities. New York: Council on Social Work Education, 1976.

Ginsberg, Mitchell I., and Bernard Shiffman. "Manpower and Training Problems in Combatting Poverty." Law and Contemporary Problems 31 (Winter 1966): 159-86.

Gissal, Elizabeth E. A. "Truly Rural." The Family 14 (July 1933): 156-58.

Goldston, Robert. The Great Depression. Greenwich, Conn.: Fawcett, 1968.

"Good Life for Rural People Is Goal of New Organization." Rural America 1 (October 1975): 1.

Gore, Peter H. "Quality of Life Assessment." Paper presented at the World Congress of Rural Sociology, Torun, Poland, August 1976. U.S. Educational Resources Information Center, ERIC Document ED 137 026, 1976.

Granger, Lester B. "The Rights of Social Workers." Social Work Journal 29 (October 1948): 145-48.

_____. "Techniques in Race Relations." Survey 79 (December 1943): 323-26.

"The Great Informer: Appalachian New York's People Mobile Project." Appalachia 8 (December 1974-January 1975): 18-27. U.S. Educational Resources Information Center, ERIC Document ED 116 454.

Hagerty, James. The Training of Social Workers. New York: Russell Sage Foundation, 1931.

Hansen, Niles M. "Regional Development and the Rural Poor." Social Welfare in Appalachia 2 (1970): 41-49.

Harper, Ernest B. "Accomplishments and Aims of NASSA." Paper presented at the National Conference on Social Work, 75th Annual Session, Atlantic City, N.J., April 19, 1948. New York: Council on Social Work Education Archives, National Association of Schools of Social Administration Files. Mimeographed.

Harrington, Michael. The Other America: Poverty in the United States. New York: Macmillan, 1963.

Hathaway, Marion. "The Constructive Role of Social Work." Social Work Today 8 (May 1941): 8-10.

Hauton, Sharon. "A Case for the Generalist Social Worker: A Model for Service Delivery in Rural Areas." Mimeographed. Bozeman: Montana State University, 1978.

Hayes, Sherrill W. Tennessee Annual Rural Manpower Report, 1973. Nashville: Tennessee State Department of Employment Security. U.S. Educational Resources Information Center, ERIC Document ED 097 180.

Hendricks, Hazel A. "The Rural Plus in Social Work." Paper presented at the National Conference on Social Work, Buffalo, N.Y., June 23, 1939. New York: Council on Social Work Education Archives, American Association of Schools of Social Work, Curriculum Committee Files.

_____. "Training for Rural Social Work." Survey 75 (November 1939): 338-39.

Hickox, Alice Gray. "Along a Country Road." The Family 11 (May 1930): 79-81.

Hightower, Jim. Hard Tomatoes, Hard Times. Washington, D.C.: Agribusiness Accountability Project, 1972.

Hines, Fred K., David L. Brown, and John M. Zimmer. Social and Economic Characteristics of the Population in Metro and Non-Metro Counties, 1970. Washington, D.C.: U.S. Department of Agriculture, Economic Research Service, 1975.

Hirth, William. "Squaring Away for the Big Presidential Contest."
Missouri Farmer 24 (March 1, 1932): 1, 4.

Hollis, Ernest V., and Alice L. Taylor. Social Work Education in
the United States. New York: Columbia University Press, 1951.

Holman, Charles W. "Focusing Social Forces in the Southwest."
Survey 26 (September 23, 1911): 866-68.

Hookey, Peter. "Rurally Oriented Components of the Social Work
Education Curricula: The Report of the 1977 HSITRE Reader-
ship Survey." Human Services in the Rural Environment 3
(October 1978): 1-19.

Hopkins, Harry L. "The Developing National Program of Relief."
Proceedings, National Conference on Social Work, 60th Annual
Session. Detroit, 1933, pp. 61-71.

Horejsi, John, and Thomas Watz. Working in Welfare: Survival
through Positive Action. Iowa City: University of Iowa School
of Social Work, 1977.

Hosch, Louis E. "The Rights of People Served." Social Work Journal 29 (October 1948): 141-49.

"How Goes the War on Poverty?" Economist 216 (September 4, 1965):
878-84.

Hyde, Henry. "Rural Development: What's Coming—What's Needed."
Human Services in the Rural Environment 3 (October 1978):
26-31.

"Impact of Supreme Court on Civil Rights Issue." Congress and the
Nation, 1945-1964, vol. 1. Washington, D.C.: Congressional
Quarterly Service, 1964, pp. 1606-8.

Jans, Paul. "Race Relations at the Grass Roots." Survey 82 (January 1946): 11-13.

Jarrett, Herbert H., and Allie C. Kilpatrick. "Off-Campus Based
Rural Field Instruction." Roundtable paper, Annual Program
Meeting, Council on Social Work Education, New Orleans, Feb-
ruary 1978, pp. 1-11.

Johnson, Charles S. Into the Main Stream: A Survey of Best Practices in Race Relations in the South. Chapel Hill: University of North Carolina Press, 1947.

_____. "The South's Human Resources." Proceedings, National Conference on Social Work, 69th Annual Session. Louisiana, 1942, pp. 92–108.

Johnson, Gerald. "Behind the Monster's Mask." Survey 50 (April 1, 1923): 20–22, 55–56.

Johnson, Lee F. "Housing: A 1950 Tragedy." Survey 86 (December 1950): 551–55.

"Johnson's Anti-Poverty Bill Coordinated Several Programs." Congress and the Nation, 1945-1964, vol. 1. Washington, D.C.: Congressional Quarterly Service, 1964, pp. 1326–31.

Johnston, Ross B. "Rural Clubs for Boys and Girls." Survey 43 (January 24, 1920): 457–58.

Jones, Lewis W. "Social Centers in the Rural South." Phylon 12 (1951): 279–84.

Kahn, Kathy. Hillbilly Women. Garden City, N.Y.: Doubleday, 1973.

Keller, Morton, ed. The New Deal: What Was It? New York: Holt, Rinehart and Winston, 1963.

Kelley, Florence. "Our Newest South." Survey 62 (June 15, 1929): 342–44.

Kelso, J. J. "Children in Rural Districts." Survey 27 (October 21, 1911): 1054–56.

King, Anna. "Home Service and Civilian Charities." Survey 42 (April 26, 1919): 139–40.

King, Joe J. "Cooperatives among Small Farmers." Sociology and Social Research 29 (March–April 1945): 304–6.

_____. "Sheltering Migratory Agricultural Laborers in the Pacific Northwest." Sociology and Social Research 26 (January–February 1942): 250–64.

Kirkpatrick, E. L. "Basic Elements of Rural Life." Survey 69 (November 1933): 398.

Kleibard, Herbert. "Bureaucracy and Curricular Theory." Freedom, Bureaucracy and Schooling. Washington, D.C.: Association for Supervision and Curriculum Development, 1971, pp. 74-94.

_____. "Curricular Objectives and Evaluation: A Reassessment." High School Journal 51 (June 1968): 241-47.

_____. "The Curriculum Field in Retrospect." In Technology and the Curriculum, edited by Paul W. F. Witt. New York: Teachers College Press, 1968, pp. 69-84.

_____. "Reappraisal, the Tyler Rationale." School Review 78 (February 1970): 259-73.

_____. "The Rise of Scientific Curriculum Making and Its Aftermath." Curriculum Theory Network 5 (1975): 27-38.

_____. "Sources of Curriculum Theory." Paper presented at the field conference Toward the Reconstruction of the Curriculum, Temple University, Philadelphia, May 10-11, 1973. Mimeographed.

Koch, William H., ed. A Symposium: Planning and Delivery of Social Services in Rural America: Three Papers. Madison: University of Wisconsin Press, 1973.

Kopetzky, Samuel J. "Health for Rejectees." Survey 78 (January 1942): 9-10.

La Follette, Robert M., Jr. "Agricultural Migration—Past, Present and Future." Proceedings, National Conference on Social Work, 68th Annual Session. Atlantic City, N.J., 1941, pp. 145-53.

"Labor Relations Law." Congress and the Nation, 1945-1964, vol. 1. Washington, D.C.: Congressional Quarterly Service, 1965, pp. 761-62.

Lambert, Virginia. "Community Problems in Five West Central Counties in Northwestern Wisconsin." Report no. 7 of a Series on Quality of Life and Development in Northwest Wisconsin, February 1976. U.S. Educational Resources Information Center, ERIC Document ED 135 574.

_____. "Preferences for Expansion of Public Services in Five West Central Wisconsin Counties." Report no. 8 of a series on Quality of Life and Development in Northwest Wisconsin, February 1976. U.S. Educational Resources Information Center, ERIC Document ED 135 575.

Lancaster, Lane W. Government in Rural America. New York: Van Nostrand, 1937.

Landis, Benson Y., ed. Handbook of Rural Social Resources. Vols. 1 and 2. Chicago: University of Chicago Press, 1928.

_____. "Rural Social Work." Rural America 8 (June 1930): 2.

_____. "Social Shortages of Rural Life." Rural America 6 (November 1928): 2.

_____. "Will Social Workers Cooperate?" Rural America 8 (February 1930): 2.

Landis, Paul H. "If I Were a County Relief Director." Survey 71 (July 1935): 208-9.

_____. Rural Life in Process. New York: McGraw-Hill, 1940.

Lasker, Bruno. "Five Outlooks from Hill-Tops." Survey 45 (December 25, 1920): 459-61.

Leadley, Tom A., and Louis W. Home. "Riding the Range Again." Survey 79 (September 1943): 241-42.

Leevy, Roy J. "Open Country Neighborhoods." Sociology and Social Research 27 (September-October 1942): 22-30.

Lerrigo, Ruth A. "The Test of the Training." Survey 71 (October 1935): 297-98.

Leuchtenburg, William E. Franklin Roosevelt and the New Deal, 1932-1940. New York: Harper Torchbooks, 1963.

Levine, Abraham S. " 'Yesterday's People' and Tomorrow's Programs." Welfare in Review 7 (July-August 1969): 8-12.

Levitan, Sar A. "The Steps for Right Now." New Generation, Summer 1968, p. 17.

Lilienthal, David E. "Statement before the Congressional Committee on Atomic Energy." Social Work Journal 29 (October 1948): 139-40.

Linn, J. Gary. "Residential Location, Size of Place, and Community Satisfaction in Northwest Wisconsin." Report from National Institute of Mental Health Grant no. Rol-MH25266-01, 1976. Mimeographed.

Longres, John. Perspectives from the Puerto Rican Faculty Training Project. New York: Council on Social Work Education, 1973.

"A Look at Rural Realities." Perspectives on Aging 7 (January-February 1978). Special issue.

Loomis, Charles Price. Rural Social Systems: A Textbook in Rural Sociology and Anthropology. New York: Prentice-Hall, 1950.

Loomis, Charles Price, and J. Allan Beegle. A Strategy for Rural Change. New York: Wiley, 1975.

Lorge, Irving. "Farmers on Relief." Survey 73 (November 1938): 348-49.

Lubove, Roy. The Professional Altruist: The Emergence of Social Work as a Career, 1880-1930. Cambridge, Mass.: Harvard University Press, 1965.

Lund, Henrietta L. "Casework in Rural Communities." The Family 2 (March 1921): 12-14.

McCauley, John S. "Manpower Development in Rural Areas." Employment Service Review 5 (March-April 1968): 10-25.

McConnell, Beatrice. "The Employment of Minors in Wartime." Proceedings, National Conference on Social Work, 70th Annual Session, War Regional Conferences. New York, St. Louis, Cleveland, 1943, pp. 158-69.

McCord, Elizabeth. The Emergency Worker in Unemployment Relief. New York: Family Service Association of America, 1932.

McDonagh, Edward C. "Ethnic Legislation in Review: 1948." Sociology and Social Research 33 (May-June 1949): 372-78.

Macdonald, James B. "Curriculum Development in Relation to Social and Intellectual Systems." The Curriculum: Retrospect
and Prospect, 70th Yearbook. Chicago: National Society for
the Study of Education, 1971, pp. 95-112.

_____. "An Evaluation of Evaluation." Urban Review 7 (January
1973): 3-14.

_____. "Myths about Instruction." Educational Leadership 22 (May
1967): 571-76, 609-12, 615-17.

_____. "Responsible Curriculum Development." In Confronting Cur-
riculum Reform, edited by Elliot W. Eisner. Boston: Little,
Brown, 1971, pp. 120-42.

Macdonald, James B., and Robert R. Leeper. Language and Meaning. Washington, D.C.: Association for Supervision and Curriculum Development, 1966.

Macdonald, James B., Bernice J. Wolfson, and Esther Zaret. Re-
Schooling Society. Washington, D.C.: Association for Supervision and Curriculum Development, 1973.

Machlachlan, John M. "Civil Service Opportunities for Undergraduate
Trained Workers in Social Welfare and Allied Fields." Paper
presented at the 26th Annual Meeting of the American Association of Schools of Social Work, January 26, 1945. Mimeographed.

Mackey, John E. American Indian Task Force Report. New York:
Council on Social Work Education, 1973.

McMillan, Robert T. "Comparisons of Veterans and Nonveterans on
Oklahoma Farms." Southwestern Social Science Quarterly 29
(December 1948): 214-20.

McNeil, John D. "Forces Influencing Curriculum." Review of Educational Research 39 (1969): 293-313.

McPheeters, Harold L., and Robert M. Ryan. A Core Competence
for Baccalaureate Social Welfare and Curricular Implications.
Atlanta: Southern Regional Education Board, 1971.

"Major Civil Rights Incidents from Montgomery to Selma." Congress
and the Nation, 1945-1964, vol. 1. Washington, D.C.: Congressional Quarterly Service, 1964, pp. 1600-6.

Mangus, A. R. Changing Aspects of Rural Relief. Works Progress Administration, Division of Social Research. Washington, D. C.: U. S. Government Printing Office, 1938.

_____. "Spotlight on Rural Needs." Survey 83 (July 1947): 203-4.

Matthews, Harold J. "Special Problems of Rural Social Work." Social Forces 6 (September 1927): 67-73.

Maxted, Mattie Cal. "Don't Forget Your Country Cousins." Survey 82 (September 1946): 219-20.

_____. "The Need for Undergraduate Trained Social Workers in Arkansas." Paper presented at the 26th Annual Meeting of the American Association of Schools of Social Work, Chicago, January 26, 1945.

_____. "Social Service in Relation to the Rural Rehabilitation Program." Paper presented at the Rural Rehabilitation Training School, Oklahoma City, December 1934. Mimeographed.

"Mental Health Act." Congress and the Nation, 1945-1964, vol. 1. Washington, D. C.: U. S. Government Printing Office, 1964, p. 1130.

Mental Health Reports, no. 6. Bethesda, Md.: National Institute of Mental Health, 1973.

Mermelstein, Joanne, and Paul Sundet. "Epilogue." In Pioneer Efforts in Rural Social Welfare: First Hand Views since 1908, edited by Emilia E. Martinez-Brawley. University Park: Pennsylvania State University Press, 1980, pp. 457-63.

_____. "Issues in Campus Based Field Instruction in Rural Social Work Education." Roundtable paper, Annual Program Meeting, Council on Social Work Education, New Orleans, 1978, pp. 1-9.

"Mexican Foreign Worker Programs." Congress and the Nation, 1945-1964, vol. 1. Washington, D. C.: Congressional Quarterly Service, 1964, pp. 762-67.

Middleton, Fred C. "Think Together, Work Together, Play Together: Community Clubs in Manitoba." Proceedings, National Conference on Social Work, 46th Annual Session. Atlantic City, N. J., 1919, pp. 556-61.

Mitchell, Broadus. Depression Decade: From New Era through New Deal, 1929-1941. New York: Rinehart, 1947.

_____. Economic History of the United States: Depression Decade. New York: Rinehart, 1947.

Mitchell, H. L. Mean Things Happening in This Land. Montclair, N.J.: Allanheld, Osmun, 1979.

Mohr, Irma. "Training Apprentice Workers in a Rural Agency." The Family 10 (February 1930): 287-300.

Morris, Robert. "Social Work Function in a Caring Society: Abstract Value, Professional Preference and the Real World." Journal of Education for Social Work 14 (Spring 1978): 82-89.

Morrisroe, Barry. Conversation between the writer and Barry Morrisroe, former Director of Rural Office, Department of Health, Education and Welfare, September 6, 1978.

Morse, Hermann N. "The Underlying Factors of Rural Community Development." Proceedings, National Conference on Social Work, 46th Annual Session. Atlantic City, N.J., 1919, pp. 552-54.

Mueller, Eva, and Jane Lean. "The Case against Migration." New Generation, Summer 1968, p. 7.

Munson, Carlton E. "Social Work Manpower and Social Indicators: Rural and Urban Differences." Paper presented at the Annual Program Meeting, Council on Social Work Education, New Orleans, February 1978, pp. 1-16. Mimeographed.

Munson, Carlton E., and Catherine S. Hull. "A Study of Rural Health Services Utilization and Advocacy Social Work Practice." ARETE 5 (Spring 1978): 11-21.

NASW News 20 (July 1977): 38-39.

National Advisory Commission on Rural Poverty. The People Left Behind. Washington, D.C.: U.S. Government Printing Office, 1967.

National Rural Center. A Concept and a Program. NRC brochure.

_____. A Directory of Rural Organizations. Washington, D. C.: NRC, 1977.

Nelson, Lowry. Rural Sociology: Its Origin and Growth in the United States. Minneapolis: University of Minnesota Press, 1969.

Odum, Howard W. "The County as a Basis of Social Work and Public Welfare in North Carolina." Proceedings, National Conference on Social Work, 53rd Annual Session. Cleveland, 1926, pp. 461-67.

Olson, Louise, and Ruth Schrader. "The Trailer Population in a Defense Area." Sociology and Social Research 27 (March-April 1943): 294-302.

"Operation Hitchhike." Rural Manpower Developments 3 (October 1972): 13-16. U.S. Educational Resources Information Center, ERIC Document ED 067 121.

Oregon State Department of Employment. 1973 Annual Rural Manpower Report, State of Oregon. U.S. Educational Resources Information Center, ERIC Document ED 096 035.

Osgood, Mary H. "Rural and Urban Attitudes toward Welfare." Social Work 22 (January 1977): 41-47.

Peele, Catherine Groves. "In Times Like These: Evacuation of Farm Families." The Family 23 (March 1942): 274-76.

Pekarsky, Herman H. "Rural Training for Rural Workers." Survey 72 (April 1936): 104-5.

Pennypacker, E. Kathryn. "No One Can Do Everything." Survey 75 (December 1939): 369-71.

_____. "They Do Care." Letter to the Editor. Survey 76 (March 1940): 115.

Persons, Frank W. "Home Service in One Rural County." Survey 40 (June 29, 1918): 370-71.

Pinar, William. Heightened Consciousness, Cultural Revolution and Curriculum Theory. Berkeley, Calif.: McCutchan, 1974.

Pinchot, Gifford. "The Case for Federal Relief." Survey Graphic 67 (January 1, 1932): 347-49.

Pincus, Allen, and Anne Minahan. Social Work Practice: Model and Method. Itasco, Ill.: F. E. Peacock, 1973.

Polansky, Norman A., Christine De Saix, Mary Lou Wing, and John D. Patton. "Child Neglect in a Rural Community." Social Casework 49 (October 1968): 467-74.

"Poverty amidst Affluence." Monthly Labor Review 88 (July 1965): 836-40.

Pratt, Vocille M. "The Significance for the Caseworker of Rural Cultural Patterns." The Family 19 (March 1938): 14-19.

Pyles, Mary Lois. "Learning with our FERA's." The Family 16 (January 1936): 281-84.

Rainey, Kenneth D. "Public Services in Rural Areas." U.S. Educational Resources Information Center, ERIC Document ED 092 308.

"Recommendations to Promote Growth in Virginia's Rural Areas." Appalachia 3 (February 1970): 1-5. U.S. Educational Resources Information Center, ERIC Document ED 016 967.

Reeves, Margaret. "The Indirect Responsibility of a State Department for Children." The Family 8 (July 1927): 168-71.

"Regional Commissions: Commissions Given New Powers for Regional Development Aid." National Journal 1 (November 15, 1969): 130-31.

Rein, Martin, and Frank Riessman. "A Strategy for Antipoverty Community Action Programs." Social Work 11 (April 1966): 3-12.

"Relief in Rural Counties." Survey 69 (March 1933): 125.

"Report from the Rural Social Work Caucus." Human Services in the Rural Environment 3 (October 1978): 20.

"Report of the Commission on Country Life—A Summary." Rural America 7 (January 1929): 5-8.

Rettig, Marilla. "Why I Do Not Think I Would Make a Good Rural Case Worker." Survey 72 (January 1936): 15.

Reynolds, Berthe. Learning and Teaching in the Practice of Social Work. New York: Farrar and Rinehart, 1942.

Rhodes, Alfred H. "Rural Mississippi." Proceedings, National Conference on Social Welfare, 96th Annual Session. New York: Columbia University Press, 1969, pp. 149-61.

Richmond, Mary Ellen. "The Need of a Training School in Applied Philanthropy." Proceedings, National Conference on Charities and Corrections, 24th Annual Session. Toronto, 1897, pp. 181-88.

_____. Social Diagnosis. New York: Russell Sage Foundation, 1917.

Robinson, Virginia. "Educational Problems in Preparation for Social Casework." Mental Hygiene 14 (October 1930): 828-36.

Rodgers, Augustus, and G. Robert Whitcomb. "Evaluating a Course in Rural Social Work: A Systems Approach." Paper presented at the Annual Program Meeting, Council on Social Work Education, New Orleans, February 1978, pp. 1-20. Mimeographed.

Rogers, David L., and Larry Whiting, eds. Aspects of Planning for Public Services in Rural Areas. North Central Regional Center for Rural Development, Iowa, 1976. U.S. Educational Resources Information Center, ERIC Document ED 125 805.

Rogers, Everett M., and Rabel Burdge. Social Change in Rural Societies. 2d ed. New York: Appleton-Century-Crofts, 1972.

Rogers, John. "Poverty behind the Cactus Curtain." Progressive 30 (March 1966): 23-25.

Rogers, Mary L. "Geechee Case Record." Survey 75 (December 1939): 372-73.

Roosevelt, Theodore. "The Roosevelt Commission Report Special Message, February 9, 1909." Rural America 7 (January 1929): 3-5. Reprint from Senate Document no. 705, 60th Cong., 2d sess., 1909.

Rumics, Elizabeth. "Oral History: Defining the Term." Wilson Library Bulletin 40 (March 1966): 602-5.

Rural America. 3 vols. 1975 to 1978.

Rural American Women. Stepping Out of Obscurity into Involvement. Washington, D. C.: RAW.

"Rural Development Act." Congress and the Nation, 1969-1972, vol. 3. Washington, D. C.: Congressional Quarterly Service, 1972, pp. 347-49.

"Rural Leaders and Their Problems." Survey 30 (August 30, 1913): 655-56.

Rural Poverty and Welfare. Rural America and Rural Housing Alliance, Washington, D. C., April 1975. U. S. Educational Resources Information Center, ERIC Document 104 584.

"Rural Social Workers Meet." Survey 26 (August 19, 1911): 747-49.

"The Rural Worker in America." Monthly Labor, vol. 91 (June 1968). Special issue.

Russell Sage Foundation Library. Rural Life from the Aspect of the Social Worker. Bulletin no. 98, 1929.

Sampson, Timothy J. Welfare: A Handbook for Friend and Foe. Philadelphia: United Church Press, 1973.

Sanderson, Dwight. "The Community as an Administrative Unit." Rural America 8 (March 1930): 5-9.

_____. "Disadvantaged Classes in Rural Life." Rural America 16 (December 1938): 3-9.

_____. "Trends and Problems in Rural Social Work." Rural America 8 (January 1930): 3-6.

Sanford, Terry. "Poverty: The Challenge to the States." Law and Contemporary Problems 30 (Winter 1966): 77-89.

Schaupp, Karl L. "Medical Care Experience of the Farm Security Administration in California." Proceedings, National Conference on Social Work, 68th Annual Session. Atlantic City, N. J., 1941, pp. 494-501.

Schorr, Burt. "Suicidal Rural Gap in the Poverty War." Wall Street Journal, February 20, 1968, p. 16.

Schuck, Peter H. "Black Land Grant Colleges—Discrimination as Public Policy." Saturday Review 55 (June 24, 1972): 46–48.

Schultz, Theodore W. "Our Welfare State and the Welfare of Farm People." Social Science Review 38 (June 1964): 123–29.

Schwarzweller, Harry K. Mountain Families in Transition. University Park: Pennsylvania State University Press, 1971.

Schweinitz, Karl de. "Social Values and Social Action—The Intellectual Base as Illustrated in the Study of History." Social Science Review 30 (June 1956): 119–29.

Segal, Julius, ed. The Mental Health of Rural America: The Rural Programs of the National Institute of Mental Health. Washington, D. C.: U.S. Department of Health, Education and Welfare, DHEW publication no. ADM76-349, pp. 35–48.

Shafer, Carol L. "This Rural Social Work." Survey 75 (May 1939): 136–37.

Shea, Alice Leahy. "Schools of Social Work Take Stock." Survey 75 (March 1939): 78.

Shenkin, Budd N. Health Care for Migrant Workers: Policies and Politics. Cambridge, Mass.: Ballinger, 1974.

Silva, Dolores. "Components in Program Development." American Journal of Occupational Therapy 30 (October 1976): 568–75.

_____. "A Search-Paradigm for the Description of Problem Solving Processes." Educational Technology 13 (August 1973): 36–39.

_____. "Self-Organization: Implications for Education." American Journal of Occupational Therapy 28 (November–December 1974): 602–5.

_____. "Toward Collaboration in Program Development for Teacher Preparation." American Journal of Occupational Therapy 31 (March 1977): 169–73.

_____. "Toward Program Development." American Journal of Occupational Therapy 30 (August 1976): 441–43.

Simon, Rita James. As We Saw the Thirties. Urbana: University of Illinois Press, 1967.

Slater, Eleanor, American Friends Service Committee. Letter to Marion Hathaway, Secretary of the Rural Subcommittee of the American Association of Schools of Social Work, July 10, 1939. Council on Social Work Education Archives, American Association of Schools of Social Work, Curriculum Committee Files, New York.

Smick, A. A. "Training for Rural Social Work." Sociology and Social Research 22 (July 22, 1938): 538-44.

Smith, Raymond C. "Rural Resources." Proceedings, National Conference on Social Work, 67th Annual Session. Grand Rapids, Mich., 1940, pp. 270-79.

Smyth, Wilma. "The Rural Child Welfare Worker in Action." Social Casework 36 (November 1955): 406-12.

Sobey, Francine. Changing Roles in Social Work Practice. Philadelphia: Temple University Press, 1977.

"Social Work at the Grass Roots." Survey, vol. 77 (February 1941). Special issue.

Social Work Yearbook, 1935. New York: Russell Sage Foundation, 1935.

Social Work Yearbook, 1938. New York: Russell Sage Foundation, 1938.

Social Work Yearbook, 1943. New York: Russell Sage Foundation, 1943.

Sotomayor, Marta, and Philip D. Ortega y Gasco, eds. Chicano Content and Social Work Education. New York: Council on Social Work Education, 1975.

Spivak, Jonathan. "Poverty Foes Launch Idea to Use Rural Poor to Beautify Roadsides." Wall Street Journal, February 9, 1966, pp. 10, 16.

Springer, D. G., and N. Springer. "Counties Are Different." Survey 77 (February 1941): 41-45.

_____. "The Education of Mr. Wyat." Survey 77 (February 1941): 45-48.

Springer, Gertrude. "Partners in a New Social Order." Survey 69 (July 1933): 243-50.

_____. "In Predominantly Rural Areas." Survey 77 (February 1941): 37-40.

_____. "Some Scars Remain." Survey 78 (January 1942): 13-15.

Steiner, Jesse Frederick. "Education for Social Work in Rural Communities: Rural Sociology—Indispensable or Merely Desirable?" Proceedings, National Conference on Social Work, 54th Annual Session. Des Moines, Iowa, 1927, pp. 587-93.

_____. "An Experiment in Rural Social Organization." Social Forces 5 (June 1927): 634-38.

_____. "Interrelation between City and Rural Life." Proceedings, National Conference on Social Work, 54th Annual Session. Des Moines, Iowa, 1927, pp. 345-51.

Stephenson, John B. Shiloh: A Mountain Community. Lexington: University of Kentucky Press, 1968.

Stinson, M. B. "I am a County Relief Director." Survey 71 (October 1935): 296-97.

Stokdyk, E. A., and Charles H. West. The Farm Board. New York: Macmillan, 1930.

Strode, Josephine. "Beef, Prunes and Ink Blots and Other Aspects of Aid to Dependent Children." Survey 75 (March 1939): 76-77.

_____. "Getting Along with the Bosses." Survey 75 (January 1939): 13-14.

_____. "Learning from the Job." Survey 74 (December 1938): 380-81.

_____. "Old Folks Are Like That." Survey 75 (February 1939): 41-42.

_____. "An Open Letter to Miss Bailey." Survey 74 (October 1938): 307-9.

_____. "Publicity by Way of the Barn Door." Survey 74 (November 1938): 345-47.

_____. "Rural Social Workers Do Everything." Survey 74 (October 1938): 308-9.

_____. "Social Work at the Grass Roots." Survey 74 (October 1938): 307.

_____. "Swinging the Depression with the Killer-Dillers, Hot-Shots, and Alligators." Survey 75 (April 1939): 108-10.

_____. "Tighten the Corner Where You Are." Survey 75 (May 1939): 138-39.

Swanson, Merwin S. "The American Country Life Movement, 1900-1940." Ph.D. dissertation, University of Minnesota, 1972.

_____. "Professional Rural Social Work in America." Agricultural History 46 (October 1972): 514-26.

Swift, Wiley H. "A Redefining of the Scope and Functions of the Juvenile Court, in Terms of the Rural Community." Proceedings, National Conference on Social Work, 48th Annual Session. Milwaukee, 1921, pp. 89-92.

Taylor, Carl C. Rural Life in the United States. New York: A. A. Knopf, 1949.

Taylor, Graham. "The County: A Challenge to Humanized Politics and Volunteer Co-operation." Survey 32 (May 30, 1914): 240-44.

Taylor, R. Sweatshops in the Sun: Child Labor on the Farm. Boston: Beacon, 1973.

Tessari, John. "Training and the War Effort." Proceedings, National Conference on Social Work, 70th Annual Session, War Regional Conferences. New York, St. Louis, Cleveland, 1943, pp. 32-46.

Tetreau, E. D. "Wartime Changes in Arizona Farm Labor." Sociology and Social Research 28 (May-June 1944): 385-96.

Thompson, Raymond. "Rural Relief Administration in the Northwest." The Family 16 (June 1935): 117-18.

Tigert, John L., Chairman, National Association of Schools of Social Administration. Letter to Leona Manoth, Executive Secretary of the American Association of Schools of Social Work, July 19, 1946. Council on Social Work Education Archives, National Association of Schools of Social Administration Files, New York.

Towle, Charlotte. "The Distinctive Attributes of Education for Social Work." Social Work Journal 33 (1952): 63-72, 94.

"Training for Home Service." Survey 42 (May 10, 1919): 250.

Tropman, Elmer J. "Agency Constraints Affecting Links between Practice and Education." Journal of Education for Social Work 13 (Winter 1977): 8-14.

Tufts, James H. Education and Training for Social Work. New York: Russell Sage Foundation, 1923.

Turabian, Kate L. A Manual for Writers of Term Papers, Theses, and Dissertations. 4th ed. Chicago: University of Chicago Press, 1967.

Twente, Esther E. "The Challenge of Social Casework in Smaller Communities." The Family 10 (November 1929): 201-3.

_____. "Social Case-Work Practice in Rural Communities." Proceedings, National Conference on Social Work, 65th Annual Session. Seattle, 1938, pp. 122-32.

Tweton, D. Jerome. "Progressivism Discovers the Farm: The Country Life Commission of 1908." North Dakota Quarterly 39 (Summer 1971): 58-67.

Tyler, Ralph W. "Distinctive Attributes of Education for the Professions." Social Work Journal 33 (April 1952): 55-62, 94.

_____. "New Dimensions in Curriculum Development." Phi Delta Kappan 48 (September 1966): 25-28.

_____. Perspectives of Curriculum Evaluation. New York: Rand McNally, 1967.

_____. "A Talk with Ralph Tyler." Phi Delta Kappan 49 (1967): 75-77.

"Undergraduate Training and Social Work." The Family 24 (May 1943): 112-15.

U.S., Congress, Senate, Committee on Labor and Public Welfare, Subcommittee on Migratory Labor. Farm Workers in Rural Poverty, 92d Cong., 1971-72, pt. 1.

_____. Land Ownership, Use and Distribution, 92d Cong., 1971-72, pt. 3.

U.S., Department of Agriculture. "Rural America Poverty and Progress: Rural Development Policy Issues." Discussion paper, Rural Development Policy Study, December 1977.

U.S., Department of Agriculture, Economic Research Service. The Economic and Social Condition of Rural America in the 1970's, vol. 3. Washington, D.C.: Government Printing Office, 1971.

U.S., Department of Health, Education and Welfare. A New Day in Rural Mental Health. DHEW publication no. ADM78-690, 1978. Washington, D.C., 1978.

Vaile, Gertrude. "The Contribution of Rural Sociology to Family Social Work." The Family 14 (June 1933): 106-10.

_____. Letter to Elizabeth Wisner re the Subcommittee on Materials from Rural Fields, February 3, 1941. Council on Social Work Education Archives, American Association of Schools of Social Work Curriculum Committee Files, New York.

_____. Letter to Marion Hathaway, June 14, 1939. Council on Social Work Education Archives, American Association of Schools of Social Work Curriculum Committee Files, New York.

_____. Memo on Material from and about Rural Social Work, January 30, 1941. Council on Social Work Education Archives, American Association of Schools of Social Work Curriculum Committee Files, New York.

_____. Memo to Directors of Member Schools re the Subcommittee on Adaptation of Materials from the Rural Field, July 28, 1939. Council on Social Work Education Archives, American Association of Schools of Social Work Curriculum Committee Files, New York.

_____. Memo to Member Schools to Consider Adapted Materials from the Rural Field, June 12, 1939. Council on Social Work Education Archives, American Association of Schools of Social Work Curriculum Committee Files, New York.

_____. Memo to Members of Subcommittee on Rural Materials of the American Association of Schools of Social Work, May 19, 1939. Council on Social Work Education Archives, American Association of Schools of Social Work Curriculum Committee Files, New York.

_____. Memo to Members of the Subcommittee on Rural Materials, January 20, 1941. Council on Social Work Education Archives, American Association of Schools of Social Work Curriculum Committee Files, New York.

Vanzand, Sally, and Susan Bosworth. "Day Care Problems and Needs in Rural Areas." Public Welfare 26 (July 1968): 219-22.

Vasey, Wayne. "Public Welfare in a Rapidly Growing Community." Proceedings, National Conference on Social Work, 74th Annual Session. San Francisco, 1947, pp. 184-93.

Vidich, Arthur J., and Joseph Benseman. Small Town in Mass Society: Class, Power and Religion in a Rural Community. Princeton, N.J.: Princeton University Press, 1958.

Vinson, Elizabeth A., and Kate M. Jesberg. The Rural Stake in Public Assistance. Washington, D.C.: National Rural Center, 1978.

Von Tungeln, George H. "Rural Social Research—Methods and Results." Proceedings, National Conference on Social Work, 54th Annual Session. Des Moines, Iowa, 1927, pp. 331-40.

Vrede, Jane Van de. "Social Health Problems in Rural Communities." Proceedings, National Conference on Social Work, 50th Annual Session. Washington, D.C., 1923, pp. 64-68.

Wagenfeld, Morton O., and Stanley Robin. "The Social Worker in the Rural Community Mental Health Center." In Social Work in Rural Communities: A Book of Readings, edited by Leon Ginsberg. New York: Council for Social Work Education, 1976, p. 71. U.S. Educational Resources Information Center, ERIC Document ED 111 583, 1975.

Walker, Sydnor H. Social Work and the Training of Social Workers. Chapel Hill: University of North Carolina Press, 1928.

Wallace, Henry A. "Economic Problems of the Farm." Proceedings, National Conference on Social Work, 54th Annual Session. Des Moines, Iowa, 1927, pp. 19-26.

_____. "The Farmer and Social Discipline." Rural America 12 (January 1934): 3-7.

Warner, W. Keith. "Rural Society in Post-Industrial Age." Rural Sociology 39 (Fall 1974): 306-18.

Weaver, W. W. "A Preface to Rural Social Work." Rural America 10 (January 1932): 5-6.

Weber, Gwen. "Preparing Social Workers for Practice in Rural Social Systems." Journal of Education for Social Work 12 (Fall 1976): 108-15.

Webster, L. Josephine. "Undifferentiated Casework for a Rural Community." The Family 10 (November 1929): 216-17.

Webster, Stephen A. "A Report from the Rural Social Work Caucus." Mimeographed. Madison: University of Wisconsin, February 27, 1977.

Weller, Jack E. Yesterday's People. Lexington: University of Kentucky Press, 1965.

Wells, Frederick. "Is an Organized Country Life Movement Possible?" Survey 29 (January 4, 1913): 449-56.

Wellstone, Paul David. How the Rural Poor Got Power: Narrative of a Grass-Roots Organizer. Amherst: University of Massachusetts Press, 1978.

Wessel, Rosa. "The Meaning of Professional Education for Social Work." Social Service Review 35 (June 1961): 153-60.

West, Walter M. "The Relief-State-of-the-Nation." Survey 69 (February 1933): 51-57.

Westbrook, Lawrence. "Getting Them Off Relief." Proceedings, National Conference on Social Work, 62nd Annual Session. Montreal, 1935, pp. 618-25.

Wheeler, John H. "Civil Rights Groups—Their Impact upon the War on Poverty." Law and Contemporary Problems 31 (Winter 1966): 152–58.

Wilson, Warren W. "Farm Cooperation for Better Business Schools of Churches." Survey 36 (April 8, 1916): 50–53.

Wisconsin, State Department of Industry, Labor and Human Relations. "Wisconsin Migrant and Rural Services Annual Report, 1975." U. S. Educational Resources Information Center, ERIC Document ED 127 105.

Wisner, Elizabeth. "Edith Abbott's Contribution to Social Work Education." Social Service Review 32 (1958): 1–10.

Woods, Robert A. "Social Work: A New Profession." International Journal of Ethics 16 (1905): 25–39.

Woofter, T. J., Jr. "Rural Relief and the Back to the Farm Movement." Social Forces 14 (March 1936): 381–88.

Wright, Caroline. "What It Takes." Survey 76 (March 1940): 115.

Wrigley, Robert L. "Small Cities Can Help to Revitalize Rural Areas." The Annals. Philadelphia: American Academy of Political and Social Sciences, 1973, pp. 55–74.

Wylie, Mary. "Social Planning in Non-Metropolitan America." In A Symposium: Planning and Delivery of Social Services in Rural America: Three Papers, edited by William H. Koch. Madison: University of Wisconsin, 1973, p. 23.

Youngdahl, Benjamin E. "Civil Rights versus Civil Strife." Proceedings, National Conference on Social Work, 76th Annual Session. Cleveland, 1949, pp. 21–37.

_____. "Community Organization in Rural Child Welfare Services." Proceedings, National Conference on Social Work, 70th Annual Session, War Regional Conferences. New York, St. Louis, Cleveland, 1943, pp. 170–215.

_____. "The Effect of Administrative Procedures on Casework in a Rural Setting." Proceedings, National Conference on Social Work, 67th Annual Session. Grand Rapids, Mich., 1940, pp. 280–88.

INDEX

Abbott, Grace, 25
Abrams, Harvey, 94
accreditation and social work, 55–56 (see also rural social work, training for; social work, training for)
Addams, Jane, 14
advocacy, 197–201
agrarianism, 221
Agricultural Adjustment Act (AAA), 28, 29, 30, 31, 118, 124
agricultural and mechanical colleges, 1, 54, 56, 180; Massachusetts, 4
Agriculture, Department of (USDA), 4, 58, 86, 105, 180, 190, 192, 193, 194, 196; agents, 144, 194; extension service, 148, 175, 193; home economists, 144
Aid to Families with Dependent Children (AFDC), 118, 123, 125, 155, 157, 158
Alabama, Morgan County, 132, 135
Alaska Redevelopment Commission, 92
Allen, Frederick Lewis, 24
American Association of Schools of Social Work (AASSW), 55, 56, 57, 163
American Friends Service Committee, 57
American Medical Association, 203, 213
American Missionary Association, 187
American Public Health Association, 202, 205, 206, 212
American Red Cross, 7, 8, 15
American Rural Health Association, 106

antipoverty: in Alabama, 86; in California, 85; expenditures for, 90; in Minnesota, 87; in Mississippi, 86; in New Jersey, 85; in North Carolina, 85; programs under, 90–91; and social workers, 95–96
Appalachia, 91–92; people of, 76, 92, 93; southern, 5, 93, 225
Appalachian Redevelopment Act of 1965, 91–92
Appalachian Redevelopment Commission (see Appalachian Redevelopment Act of 1965)
Arkansas, 164, 165–69
Armenians, 177
Association for Rural Mental Health, 106
Association of State and Territorial Health Officials (ASTHO), 212
Atkinson, Mary Irene, 32–34
Atomic Energy, Congressional Committee on, 77
Axinn, June, 22

Bailey, Liberty Hyde, 2–3
Bailey, "Miss," 117–19, 121–25
Basques, 70
Bast, David, 107
Beale, Calvin L., 222, 224
Berea College, 76
black land-grant colleges, 190–92
black students, 190, 191
blacks: in Alabama, 77; in the army, 72; in the cotton fields, 70; and FERA, 35; in Kentucky, 76; in rural areas, 177–80; in the rural south, 35, 71, 74; in USDA, 78, 180

ABOUT THE AUTHOR

EMILIA E. MARTINEZ-BRAWLEY, Ed.D., ACSW, is Assistant Professor of Social Welfare at The Pennsylvania State University. Dr. Brawley received her Ed.D. from Temple University and her M.S.S. from Bryn Mawr College, both in Pennsylvania. She edited <u>Pioneer Efforts in Rural Social Welfare: First Hand Views since 1908</u> (University Park: Pennsylvania State University Press, 1980) and has written numerous articles on rural social work, which have appeared in such publications as <u>Human Services in the Rural Environment</u>, <u>Sociology and Social Welfare</u>, and <u>Arete</u>. In addition to her research interests in the United States, Dr. Brawley has conducted cross-cultural studies in rural social welfare in the United Kingdom, Ireland, and Latin America. She is an active member of NASW, CSWE, and the National Rural Social Work Caucus.